For Notre Dame

**Other titles of interest from St. Augustine's Press**

Charles E. Rice, *What Happened to Notre Dame?*

Charles E. Rice, *Right or Wrong?*

Charles E. Rice & Theresa Farnan, *Where Did I Come From? Where Am I Going? How Do I Get There?*

Gerhart Niemeyer, *The Loss and Recovery of Truth*

Gerhart Niemeyer, *Between Nothingness and Paradise*

Ralph McInerny, *Some Catholic Writers*

Ralph McInerny, *Defamation of Pius XII*

Christopher Kaczor, ed., *O Rare Ralph McInerny*

Gerard V. Bradley, *Unquiet Americans*

Gerard V. Bradley, *Essays on Law, Religion, and Morality*

Jeffrey Langan, *The French Revolution Confronts Pius VI* (I)

Thomas Aquinas, *Treatise on Law,* trans., A. J. Freddoso

Thos. Aquinas, *Treatise on Human Nature,* tr., A.J. Freddoso

Thomas Aquinas, *Disputed Queswtions on Virtue,* trans. Ralph McInerny

John of St. Thomas, *Introduction to the Summa Theologiae of Thomas Aquinas,* trans. Ralph McInerny

Joseph Bobik, *Veritas Divina*

Florent Gaboriau, *The Conversion of Edith Stein,* trans., Ralph McInerny

Plato, *Symposium of Plato,* ed., intro. David O'Connor

Otto Bird & Katharine Bird, *From Witchery to Sanctity*

Josef Pieper, *The Christian Idea of Man*

Josef Pieper, *Happiness and Contemplation*

Rémi Brague, *On the God of the Christians*

Rémi Brague, *Eccentric Culture*

# For Notre Dame

## Battling for the Heart and Soul of a Catholic University

Wilson D. Miscamble, C.S.C.

Foreword by David Solomon

ST. AUGUSTINE'S PRESS
South Bend, Indiana

Manufactured in the United States of America

1 2 3 4 5 6    19 18 17 16 15 14 13

**Library of Congress Cataloging in Publication Data**
Miscamble, Wilson D., 1953–
For Notre Dame : battling for the heart and soul of a Catholic university / Wilson D. Miscamble, C.S.C.;
introduction by David Solomon.
pages   cm
Includes index.
ISBN 978-1-58731-265-6 (paperbound : alk. paper)
1. University of Notre Dame – History. 2. Catholic universities and colleges – United States – History.  I. Title.
LD4113.M57 2013
378.772'89 – dc23        2013008873

∞ The paper used in this publication meets the minimum requirements of the American National Standard for Information Sciences – Permanence of Paper for Printed Materials, ANSI Z39.48-1984.

St. Augustine's Press
www.staugustine.net

To the Memory of


Bishop John M. D'Arcy (1932–2013)
Bishop of Fort Wayne-South Bend (1985–2009)

&

for
Bill and Mary Dempsey and the men and women of
the Sycamore Trust

With deep gratitude for
their commitment to and love for Notre Dame

# Table of Contents

## Table of Contents

# Acknowledgments

This book has been in preparation, in a certain sense, over the past twenty years during which these various articles or talks were either written or delivered. I thank all those who have instructed me regarding the issues involved and helped me understand better what is at stake in the battle for the heart and soul of Notre Dame. I am especially grateful to those who have given me their friendship over this time and joined in the endeavor to shape Notre Dame as a Catholic university. Whatever the limitations of our efforts we assuredly have been engaged in a good and worthy fight.

In the specific preparation of the book I must extend special thanks to three wonderful women and two stalwart men. In the earliest stages of the project I enlisted the invaluable assistance of Claire Gillen Cousino. In her tough but gracious way Claire forced me to select the contents more carefully. She then worked on the manuscript at every stage organizing it effectively and improving it notably. St. Augustine's Press recruited Pam Bradley to edit the manuscript, and she brought her astute eye to bear on the full manuscript and improved the clarity of it. Madeline Gillen aided me with genuine thoughtfulness on various research and writing projects over this past year but lent key support in dealing with the various details involved in getting what we called "FND" into its final shape.

I am truly grateful to Bruce Fingerhut of St. Augustine's Press for his generous support of my idea for this book from the outset and for all he has done to produce the fine volume the reader now holds. I can only hope and pray that the book sells some copies to reward his faith in it! My deep regard for David Solomon and for his accomplishment at the Notre Dame Center for Ethics and

Culture is expressed in one of the entries in this book. Let me simply thank him here for providing the foreword and for his comradeship at Notre Dame on many of the matters addressed in this book. He is a true friend and a man of character and, as a confirmed Aristotelian, he knows all that I mean by this.

I must thank the talented Matt Cashore for his arresting cover photograph. I also am grateful for the encouragement of the editors of the various publications where I first placed some of the pieces in this volume, especially Drew Christiansen, S.J., of *America* and the great *Irish Rover* trio of Gabby Speach, Claire Gillen and Bob Burkett. Furthermore, in a general way I must also express my sincere thanks to loyal friends who have generously supported my work over the years, especially Dan and Mary Ann Rogers, Brian and Nancy Sullivan, and Terry Seidler. I truly appreciate their kindness. I am fortunate to be a member of the Moreau Seminary community at Notre Dame and I value the fraternity of my Holy Cross confreres there. Of course, I also extend my thanks to my family in Australia—my devoted parents and my treasured sister and brother—who have heard so much about Notre Dame in the last quarter century and offered me unfailing love and support throughout my priestly ministry at Our Lady's school.

This book is dedicated with great admiration and deep gratitude to Bishop John D'Arcy and to Bill and Mary Dempsey and the men and women of the Sycamore Trust. These remarkable folk have understood well what is at stake at Notre Dame and have been courageous in calling Notre Dame to fulfill its true mission as a Catholic university. Their witness and commitment have served to inspire me. The dedication is but a token of my regard and respect.

Wilson D. (Bill) Miscamble, C.S.C
Solemnity of Mary, the Mother of God, 2013.

# Foreword

It is easy to spot Father Miscamble on the Notre Dame campus. He is tall, sandy-haired and he moves quickly. His presence, pretty distinctive when he is still, is impossible to miss when he is on the move–head bobbing up and down, turning from side to side, his face wreathed in an engaging smile, looking for someone to greet or to talk to. Students know him from his sold-out classes on Australian history ("it's not just beer and beaches") and American foreign policy, the countless masses he celebrates in dorm chapels or in the Basilica, and the spiritual counseling for which he is always in demand. Faculty know him from his engagement in intellectual conversations at conferences, lectures and receptions on campus—and the significant , agenda-shaping roles he has played in such organizations as the Faculty Senate, the local chapter of University Faculty for Life, and the "conversation on the Catholic Character of Notre Dame" of a couple of decades ago. It goes without saying that everyone in the administration knows him since he has been the unofficial leader, one might say, of the loyal opposition at Notre Dame in recent years. And there is no question of either his Loyalty or his Opposition! Father Miscamble is not a half-way or luke-warm guy. He loves Notre Dame and everybody knows it. He also thinks that some important things have gone wrong at Notre Dame—especially with regard to faculty hiring—and everybody knows that as well.

This collection chronicles Father Miscamble's engagement with the contemporary debate about the future of Catholic higher education, especially as this debate is being played out on the campus of the richest and most influential Catholic university in the world. The reader will find collected here the articles, talks, and columns that together constitute Father Miscamble's indictment of wrong-headed policies that have all too often prevailed at Notre Dame recently. One will also find an alternative vision of the university, hopeful and inspiring, around which many of Father Miscamble's admirers have rallied. Father Miscamble has explored the indictment, as well as the alternative vision, in the pages of national Catholic magazines and local students newspapers, in talks to students and to alumni groups, in homilies and in after-dinner reflections. Although the pieces collected here have appeared in diverse venues and were intended for sometimes quite different audiences, they are of a piece and they constitute a single vision.

It is quite remarkable that Father Miscamble has had time to become the leader at Notre Dame in raising these issues given the many other roles he plays at the University. He was for some years the head of the seminary at Notre Dame with the direct responsibility for the formation of a generation of Holy Cross priests, a group of men fiercely loyal to him and to his vision of Notre Dame. Before that he served as chairman of the history department in a difficult and demanding period in the history of that department. His term as chairman is perhaps most memorable for his ability to disagree sharply with some of his colleagues while retaining their friendship and trust. He is also certainly the most distinguished scholar among his generation of Holy Cross priests, with two widely-praised scholarly books (along with many articles) about the intricacies of American foreign policy in the early years of the Cold War. He has emerged as one of the leading contemporary scholars of the foreign policy of Harry Truman (one of his great personal heroes) and George Marshall, appearing regularly on prestigious scholarly panels on American foreign policy, as well as commenting on these matters in more popular media. He has won all of the major teaching awards at Notre Dame and is besieged by students who want to work with him—or just hang around him. He is also attentive to his many pastoral duties, traveling frequently to preside at weddings, baptisms, or funerals for his friends, his students, or Notre Dame alums whom he has come to know. In addition to all this, he has the energy remaining to be at the center of a circle of close friends (among whom I count myself) to whom he is attentive and with whom he always finds time to share himself.

Father Miscamble clearly belongs to that class of priests who seem to draw an extra portion of energy and endeavor from their priestly vocation. They are more alive than the rest of us. Notre Dame has been fortunate to have had many such priests. Father Marvin O'Connell's magisterial biography of Father Sorin makes clear that Notre Dame's founder set a standard for lives of this sort, and many others have followed in his wake. Father Hesburgh, with his massive accomplishments, must stand at the head of the list among contemporary Holy Cross priests, but many others, including contemporaries of mine such as Father Tim Scully and Father David Burrell, join Father Miscamble in demonstrating to us all how much good can be accomplished by priests who are "all-in" for Notre Dame and the community of Holy Cross. We have all been told that part of the point of priestly celibacy is to make it possible for priests to live wholly for others. When one witnesses the lives of those like Father Miscamble and the others I have mentioned, one sees what it is like when that ideal is fully realized.

Father Miscamble, almost by accident it sometimes seems, has become the spokesperson (or at least the rallying point) for a relatively small group of faculty, students, and administrators at Notre Dame (as well as for a quite large group of Notre Dame alums) who are deeply dissatisfied with important aspects of the direction Notre Dame has taken in recent years—while still believing that this university is the best hope for Catholic higher education. This volume collects a number of his essays and talks that express the views which have earned him this leadership role. His position as our leader was solidified when he gave the opening talk at the rally held on the South Quad of the University on the Sunday on which President Obama was being given an honorary degree along with the applause and adulation of the majority of the Notre Dame community. Air Force One flew over the campus on that beautiful and sunny spring day bringing President Obama to campus as over 3500 people met on the south quad to celebrate an outdoor mass with Father Miscamble and a number of other Holy Cross priests on the altar. When he mounted the podium later in the day to speak to an even larger crowd, he invoked Notre Dame's history and the selfless, indeed frequently heroic, work of members of his religious community in an attempt to explain why it was so wrong to celebrate the most pro-abortion president in the history of our country at the commencement exercises of Our Lady's University. It was a talk that will never be forgotten by those present that day. When the much-loved late Bishop of Ft. Wayne/South Bend, Bishop John D'Arcy, followed Father Miscamble to the podium to give another rousing talk, he memorably quipped, "Coming to the podium after Father Miscamble is like coming to bat after Babe Ruth."

Father Miscamble is frequently called "a happy warrior," and the appellation is certainly appropriate for him as it was for the other great Catholic hero, Al Smith, for whom it was first coined. Although he can be quite heated in debate, his affability always shows through. He grew up in the rough-and-tumble world of Labor Party politics in Australia. His favorite sport was rugby, and he is the son of a butcher who aspired to go on cutting meat even after he lost his sight from a mid-life illness. And he clearly still enjoys a good scrap. Like those Holy Cross priests who inaugurated the Bengal Bouts on campus, however, he gives us a good example of someone who, while mixing it up, is ready with a handshake and a smile when it is over. Like Socrates and Joe Louis, he appreciates a good opponent. It makes the battle more fun.

I am glad I am Father Miscamble's friend and on his side in the great controversies that now roil the waters of Notre Dame. I would not like to have him as an opponent. An outsider to Notre Dame's situation might see things differently, however, and note that Father Miscamble's side in the current debate *seems* to be losing—indeed, *seems* to be losing quite badly. The other side seems to hold all the good cards. Not a single dean or department chairman attended our Obama protest, nor did any other member of the senior administration (except our friend Bill Kirk, then an associate vice-president, who was fired without notice within a year of his attending the Obama protest). Of the thousand or so faculty members at Notre Dame, only about 25 came forward when I asked faculty members who supported our cause to stand with me and Father Miscamble at the rally. Most faculty, all the deans and senior administrators and, of course, most students were in the Joyce Center cheering President Obama while we attended the student rally on the south quad. Father Miscamble has no significant position of bureaucratic power at Notre Dame presently. He serves on no important university committees—nor is it likely that he will be asked to do so in the near future. While he was considered for both the deanship of his college and the presidency of the University, he was rejected for both jobs. He teaches his classes, writes his books, marries, baptizes, and buries when asked to do so, reads his office each day, prays for Notre Dame, and tells the truth as he sees it about the way things are going at the most significant Catholic university in the world.

He sees more clearly than most what is at stake in the battle for the soul of Notre Dame, and he has been prepared to do what he can with a smile on his face to avert the secular future that many predict—and, alas, many more strive to bring about—for the university. People sometimes thank Father Miscamble for the sacrifices he has been prepared to make in pursuit of the cause to which he has been so committed. He rightly, and sincerely, makes light of such talk of sacrifice on his part. To be a faculty member at Notre Dame defending the project of Catholic higher education, if you believe what Father Miscamble believes, is as good as it gets. The struggle in which he is engaged is a noble one. The stakes are of the first importance both for the Catholic Church and for Christian higher education generally, and he has been providentially put in a position where his voice carries a special authority in the debate. He is yoked together with allies whose friendship and devotion he fully enjoys. His talents and charisma almost perfectly suit him for his leadership role. He hasn't chosen this battle. The battle seems rather to have chosen him.

To expend enormous amounts of time and energy, even to suffer disparagement and some mockery, seems nothing when set alongside the great goods at stake in this struggle. Father Miscamble has had opportunities to assume leadership roles at other institutions in recent years where his talents would be more appreciated than they are at Notre Dame under its present administration. He has turned all of these opportunities down, and, indeed, seems hardly to have been tempted by them. Father Miscamble is exactly where he wants to be and surely where he belongs. I am sure he regards himself as the most fortunate person in the world to have the opportunities he has to defend the truth in these matters alongside the dedicated if somewhat motley band of brothers and sisters he leads.

He has many critics, of course, but they are unconvincing to those who know Father Miscamble and understand the present state of things at Notre Dame. Indeed, the slightly nervous tone of many of the criticisms suggests that the critics themselves harbor the deep fear that Father Miscamble is right on the fundamental issues. I am sure it is difficult for his critics to reckon with Father Miscamble's confidence, fearlessness, and joy in putting forward the views in this book. They must constantly wonder how he can be so joyful when, by some measures, he appears to be so clearly losing!! How can he be so happy when he is kept so far from the levers of power at contemporary Notre Dame?

These are good questions, and the sources of Father Miscamble's joy are worth pondering for all of us. It is also worth noting first, though, that perhaps the rumors of Father Miscamble's losses are a bit exaggerated. He has won a few battles, too. While he certainly has not featured prominently in the University administration's presentation of self in recent years, there is no doubt that his efforts have made a difference at Notre

Dame. His rousing talks at the Notre Dame alumni weekend a couple of years back, raising questions about the suitability of Roxanne Martino's appointment to the Notre Dame Board of Trustees, was followed promptly by her resignation. Also, in spite of the still quite discouraging overall picture of the Catholic presence on the Notre Dame faculty, the numbers of Catholic faculty appear in the last few years to be on a slight upward curve. This comes after many years of steady decline in the percentage of Catholic faculty. Many of us are quite confident that this slight, but surely significant, shift in the trends of Catholic hiring at Notre Dame would not have occurred without the firm and persistent voice of Father Miscamble over the past two decades.

His pivotal role in founding and leading the local chapter of University Faculty for Life has also provided a vital intellectual meeting place for those who share his vision of Notre Dame's proper place in the world of higher education. And when 650 Notre Dame, St. Marys', and Holy Cross students traveled to the March for Life this year, along with over 50 faculty member, all agreed that Father Miscamble could take much credit for these unprecedentedly large numbers. His has frequently been a lonely voice, but it has clearly been heard by many above the crowd of those who disparage his vision.

It is also important, however, to reflect on the deeper source of his fearlessness and confidence in pursuing his vision of the cause of Catholic higher education. One of the pieces in this book is a little talk he gave on fear at the first in a series of undergraduate dinners entitled Breaking Bread sponsored by the Notre Dame Center for Ethics and Culture. The Center asked him to explore the meaning of Pope John Paul II's oft repeated injunction, "Be not afraid!" No one who was at that talk will ever doubt Father Miscamble's clear grasp of the distinction between what is genuinely to be feared and what is feared only by the foolish and the self-deceived.

Like Aristotle, he does not think that the key to courage is to banish fear from our lives. Rather it is to learn to fear the right things and in the right ways. He is clearly not afraid of those who currently wield power at Notre Dame insofar as their actions may have consequences for his own career or his standing at the University. He rightly sees such fear as unmanly and not worthy of those with his vocation. At the same time, he seems genuinely afraid of remaining silent from some misplaced notion of loyalty to the university while institutional decisions that destroy the possibility of Notre Dame's future as a genuinely Catholic university are being made. As a member of the religious order that founded Notre Dame and nurtured it through its tumultuous century-and-a-half history, he takes a special responsibility for speaking out against decisions and policies that threaten the very future of genuine Catholic higher education.

The pieces collected in this volume track Father Miscamble's reflections on the Catholic character issue at Notre Dame since the early 1990s. His has without question been the most important voice opposing secularizing trends at Notre Dame during this period. As important as the views expressed in his talks and essays, however, has been his personal example of faithful, joyful, and fearless commitment to the cause of Catholic higher education. In 1979 the Lenten meditations of Pope John Paul II appeared under the title *A Sign of Contradiction*. This mysterious phrase is one Father Miscamble has always borne in mind, as he has labored to serve the Jesus who said, at the end of his life, "I have come to bear witness to the truth."

*David Solomon*
*University of Notre Dame*

# Introduction:
# Beyond Country and Career
# to a Calling at Notre Dame

This is a book for all those who love Notre Dame and are interested in its past, present, and future. It is a book that asks its readers to reflect deeply about the ongoing struggle to determine the university's present mission and future course. This struggle is not readily apparent to those who visit the campus briefly and experience its picture-postcard beauty and then participate in a wonderful liturgy or a well-staged academic conference. It is also well disguised by the university's relentless institutional self-promotion. It is not even always obvious to many of the undergraduates who blithely enjoy their four years under the dome. Nonetheless, the struggle is very real, and its outcome will shape whether or not Notre Dame will be a Catholic university in a meaningful sense in future decades.

Notre Dame's mission as a Catholic university has been the subject of significant debate and dispute for at least the past four decades. This book raises serious questions about the path that Notre Dame has pursued and presently follows. It holds that the Catholic mission and identity of Notre Dame have suffered and, indeed, are at risk. This view will not receive the approbation of the Notre Dame public relations machine and those it serves. No doubt the book will attract some censure from those who resent any criticism of the university, however well grounded. But I do not aim to placate those who bear responsibility for Notre Dame's current situation. Instead, I seek to deepen understanding of the university so that its fundamental challenges can be faced honestly and a better course charted for it. The debate also relates to and is in some ways a microcosm of larger conflicts in the culture, the church, and Catholic higher education. Tracking the debate at Notre Dame casts some light on elements of those broader areas.

I have been a participant, to some extent, in what I call the battle for the heart and soul of Notre Dame for well over two decades, and this collection brings together some of my written and spoken contributions to this debate. Read together, I trust these essays and talks will provide insight not only for those—both friend and (metaphorical) foe alike—who have contributed in various ways to the debate, but also to those who come to it afresh with true concern for Notre Dame. Understanding important aspects of the debate and its history hopefully will inform future discussions of the critical issues that presently confront Notre Dame.

As I acknowledge in the pages that follow, Notre Dame is blessed with real strengths as a Catholic university. Yet without major actions to bolster its essential institutional commitment the university's strengths are insufficient to ward off the dangers that threaten its Catholic mission. Over the years those who exhibit tendencies towards naiveté and gullibility have occasionally pronounced that Notre Dame had its course right or was back on track, but they regularly are disappointed. It is little consolation to claim that Notre Dame is much "better" in facing Catholic mission issues than the major Jesuit universities.

I argue that Notre Dame must hold itself to a much higher standard as a Catholic university than contemporary Georgetown. To do so, the university must be prepared to be a Catholic university at its heart, in the center of university life, and not just at the periphery. The debate between these two approaches persists. How the contest is resolved in practice will determine the long-term direction of Notre Dame. Will we merely settle for a Catholic "gloss" on or around Notre Dame? My philosopher colleague Fred Freddoso addressed the essential problem when he described Notre Dame as "a public school in a Catholic neighborhood." If this model prevails, the basilica, the chapels in each dorm, the lady on the dome and in the grotto, and other religious symbols might remain on campus, but the central academic project would not be guided by Catholic principles or by the call of Christ.

Much is at stake in the debate, and I hope and pray that readers will find my perspective and positions to be persuasive. They should also understand why I first entered this debate and something of my commitments and contributions at the university that have influenced my participation in it. I trust the following brief and inevitably incomplete account of my Notre Dame journey provides background for the various articles and talks gathered in this collection. I hope it also sheds some light on the larger Notre Dame story—both its history and its current challenges.

I am a Catholic priest at Notre Dame and a member of the Congregation of Holy Cross. I am also an Australian, a teacher, and a historian. How I came to Notre Dame and have ended up serving there as a priest for almost a quarter century occasionally baffles me. I suspect it occasionally baffles others. I cannot tell my story or reflect on my life without seeing the importance of my nationality and its meaning for me. I am an Australian and proud of it. Dare I admit it that I once had some hopes of influencing Australia directly as a politician or policymaker. This notion was certainly still with me when I first came to Notre Dame to study for my doctorate in history in 1976. I studied American diplomatic history and international relations, moved, as I recall, by some vague notion that I might help determine how Australia should make its way in the world and how it should relate to its "great and powerful friend"—the United States. My choice of American history, nonetheless, still strikes me as a little surprising. I had been interested in Australian history from an early age. But due to a friendship with a teacher, a young American professor, as well as from enjoying and doing well at American history as an undergraduate at the University of Queensland, I left the rich field of Australian history behind and turned to explore American foreign relations in the twentieth century. In retrospect, this was a decisive choice in my life.

I found my time in graduate studies at Notre Dame intellectually stimulating and rather enjoyable, but it did not negate my desire to return to Australia. And that is what I did after completing my dissertation at the end of 1979. I took a position in the Office of National Assessments of the Prime Minister's Department in Canberra, where I tried (and let me emphasize "tried") to analyze developments in American foreign policy for Australian policymakers. This was exciting and challenging work, and yet it did not feel quite right for me. I sensed a deeper call. I had come to Notre Dame in 1976 for an education which would further my career. Instead, I discovered a calling—the vocation to which God summoned me.

I initially chose to come to Notre Dame for my graduate work in history because of the intervention of a Notre Dame professor, my eventual mentor and treasured friend, Vincent P. De Santis, who was in Australia on a Fulbright fellowship. I knew little about the place beyond what he told me. Being a rugby fan, I wasn't all that interested in Notre Dame's fabled football tradition. I already knew that I followed the superior brand of football, one in which such accessories as helmets and pads were not required! Being a practicing Catholic I was somewhat intrigued by the notion of a Catholic university. (Australia at that time had no church-related universities.) But this was not enormously influential in my decision to come to Notre Dame. Truth be told, I came there primarily to get my Ph.D. as quickly as possible and to go home to pursue my career.

While at Notre Dame in the late 1970s, prompted by the example of some of my graduate student friends and my teachers, my own faith life deepened. I became much more conscious of my call to discipleship and of being on a mission as a Christian. I gained a deeper appreciation that authentic living involved making a journey in the Spirit and that to avoid this journey would be only to exist. Indeed it would be a recipe for the spiritual emptiness and general cynicism that I had observed at times among academics in Australia—and, subsequently, observed among some American scholars.

At Notre Dame I began to think of teaching in a different way. I came there imagining that I might someday teach at the university level as a way-station along the road to other more 'significant' possibilities. It was a career path. But at Notre Dame, and specifically within the department of history, I observed and/or studied with an extraordinary group of teacher-scholars who conveyed with their lives that teaching was a special calling.

But more happened at Notre Dame than the deepening of my appreciation for teaching as a vocation. I was guided to an even more distinct calling. At Notre Dame, I had modeled for me, especially by my teacher and now long-time colleague Fr. Thomas Blantz, a way of being a priest—that of the priest/scholar/teacher—that with God's grace brought me back to enter the Congregation of Holy Cross. In August of 1982, after much prayer and thought, I returned to enter Moreau Seminary at Notre Dame. This decision was for me rather gut-wrenching. It involved my separation from family and country. Eventually, as I moved through to ordination as a priest in 1988 and my assignment to teach at Notre Dame, it meant some surrender of my naive but nonetheless real hopes and dreams that I would play some part for the good in the Australian story. It involved some letting go of my claims upon Australia.

Yet despite the seeming strangeness of my decision—"Don't you have seminaries in Australia?" I once was asked—I sensed from the outset of my time in Holy Cross that I was responding to the Lord's call to me. I knew deeply that within this community and its ministry of higher education, I might proclaim the Good News. Subsequently, I grew to appreciate that I exercised my ministry as a priest as part of the larger apostolic effort of my religious order. In the Congregation of Holy Cross I sought to utilize my training as a historian, and whatever my gifts for teaching, as a part of my calling as a priest. I also preached the Word of God, presided over the liturgy, and struggled to build up the community. I tried to listen sympathetically, to counsel intelligently, and to console lovingly. I never saw myself as having a bifurcated calling in which I switched hats from "teacher" at one moment to "priest" at another. My teaching and scholarship from the outset were subsumed within that basic calling.

I was ordained a priest on April 9, 1988, and was assigned (in the words of my religious superior's letter of obedience) "to reside and assist at the University of Notre Dame." I began my teaching with a strong sense that I was engaged upon an evangelical and spiritual work. I knew that I was not only to improve minds but also to shape souls; that I was called to nurture not only the intellectual lives of my students but also their religious and moral lives and, indeed, to aid them in integrating the two. I regret that I have not done this better over my years of teaching, and yet I have been extremely blessed in my teaching ministry at Notre Dame. I possessed certain natural gifts for teaching and worked zealously to develop them. Able students signed up for my courses and, in the main, we drew the best from each other. I was fortunate to have my teaching recognized with awards bearing the names of legendary Notre Dame figures such as Frank O'Malley and Fr. Charles Sheedy, C.S.C. I include my address accepting the Sheedy Award in this volume as it provides some insight into my approach to teaching as a priest.

I exercised my teaching ministry in conjunction with an active pastoral ministry, especially in the residence halls. For a rather brief period I might even have been counted as one of those proverbial "popular young priests" who emerge regularly at Notre Dame. I certainly was asked to give a variety of talks and presentations on campus. These covered a range of topics but I focused especially on the themes of calling my student audiences to live out their vocation as Christian disciples to make a difference in the world. Such themes are certainly evident in the addresses included here which I gave when honored as the senior class fellow in 1992 and when called to offer a charge to the graduating class at their last visit to the Grotto in 1995.

In addition to establishing some kind of decent reputation

for my teaching I worked hard in my initial years as a full-time faculty member to establish some record as a scholar. My efforts reached fruition in 1992 when Princeton University Press published my book *George F. Kennan and the Making of American Foreign Policy, 1947–1950*. This book—still in print and available for purchase!—cast light on the origins of the Cold War and traced how the Truman administration determined the major elements of the American response to the Soviet Union during the crucial postwar years, initiatives such as the Marshall Plan and the North Atlantic Treaty. The book was well received, and it assured my promotion to associate professor with tenure at Notre Dame. A clever academic would have moved quickly to a second major writing project and earned further professional recognition. But by the time the reviews appeared on my book I devoted much of my energies to two other areas to which I judged I was called—the administration of the history department and the broader debate over the Catholic mission and identity of Notre Dame.

I began my service on the faculty of Notre Dame just as the leadership of the university passed from Fr. Theodore Hesburgh to Fr. Edward "Monk" Malloy. I had served as deacon at Monk's inauguration Mass in 1987, and I knew him quite well. His initial years in office coincided with enhanced discussion of Notre Dame's mission as a Catholic university. The promulgation of Pope John Paul II's apostolic constitution on Catholic colleges and universities, *Ex Corde Ecclesiae* (From the Heart of the Church) in August 1990 gave a pointed focus to campus deliberations. Much of this discussion emerged in the debates surrounding the university-wide self study known as *The Colloquy for the Year 2000,* which Fr. Malloy initiated and which did the bulk of its work in 1992. The Colloquy's draft mission statement for the university provoked considerable dispute, most notably over its clear expression (in accord with *Ex Corde Ecclesiae)* that "the Catholic identity of the University depends upon, and is nurtured by, the continuing presence of a predominant number of Catholic intellectuals."

Resistance to this laudable and deeply responsible goal was significant, especially in the College of Arts and Letters. At the time there existed a sizable group of faculty, mainly hired in the 1970s and 1980s, who operated behind the 'cover' of seeking Notre Dame's academic advancement so as to reduce the meaning of Notre Dame's Catholic identity. Many of these faculty members seemed embarrassed by Notre Dame's clear religious mission. They spoke of the importance of Notre Dame following the example of aspirational peers like Northwestern University or Duke University. They implied that Notre Dame's Catholicism prevented the university from realizing its full academic potential. Under the guise of diversity, they argued that Notre Dame should hire the "best" faculty without regard to religious commitment, while hardly tolerating candidates who might contribute to intellectual diversity vis-à-vis their own views. The somewhat superior tone of some of these colleagues barely disguised a deep anti-Catholic disposition.

Capable faculty willing to combat and contest this dangerous force seemed surprisingly few and not well organized. For too long committed faculty had simply expected the university administration to hold the line, but the declining percentage of Catholic faculty over the past decade had revealed the flaw in that tactic. Warnings of impending secularization appeared regularly but prompted little effective response. The historian George Marsden notably clarified the sad process of the de-Christianization of the major Protestant universities and it required little imagination to speculate how far a similar process already had progressed at Catholic universities like Notre Dame. But this speculation hardly led to considered actions to avoid the regrettable course towards agnosticism and non-belief.

In such circumstances in the spring of 1992 four faculty members—two laymen and two priests—gathered for lunch to discuss the worrying situation with the intent of at least doing *something* so as to strengthen the administration's commitment in the colloquy to hold strong on Catholic mission. Craig Lent, a brilliant electrical engineer, and Al Plantinga, a renowned philosopher and devout Protestant, joined Fr. Tim Scully from the Government Department and myself. We agreed that we had to engage and stir faculty concerned with the broad question of Notre Dame's Catholic identity. A larger meeting then followed and so the Conversation on the Catholic Character (of Notre Dame) began. I served as the coordinator of the group, which brought together impressive groups of faculty for serious and lively reflection on Notre Dame's Catholic identity over the following two years.

The deliberations of the colloquy and of the Conversation on Catholic Character (CCC) provided the context for an intervention on my part in February 1993. I distributed a memorandum outlining a series of very practical measures to recruit Catholic faculty in response to the report of the Academic Life Committee of the Colloquy drafted by the then-provost Timothy O'Meara, which I judged to be "far too limited and weak." This document, the first piece included in this volume, was titled "Constructing a Great Catholic University: Some Specific Proposals" but soon became branded as the "Miscamble Memo." It stirred considerable public response, most of which was negative. The most extreme reaction came from noted biology professor George Craig—an expert on mosquitoes—who alleged that I wanted to turn Notre Dame into an equivalent of Bob Jones University and, for rhetorical flourish, asserted that I favored some version of "ethnic cleansing" of non-Catholic faculty. Craig's scurrilous comments were joined by more 'polite' responses which claimed I was merely either intolerant or a Catholic extremist.

Fortunately I had some experience in Labor Party politics in Australia in my undergraduate days and had learned not to be intimidated by mere name-calling. The fevered reaction to the very modest suggestions of my memo nonetheless convinced me of the determination of certain faculty to emasculate Catholicism's role in the academic heart of the university. I resolved to oppose their efforts. I responded vigorously to criticisms and, according to the account provided by Kevin Coyne in his book *Domers*, at a charged meeting of the CCC soon afterward I rejected the notion that my position was extreme. Instead, I assigned the "extremist" label to "those who say that Notre Dame is already too far down the path to secularization to be redeemed." I also claimed a "special responsibility as a member of the [Holy Cross] order to ensure that this place will be Catholic in a meaningful way in ten years' time." That truly is what I sought to do in subsequent years.

I gathered my thoughts about "mission and method" in constructing a great Catholic university in my contribution to *The Challenge and the Promise of a Catholic University*, the volume that Fr. Hesburgh edited in 1994 which collected essays from most of those who had given CCC presentations. My extended essay proved a point of departure for much of my later reflection on the mission and identity of a Catholic university. Here and in talks I gave in the following years at Notre Dame and elsewhere I focused on the crucial matter of faculty hiring. The address I delivered in 1996 on this subject at the University of St. Thomas in Saint Paul, Minnesota, captures my conviction of the central importance of recruiting and retaining faculty supportive of a university's Catholic mission.

My speaking and writing on the subject, however, necessarily took a back seat during the five years I served as chair of the history department in the 1990s. In that capacity I tried to put into practice on a departmental level the broader vision I had for Notre Dame. I sought to recruit faculty—Catholic and non-Catholic alike—who supported the distinct mission of the university. I worked to develop specific departmental academic strengths, which melded well with Notre Dame's Catholic identity, and I tried to keep the cultural studies 'blight' which then was savaging the humanities at bay. The myriad duties of a capable department chair make it one of the more challenging roles in a university but I welcomed the challenge and approached my duties energetically. I argued vigorously for greater resources for the department and pushed the strategy of targeted hires, the process through which the present dean of arts and letters at Notre Dame, John McGreevy, was recruited to return from Harvard to his *alma mater*. My department had received a critical external review in the years before I assumed the reins as chair and I worked with my colleagues to address the legitimate criticisms and to improve both the quality of our undergraduate and graduate programs. Modestly, I claim our endeavors met with genuine success and the department's external profile and general reputation were enhanced.

Whatever my accomplishments as chair of the history department, my tenure proved somewhat contentious. Disagreements occurred mainly over faculty hiring matters where I engaged in forceful argument and brought a certain Australian combativeness to the departmental deliberations. Perhaps I should have simply sought to placate my critics and occasional opponents in the department but acquiescence and appeasement on important matters did not come easily to me. I thought faculty hiring a very important matter and still do as a number of the more recent pieces included in this collection make clear.

My forceful efforts as history department chair clarified for anyone interested that I was not cut from the cloth of those, such as the liberal administrators of Georgetown University at the time, who proved content with a kind of Catholic gloss upon or patina surrounding Catholic higher education. My strong Catholic commitments also emerged publicly in a critical essay I published in the *Notre Dame Magazine* in 1993 entitled "The Tragedy of Mario Cuomo" which ripped the liberal Catholic icon's deeply flawed position on the crucial moral issue of abortion. I increasingly saw my liberal Catholic colleagues at Notre Dame such as Fr. Dick McBrien, with whom I had sparred during a purgatorial term I spent on the faculty senate, as unwilling to truly build a robust Catholic university along the model called for in *Ex Corde Ecclesiae*. Instead, they seemed obsessed with criticizing Pope John Paul II and with accommodating a broad culture which seemed increasingly anti-Christian (they always seemed to welcome an approving mention in the *New York Times*!) while neglecting the real issues that confronted Notre Dame.

My own regard for the Polish pope had always been high, especially in light of his impressive challenge to Soviet power through the 1980s and his role in overcoming communism and bringing the Cold War to an end. But it only grew in the 1990s, and I found myself inspired by the pope's powerful call for a New Evangelization. His faith, and courage and manliness served to encourage me. I also saw myself as guided by his call for renewal of Catholic higher education in *Ex Corde Ecclesiae* and never wavered in my conviction that I was living out my proper call as a priest in the Congregation of Holy Cross through my efforts to defend and enhance the Catholic identity of Notre Dame and to ensure that its profound bond to the institutional church remained strong.

Of course not all members of the ND community greeted my efforts warmly. This was made patently clear in 1997 when Nathan Hatch, by then provost of Notre Dame, kindly explained to me that I could not be seriously considered for the deanship of the college of arts and letters because my appointment would spark too much faculty opposition. My Catholic commitments, determination to act on them, and forceful personality even caused some "fear," he suggested. I recall responding that these attributes were my strongest qualifications for the position and were needed in any person who would truly lead the college well, but the decision had been made.

I confess that missing out on that position at that time caused me real disappointment. I truly wanted to follow in the footsteps of my Holy Cross forebear, Charlie Sheedy. Yet, I sensed that the upper administration of Notre Dame wanted to 'finesse' the so-called "Catholic question" but not to confront the matter head on as I knew it must be. Fortunately I possessed a certain resilience and perspective—a gift from my working class parents—and I quickly recalibrated. I resolved to re-engage my scholarly work and sought a sabbatical to work on a book exploring the meaning of the transition from Franklin Roosevelt to Harry Truman for the end of World War II and the onset of the Cold War. I planned to spend the 1998–1999 academic year at

Yale but instead, following upon the request of my Holy Cross provincial, I moved less than a mile across St. Joseph Lake to Moreau Seminary, hoping to write but also instructed to assist in the formation program there.

I did do some writing at the seminary, although not what I had planned. As I was drawn more fully into service there I put my history notes aside while completing my collection *Keeping the Faith, Making a Difference*, which challenged young Catholics to view the world through the lens of faith. I also edited and introduced *Go Forth and Do Good*—a selection of memorable Notre Dame commencement addresses—which I hoped might inspire contemporary readers to live out their Christian callings in the world. I had expected to serve a limited and supportive role at Moreau Seminary, but due to various personnel issues I was eventually asked to serve as rector of this principal formation site of the Holy Cross order in North America.

These were challenging years. I set out in 2000 intent on leading my small but dedicated seminary staff to assist the seminarians to discern well their call and to provide them with good training so that they might become zealous agents of the New Evangelization. I wanted them well equipped to proclaim the Gospel to an increasingly secular world and ready to join the veritable struggle for the world's soul by preaching Christ, yesterday, today, and forever. I was truly blessed to have some wonderful seminarians within my care during those early years of the new century. I tried to offer them support and encouragement as the sickening details of clergy sexual abuse as well as the subsequent mishandling and cover-ups by certain church officials became public. I recognize all too well the limits of my efforts, and yet I hope that the good men whom I served as a mentor and who moved on to ordination to the priesthood will play a notable role in renewing religious life in Holy Cross and also in enhancing the order's contribution to the Catholic mission of Notre Dame. I have included in this volume some pieces related to priesthood and to the Congregation of Holy Cross. Careful readers will understand how in important ways the topics addressed in these essays relate to the ultimate well-being of Notre Dame for the Holy Cross order must play a key role in preserving and enhancing the university's religious identity.

In 2004–2005 I eventually did spend a sabbatical at Yale and returned to my historical research and writing which eventually resulted in the publication of *From Roosevelt to Truman: Potsdam, Hiroshima and the Cold War* by Cambridge University Press in 2007. By the time the book appeared I had returned to my full-time teaching at Notre Dame. I resumed it with relish and with a most gratifying student response. I also picked up my efforts to engage students in various forums beyond the classroom as is evident in some of the pieces published here.

By this point Fr. John Jenkins had replaced Monk Malloy as president of the university. I had been tangentially involved in the rather farcical pre-determined "evaluation/search process" that ended Monk Malloy's tenure as president and selected John Jenkins. The poor state of the football program and Malloy's refusal to fire Notre Dame's first African-American football coach, Tyrone Willingham, evidently offended some of the oligarchy that controlled the board of trustees at the time. Anyway, they terminated Malloy and selected Jenkins.

John Jenkins inquired if I would serve as a vice president in his administration, but I quietly declined. I was not at all confident that John was resolved to take the courageous steps necessary to truly secure Notre Dame's Catholic identity. I feared that he might try to 'finesse' this central issue in the manner of past administrations, and I recognized that I could not participate easily in such a questionable approach. It would be better for me to contribute again as a Holy Cross priest/scholar/teacher in the history department and to support Notre Dame's Catholic mission by assisting the work of such lively entities as the Notre Dame Center for Ethics and Culture, which my philosopher colleague David Solomon founded in 1999. From this position in the faculty ranks I continued to raise my concerns on crucial issues like faculty hiring and the increasing corporate trend at Notre Dame, including in essays published in the Jesuit periodical *America,* as the contributions in the second part of this book reveal.

While my expectations for John Jenkins' presidency had not been especially high, I had not thought it likely that he would take actions that markedly damaged Notre Dame's reputation as a Catholic university. Surprisingly, he took a number of controversial decisions that did exactly that. In his first year he retreated from assurances given prior to his formally taking office that he would cancel performances of *The Vagina Monologues,* a play which directly attacked sound Catholic sexual ethics. Undoubtedly the worst was his decision to honor President Barack Obama at the 2009 commencement, despite the president's fulsome pro-abortion record and his undisguised determination to extend the abortion regime in the United States and beyond. Compelled to oppose such decisions, I spoke at the terrific rally protesting the honoring of President Obama that the courageous students of NDResponse organized on the university's south quad on commencement day in May of 2009. That speech and related efforts on this and other matters are included in this volume. My criticisms cast light on some of the more turbulent and contentious episodes at Notre Dame over the past decade.

My direct and public criticisms earned me a certain opprobrium in the Notre Dame community, including from some of the more liberal (and usually older) members of the Holy Cross order. Happily, my views received a more sympathetic reception from the younger members. The more recently ordained Holy Cross religious, a number of whom had passed through Moreau Seminary during my rectorship, belonged to the so-called "JP II" generation. They saw clearly what was at stake and refused to engage in denial and obfuscation regarding actions that damaged Notre Dame's relationship with the Church from whose very heart it was called to operate. Many of their older confreres held a different ecclesial outlook, and some among them seemed largely unconcerned with the pro-life cause to which I gave increased attention. I regret the distancing in relations with some community members with whom I worked shoulder to shoulder for two decades but it has been a modest cross to bear. It would have been much more painful to bear the guilt of not speaking out against actions that so hurt Notre Dame's Catholic mission and reputation and, incidentally, which offended so many loyal alumni. From the days of St. Paul there has been a place for holy conflict in Christian communities, and, dare I say, I increasingly was drawn to and inspired by the great saint.

The regrettable and avoidable missteps of the Jenkins presidency accompanied a larger failure to address effectively the primary issue facing the university. This, unquestionably, was the need to fulfill the university mission statement's clear call for a preponderance of committed Catholic faculty. The administration struggled to keep the number of nominal Catholic faculty above the fifty percent mark but appeared content with this rather misleading measure, which included substantial numbers of non-practicing and dissenting faculty members. Given their refusal to face the faculty problem honestly, it was hardly surprising that the administration would not address related key areas such as the content of curriculum.

Sadly, the Jenkins presidency lacked a "true north" to guide it and thus it proved vulnerable to faculty pressures and to an excessive concern for rankings and with aping our so-called "preferred peer" schools. While the negative publicity and serious criticism of Notre Dame by members of the hierarchy generated by the Obama affair prompted various remedial actions by the university, these measures carried the quality of a public relations campaign in damage limitation mode. The painful experience of 2009 hardly led Notre Dame to recapture its true and best communal self, as the appointment in 2011 of a trustee who had donated generously to pro-abortion organizations confirmed. I described this situation in the lengthy interview included here with Catholic journalist Kathryn Lopez, published in the *National Catholic Register* online in 2011.

The more recent and commendable action of Notre Dame in joining a number of Catholic dioceses and institutions in suing the Obama administration over its harmful implementation of the Department of Health and Human Services mandate on contraception, abortifacients, and sterilization is certainly a positive development, but of itself it does not change the essential dynamics on the campus. We can only pray that it is a harbinger of a more serious effort to secure Notre Dame's Catholic identity and that it will be followed by further resolute actions to use the university's influence to promote the common good, even in countercultural ways. Much needs to be done, as will be apparent to fair-minded readers who work through the following pages to my conclusion.

In the interview I gave to Kathryn Lopez I spoke to my own love for Notre Dame and to the important role it can play in the Catholic Church in the United States. I trust this love and hope for Notre Dame is evident in all the pages that follow. The four Notre Dame scholars—two philosophers and two historians—to whom I pay tribute in the final section of the book all helped deepen my love for and commitment to Notre Dame. I am grateful to them and others who have supported me on my journey thus far. In various ways they have guided and encouraged me neither to relent nor to retreat but to continue my work for Notre Dame.

# Part I
# The 1990's:
# Initial Positions and Arguments

# Section I: Matters Academic

## Constructing a Great Catholic University:
## Some Specific Proposals [The "Miscamble Memo"]
## 1993

*This initial foray into the debate over the Catholic identity and mission of Notre Dame was written in response to recommendations included in the report of the Academic Life Committee of the Colloquy for the Year 2000. I judged this committee's recommendations as quite insufficient and called attention to their limits. I also offered some specific suggestions regarding faculty hiring and the training of a new generation of Catholic scholars.*

### A Great Catholic University

At an early meeting of the Conversation on the Catholic Character group, Charles Wilber of the Department of Economics expressed his belief that the world did not need another Duke or Northwestern. But, he argued, "it does need a Notre Dame that is truly great in its own way." He continued, "It is its Catholic character that makes Notre Dame unique. The 'great quest' is to build a *Catholic* university—for which there are no blueprints. To simply copy the great secular universities is to abandon the quest."

Wilber's comments, emphasizing both the distinctive character of Notre Dame and the fact that there are no well-defined blueprints to guide our future course, have been repeated in one form or another by a number of recent reports and commentaries. Nathan Hatch, Vice President for Advanced Studies, surely alludes to this in a section of the provost's recent report, "Notre Dame's Quiet Revolution," entitled "Cutting Against the

Grain" where he notes that "Notre Dame's experiment in building a university of sterling quality and revitalizing Catholic intellectual life is far from complete. To realize these dreams will require renewed commitment, enormous resources, and willingness to hew an independent course." In regard to the latter he observes that "at a time of wide divorce between the academy and the church, Notre Dame intends to frame a university both authentically Catholic and accountable to the highest standards of scholarship."

The draft report of the Committee on Academic Life of the Colloquy for the Year 2000 [a university-wide self-study carried out by committees composed of faculty, staff, and students and overseen by then-president Rev. Edward A. Malloy, who submitted its final report to the university trustees in May of 1993] expresses the "Wilber view" directly. In the section entitled "The Faculty and the Intellectual Life of the University," the report states clearly: "What we intend has no exact models: to be a great university, without conceding that professionalization and insistence on quality inevitably entail secularization, which has been the experience of numerous American universities in the twentieth century; to be a great Catholic university, without conceding that allegiance to a religious identity is possible only at the level of a strictly sectarian college."

This goal to be a "great Catholic university" is thoroughly appropriate. To build Notre Dame into such an institution must be our "great quest," as Chuck Wilber puts it. The difficult issues emerge when one confronts the question of how it is to be done.

### The Academic Life Committee Report

The Academic Life Committee outlined a number of laudable objectives to achieve the great goal. Fundamental among these were attracting faculty committed to the objective and constructing an intellectual community informed by "Christian learning generally and the Catholic tradition more particularly." Responsibility for forging such a community was laid upon the academic leadership of the university and the faculty. After outlining these goals the committee report stated, "It is clear, in short, that if Notre Dame is to remain a Catholic university, committed Catholics must predominate, providing open-minded and creative intellectual leadership."

The report goes on to make a number of sensible recommendations, among them the energetic efforts by departments to hire those who would contribute to the life of a dynamic Catholic university; support for Congregation of the Holy Cross academic appointments; a faculty orientation program; the development of certain "centers of strength" which connect explicitly with Catholic intellectual life; and the requirement that each department of the university "conceive a plan, to be reviewed at the collegiate level, which reflects on its purpose within the overall mission of the University."

When a draft of the Academic Life Committee Report (ALCR) was presented to the committee of the whole by the provost, he acknowledged (according to the minutes) "vigorous debate on the Catholic identity issue [within the Academic Life Committee] but said the draft document was a unanimous one." Further, according to the minutes, the provost "noted that the draft report's discussion on the role of the faculty in maintaining the Catholic character of the University reflects similar thoughts in the COUP and PACE reports, [earlier university self-study and strategic planning documents] but goes further in that it mandates departments to state their roles 'in contributing to the animation of Catholic intellectual life.'" In effect, however, the provost admitted that the comments on the Catholic character question essentially restated the laudable goals from COUP and PACE. In the same discussion (although it is not recorded in the minutes) the provost also stated his view that this was the last major chance to "get this right." He observed, with some concern, that if this question wasn't addressed successfully now it probably would not be a matter for serious discussion in ten years' time. Notre Dame would have marched too far down the road to secularization to turn back.

*Strengthening the Academic Life Committee Report*

In light of the provost's concerns, which are confirmed by the seeming refusal of some departments to act effectively upon the rhetorical exhortations of such reports as COUP and PACE, the recommendations of the ALCR seem far too limited and weak. They will not suffice to ensure that Notre Dame preserves and enhances its Catholic commitment as it becomes a great university. Further measures are needed.

In considering the measures outlined below, the assertion of the Academic Life Committee that "there are no exact models" must be taken with the utmost seriousness. Notre Dame cannot simply continue on a "business as usual" course nor can it simply ape the procedures of the secular universities. A variety of specific measures, both large and small, must be undertaken immediately. Many of them relate to procedures for hiring of new faculty.

The leadership of the university must articulate forcefully the essential goal outlined in the report and clarify that this makes us a place different than other universities. Only if this is well understood by everyone can the following recommendations be effectively implemented.

*Recommendations on Faculty Hiring*

Notre Dame's efforts in the area of faculty hiring over the last decade have produced very mixed results. There is a clear need for procedures to be adopted for use by all departments to guarantee that the broad mission of the university is taken into account in the initial hiring process. These might include the following changes.

In all job advertisements, Notre Dame's Catholic identity should be noted and some indication given that Notre Dame seeks to employ scholars who will contribute to the intellectual community we seek to create here.

After an application is received by a relevant department, it should be acknowledged in the normal manner and the applicant sent some brief materials outlining the nature of Notre

Dame and the expectations for faculty who teach here. (This might include the mission statement or materials from the initial part of the ALCR.) An applicant might be asked to consider how he/she would contribute to this intellectual community, as well as advised that this matter will be raised in the interview stage.

At interviews this matter should be raised explicitly and without defensiveness. The candidate should be asked to discuss how he/she would contribute to Notre Dame's Catholic mission. The information gleaned from such interviews must be a formal part of the relevant Committee on Appointment and Promotions (CAP) deliberations regarding which candidate to select. It should be written up by the chair in a report which would be forwarded to the dean of the college and the provost. The dean and the provost would take this information into account in approving the appointment. (It is clear that we must move beyond "ticking a box" on the faculty questionnaire form in this regard.)

The existing program to orient new faculty to Notre Dame must be developed further. In this regard, additional meetings with new faculty might be scheduled after the first semester. (This position is supported in the ALCR.)

The ALCR presently recommends that "the University must also be prepared to authorize and fund hiring beyond the beginning ranks when outstanding scholars become available." This should be acted upon. Departments should aggressively identify scholars committed to Catholic education and attract them to Notre Dame. The ALCR rightly puts important responsibility for this matter on the department chairs and the deans. It should be made clear to those who would take on these offices that this question will be an important one used to assess their performance.

Each year following upon the departmental committee elections, the president and the provost should meet with the department chairs and all CAP members, by college, to remind them of the seriousness with which the university regards this matter and to answer any questions committee members might have concerning it. At least in the initial stages as the general "culture" on hiring changes at Notre Dame, it might be worthwhile to arrange for presentations by "units" within the university which have a good track record on this matter. It should be made very clear to departments that performance in this area will be considered as a factor in the determination of the distribution of resources, especially as regards faculty appointments.

The provost should prepare an annual report on the question of faculty hiring and the Catholic character of Notre Dame for presentation to the president, the board of trustees, and especially to the fellows of the university who, after all, are charged as part of their formal duties with maintenance of "the essential character of the University as a Catholic institution of higher learning."

### Training the Next Generation of Catholic Scholars

The above recommendations have concentrated on direct faculty hiring. (They are primarily matters of procedure requiring a change of mind and heart without any significant expenditure.) This hiring matter is of fundamental importance and must be quickly addressed, but it is not the only issue that needs attention. Other initiatives are needed and some of them require substantial resources.

All departments should reflect on their contribution to the Catholic identity and mission of Notre Dame. How does the Catholic character of the university affect areas for concentration and plans for future development? (Clearly this has greater relevance for some departments than others.)

In the admission and training of graduate students, faculty should be concerned about training the "next generation" of Catholic/Christian scholars. Notre Dame is presently one of several universities assisting in the Lilly Fellows Program in the Humanities and the Arts at Valparaiso University. This is a "fellowship program for young scholars to renew and deepen their sense of vocation within a Christian community of learning."

The two-year fellowships are designed for those preparing for leadership roles in teaching and administration in institutions of Christian higher education.

We must have a similar program based here aimed at attracting young scholars who wish to teach in institutions of Catholic/Christian higher learning. These post-doctoral fellows would provide a healthy recruiting ground for Notre Dame. We should take the best of them but the others would hopefully be well prepared to serve in other Catholic institutions. These folk also would help animate intellectual life at the university. [At least in the humanities they would be expected to do some teaching as part of their post-doc, as modeled in the program at Valparaiso; this might also help us somewhat in the teaching/class size issue.] This is an important initiative. Too often we hear the phrase "there just aren't any Catholics out there" but this program will bring them to us.

Notre Dame—for all its limitations—has a generally–recognized preeminence in American Catholic higher education. It should assume this role more forcefully and seek to aid other institutions in either reclaiming or enhancing their Catholic identities. We need to establish some kind of institute to oversee this task. It must be well-funded and led by a person of academic prestige.

This institute should take on a number of functions, perhaps including the following: foster discussion of the Catholic character of Notre Dame and facilitate meetings across departmental and college boundaries; organize for outside speakers to come to this campus to address issues related to Catholic higher education; organize an annual symposium bringing together Catholic intellectuals and thinkers from across the country and beyond to address issues related to Catholic universities. Such an institute could serve as a clearinghouse for young Catholic scholars seeking positions and for Catholic colleges and universities seeking to make appointments to their faculties. It should seek to arrange for training programs and internships for administrators of Catholic colleges and universities to better prepare them to undertake their distinctive responsibilities. It should play an advisory role for other Catholic institutions.

Finally, this institute might be Notre Dame's vehicle to encourage the development of other institutions of Catholic higher learning elsewhere in the United States and the world. (It might seem inappropriate to be undertaking to advise and encourage others but the experience of teaching suggests that when you have to explain something to others you learn it especially well yourself. Notre Dame has much to learn but we can do it while helping others.)

Serious consideration and adoption of measures such as these seem essential if Notre Dame's rhetoric of "great *Catholic* university" is to be made real. Talk, as they say, is cheap. Now is the time to act.

## Meeting the Challenge and Fulfilling the Promise: Mission and Method in Constructing a Great Catholic University 1994

*All the discussion on campus growing out of the Colloquy 2000 deliberations, especially the disputes over the mission statement and the arguments about faculty hiring, prompted a number of responses. President Emeritus Theodore M. Hesburgh believed it would be constructive to gather together reflections from a number of faculty who had dedicated their lives to the development of a Catholic university. He invited a notable group of Notre Dame faculty to reflect on the character and mission of Catholic universities at the end of the twentieth century. These reflections were then gathered into a book edited by Fr. Hesburgh, entitled* The Challenge and Promise of a Catholic University, *which the University of Notre Dame Press published in 1994. My own contribution to that volume is included below.*

*In retrospect, my essay was overly optimistic about certain matters, such as the resolve of the fellows and trustees at Notre Dame to address the issues surrounding Catholic identity. Sadly, their performance has been rather ineffective and at times cowardly. The essay is built upon the recommendations regarding faculty hiring that I had outlined in the so-called "Miscamble Memo." This piece sets the faculty issue within a broader discussion of Catholic higher education and aims to engage a larger audience.*

In 1968 Christopher Jencks and David Riesman published *The Academic Revolution*, their influential study of American higher education, in which they described the "Harvard-Berkeley model" of the research university as the academic pace-setter. When examining Catholic universities, they observed that "the important question" was not "whether a few Catholic universities prove capable of competing with Harvard and Berkeley on the latter's terms, but whether Catholicism can provide an ideology or personnel for developing alternatives to the Harvard-Berkeley model of excellence." They speculated, with some prescience, that "the ablest Catholic educators will feel obliged to put most of their energies into proving that Catholics can beat non-Catholics at the latter's game. But," they noted, "having proved this, a few may be able to do something more." Throwing down a gauntlet of sorts before Catholic educators, they asserted that "there is as yet no American Catholic University that manages to fuse academic professionalism with concern for questions of ultimate social and moral importance" and challenged Catholics to make "this distinctive contribution to the over-all academic system."[1]

It would be satisfying to report that in the ensuing quarter century a number of Catholic institutions have met the challenge put forth by Jencks and Riesman and that flourishing Catholic universities now exist that are committed to the pursuit of their distinct mission in American higher education. Alas, this is not the case. For many Catholic institutions, the past two decades have witnessed a substantial diminution of their Catholic identity. Sadly, some of the oldest and most respected Catholic schools

1    Christopher Jencks and David Riesman, *The Academic Revolution* (Garden City, N.Y.: Doubleday, 1968), 405.

are well–advanced down a path to secularization similar to the one traveled by Protestant institutions of higher learning like Duke and Vanderbilt, a path which my distinguished colleague, George Marsden, has described so well.[2] The rapaciousness of the forces for secularization—made all the more so by their complexity and subtle allure—leads to predictions of their effective triumph in the major Catholic institutions. Vestiges of Catholic identity might remain in campus ministry, residential life, or in the supposed influence of a particular religious order's tradition, but the central academic project will simply ape the "Harvard-Berkeley model." Faculties will be dominated by those who have no interest in, or allegiance to, the Catholic mission of the institutions, and who, in fact, might be deeply hostile to it.

One might undertake a *tour d'horizon* of Catholic universities and speculate on which ones have passed a virtual point of no return and are marching inexorably to complete secularization, but such an undertaking would serve no good end here. It suffices to say that no Catholic institution—neither Notre Dame nor any other—has cause for complacency about its own situation. Nor can any institution take a back-handed pleasure that another has advanced further along a secularist path. Indeed, Catholic institutions need to cooperate more effectively to support, encourage, and challenge each other. Nonetheless, there is in Catholic higher education today a "dividing line," as Peter Steinfels has put it, "between those institutions determined to face these questions [regarding secularization] and those who prefer to avoid them, proceeding with a calculated ambiguity or by simple default."[3]

The University of Notre Dame, I am thankful to say, is an institution at which the questions regarding Catholic identity and mission are still posed, whatever the limitations of the institution in settling and acting upon answers. Admittedly, facing

2    See George Marsden's *The Soul of the American University* (New York: Oxford University Press, 1994).

3    Peter Steinfels, commencement address, Fordham University, May 22, 1993, as reported in the *New York Times*, May 23, 1993.

these questions honestly is not the easiest of tasks, and the temptation to gloss over crucial issues has not always been avoided. But at Notre Dame, men and women have wrestled, at times with some intensity, with the questions and issues involved in becoming a notable Catholic university.

I merely watched this discussion as an interested observer during my time here as a doctoral student in history in the late 1970's. However, my direct involvement in the discussion has increased steadily from the mid-eighties as a seminarian in the Holy Cross order and student in the theology department to the present time, when I serve as a priest-teacher and scholar in the department of history. I understand it as part of my vocation and responsibility as a priest of Notre Dame's founding religious order to contribute to this debate and to aid in strengthening Notre Dame as a Catholic university. If God and my provincial are willing, I hope to be about this undertaking for years to come. Fortunately, this will not be a lonely work. My own involvement in the conversation on these matters at Notre Dame has revealed to me colleagues—Catholics and non-Catholics alike—who are eager for Notre Dame to fulfill its true promise as a Catholic university and to reject the easy temptation of the secularism that characterizes most American universities. They, like me, want Notre Dame to pursue its distinct mission, to avoid the essential uniformity accepted by most American private and public universities, and to contribute notably to American higher education, the Church, and society at large.

The task will not be easy but Notre Dame has some distinct advantages in its pursuit: the strong resolve of its fellows and trustees; the continuing involvement and commitment of its founding religious order; the loyalty and support of its alumni and friends; the appeal of the university to Catholic parents and students; the faith of Notre Dame's students; the special place of Notre Dame in American Catholicism; the enduring vision of Theodore M. Hesburgh, C.S.C., calling Notre Dame forth to be a truly great Catholic institution; the commitment of faculty members dedicated to the undertaking; the resources of the rich, if somewhat neglected, Catholic intellectual tradition; and the recognition that emphasis on subjects appropriate to a Catholic university means no tempering of academic excellence but instead an opportunity to achieve real intellectual distinction. (Notre Dame's focus on the philosophy of religion and on American religious history demonstrates this last point.) The very existence of these elements has given Notre Dame a special opportunity and responsibility to meet the Jencks-Riesman challenge and, in the process, to blaze a trail for other religious institutions of higher learning. Indeed, the times demand that Notre Dame thoroughly reject the timid and unimaginative path to secularization and pursue its authentic development as a Catholic university.

## *The Great Need*

It is a curious and ironic reality that some of the significant features of contemporary society and academe simultaneously present formidable obstacles to the development of Catholic universities yet reveal the desperate need for just such institutions. This is not the place to take the pulse of this society or its academic world in any detail, but a brief excursion will reveal both the necessity of Notre Dame's fulfilling its promise and its potential contribution to the world beyond its beautiful campus.

A mere recitation of the serious problems which confront our society makes for depressing reading—social disintegration and the dissolution of the family structure; rampant individualism and the decline of community; the drug, violence, and death culture; the pervasiveness of crime, alienation, and isolation; the breakdown of moral standards; materialism; limited confidence in government, and so forth. Such realities have prompted President Clinton, no less, to decry "the great crisis of the spirit that is gripping America." A Catholic university, which is concerned with questions of ultimate social and moral importance, will address such questions authentically. It will be able to diagnose more clearly the true nature of societal ills and to prescribe appropriate remedies without the restrictions which secular institutions place upon themselves. It might address the full

needs of men and women, both material and spiritual, by inject-
ing moral and religiously–grounded viewpoints into the public
square. It will speak to the development of a more just and moral
society.

The American academy is enormous, and secular research
universities, which set the direction for the whole enterprise,
have many strengths, especially in their research achievements.[4]
Major American universities benefited enormously from the
beneficence of the federal government in the Cold War era.
Large-scale collaboration between government and science and
the development of a military/industrial/academic complex (as
exemplified by an institution like MIT) helped power the great
achievements of American science and technology. American
universities also became the location for much of the nation's
intellectual life and the source of many of the ideas and proposals, both good and ill,that influenced the society. The important
place of universities in the society could hardly be contested.

Acknowledging their influence and enormous technical
accomplishments is not to deny that American universities are
beset by substantial problems. They are for the most part fragmented entities, lacking an intellectual coherence or sense of
unity and given to moral relativism and postmodern intellectual fads in which truth becomes a mere expression of power. And,
as George Marsden has argued persuasively, they "have jetti-
soned the most important of human concerns."[5] A genuine
Catholic university, with its conceptions of universal truths and
the unity of knowledge, along with its willingness to accord theological and philosophical investigations a central place, holds
out hope both of overcoming this debilitating intellectual fragmentation and examining seriously the most fundamental
moral, social, and religious issues.

4   For a good statement of the strengths in the best secular schools,
    see Jaroslav Pelikan, *The Idea of the University: A Reexamination*
    (New Haven: Yale University Press, 1992).
5   See George Marsden, "Christian Schooling: Beyond the
    Multiversity," *Christian Century*, October 7, 1992, 875.

The challenges set forth in the preceding paragraphs are much more easily outlined than met. This is especially so because we live in a time, as the liberal Yale Law School professor Stephen L. Carter recently pointed out, when the elite culture—that which dominates the national news media, policy making, the courts, and the universities—is programmed to trivialize religion.[6] Other astute observers would portray the elite as more profoundly and explicitly hostile to religion.[7] Whatever the case may be, a Catholic university cannot necessarily expect a friendly reception because its very existence, if authentic, represents an implicit critique of the intellectual presuppositions of this highly secularized elite culture. So be it. We must be aware of this situation and yet avoid a defensiveness which limits our engagement with the academy and the society at large. And, if Notre Dame pursues its course with integrity, we may be surprised at the friends and admirers located in other institutions and sectors of society who cheer for us because they recognize the importance of our venture and the need for a renewed participation by Christianity in this nation's public and intellectual discourse.

## A Mission Renewed

Most Catholic universities have mission statements of one sort or another. For the most part they are harmless and little-read documents, although each should encapsulate its university's purpose and commitments. Some Catholic universities, perhaps reflecting their approach of calculated ambiguity, have adopted increasingly tepid statements such that the astute Jesuit theologian, Michael Buckley, has observed that "the very vagueness of language and the indeterminacy of the general commitments leave one with the sense that the decline in some Catholic institutions may be already advanced, that the conjunction

6   Stephen L. Carter, *The Culture of Disbelief* (New York: Basic Books, 1993). Subtitle not necessary.
7   See Richard John Neuhaus, *The Naked Public Square: Religion and Democracy in America* (Grand Rapids, Mich.: Eerdman's, 1984).

between a vibrant Catholicism and these universities seems increasingly faint, that the vision is fading."[8] A clear statement of mission and purpose is essential, however, if a Catholic university is to hew its distinct course rather than follow meekly in the wake of the "Harvard-Berkeley model."

The final report of the Colloquy for the Year 2000, submitted by Notre Dame's president, Edward A. Malloy, C.S.C., to the trustees of the university in May of 1993, contained a mission statement for the university which, whatever its other limitations, was not received as tepid. It described Notre Dame as "a Catholic academic community of higher learning . . . dedicated to the pursuit and sharing of truth for its own sake" and set forth as one of its goals the provision of "a forum where through free inquiry and open discussion the various lines of Catholic thought may intersect with all the forms of knowledge found in the arts, sciences, professions, and every other area of human scholarship and creativity."[9] If the mission statement had been limited to such general goals, it might have been benignly received and quickly shelved. But it went further and outlined some practical requirements deemed essential to achieving these goals. Specifically, it stated that "the Catholic identity of the University depends upon, and is nurtured by, the continuing presence of a predominant number of Catholic intellectuals" and it asked that all faculty—both Catholics and non-Catholics—respect the university's objectives and willingly enter into "the conversation that gives it life and meaning." These statements gave some sense that the overall mission statement might be more than mere words.

These more practical objectives have prompted debate. The revelation that the mission of the university might have implications for matters such as faculty hiring provoked a negative reaction among certain faculty members, who gave evidence of

8    Michael J. Buckley, "The Catholic University and Its Inherent Promise," *America*, May 29, 1993, 14.
9    Edward A. Malloy, C.S.C., Colloquy for the Year 2000, Final Report, May 7, 1993, in *Notre Dame Report*, June 18, 1993.

being embarrassed to be part of a Catholic university which takes its commitments seriously. Such individuals apparently assumed, perhaps as a result of confusing earlier signals from the university administration, that Notre Dame would maintain at most a calculated ambiguity towards its Catholic identity.

The debate at Notre Dame over the mission statement, and especially over the matters of faculty commitment and faculty hiring, has for the most part been healthy. The issue was at least raised to what John Courtney Murray termed "the level of disagreement." The debate over the mission statement, however, revealed that while this document serves as a statement of intention and a guidepost of sorts, it still needs to be fully owned and internalized. Commitment to the mission of the university will be essential for Notre Dame to fulfill its real promise. Only when the mission has been successfully embodied in its central components will the identity of a Catholic university be firmly established. This is why the leadership of the university must forcefully articulate the essential and distinctive goals of the university. The vision of Notre Dame as a great Catholic university must capture the loyalty of all its elements. The religious character of the institution should come as no surprise to any who would study or teach here. Indeed, it should influence the decisions of all, from freshman students to endowed chairholders, who seek to enter this intellectual community.

## Theory and Practice

Preparing a mission statement is relatively easy compared to the task of implementing it in the life of the university. It is in this area of implementation—of devising strategies which answer the question, "How?," that Catholic universities have been especially confused and weak in recent years. Reasons for this situation are not hard to identify. Since the collapse of the neoscholastic synthesis in the 1960's, no overarching theory has emerged to replace it as a source for intellectual coherence for Catholic universities and as a method for faith and reason to engage.[10] Catholic universities have manifested rather poorly the unity and integration of knowledge claimed in their self-definitions.

The story of this intellectual failure is undoubtedly a complex one, but surely it can be attributed in part to the failure of contemporary theology to serve the Catholic university well. Pope John Paul II's apostolic constitution on Catholic universities, *Ex Corde Ecclesiae*, accords theology "a particularly important role in the search for a synthesis of knowledge as well as in the dialogue between faith and reason." Theology is called to serve "all other disciplines in their search for meaning, not only by helping them investigate how their discoveries will affect individuals and society, but also by bringing a perspective and an orientation not contained within their own methodologies." But, if Notre Dame is any guide, theology has assumed a rather insular posture within the Catholic university. It operates rather like any other discipline and contributes little to intellectual synthesis or integration. The fundamentally incarnational and sacramental nature of Catholic theology is occasionally mentioned but is rarely explicated effectively by theologians in a way that a physicist or architect or historian would note or care about. I hasten to add that the cupboard is not completely bare, however. In sharp contrast to the relative barrenness of theology stands the Catholic philosopher Alasdair MacIntyre, whose provocative argument that all universities teach out of a particular intellectual tradition and whose powerful presentation of the Thomist mode of inquiry provides much fuel for reflection for serious Catholic universities.[11]

10  On this, see Philip Gleason's *Keeping the Faith: American Catholicism Past and Present* (Notre Dame, Ind.: University of Notre Dame Press, 1987); and Gleason's essay "American Catholic Higher Education, 1940–1990: The Ideological Context," in *The Secularization of the Academy*, ed. George M. Marsden and Bradley Longfield (New York: Oxford University Press, 1992).

11  Alasdair MacIntyre, *Three Rival Versions of Moral Enquiry: Encyclopaedia, Genealogy and Tradition* (Notre Dame, Ind.: University of Notre Dame Press, 1990).

The present absence of an overarching synthesis to serve as detailed guide for Catholic universities need not paralyze us. There is no need to wait for a great architect to come along to provide specific plans and instructions for building the structure of a Catholic university. The university is a living entity and an evolving one. Fortunately, if the appropriate and willing on-site artisans can be assembled and can converse and cooperate, they can build on the established foundations and fashion in remarkable ways an educational institution prepared to face ultimate social and religious questions. In this sense, willing faculty contributors in the venture are an essential component. They can compensate effectively, if you will, for the absence of a guiding theory. With the guidance of the Spirit, their discussion and debate—their conversation—will aid in forging a new synthesis. For this reason Notre Dame must enlist men and women willing to commit their lives to the undertaking. Recruiting and retaining such a faculty is the most important task which Notre Dame faces at present.

### Faculty Hiring: The Crucial Issue

The faculty is located at the heart of a university. When a faculty is hostile to the mission of the institution, its attenuation is likely. When a faculty is passive, the mission is likely to be anemic. When a faculty is committed, there is every likelihood that the mission will be fulfilled.[12] These observations are so obvious as to be banal. Yet it is surprising how many Catholic institutions have ignored these commonsense insights over the past two decades. Engaged in a needed effort to improve their quality and eager to gain a form of academic respectability, Catholic universities, across most departments, increasingly hired in a manner similar to their secular peers. Sizable numbers of scholars joined the faculty ranks who had little or no interest in the university's mission. At Notre Dame, the majority of these individuals have

12  This formulation relies upon, and is influenced by, the analysis in Burton R. Clark, *The Distinctive College: Antioch, Reed, and Swarthmore* (Chicago: Aldine Publishing Co., 1970), 246–48.

been passive towards the university's mission; a few have been hostile and appear to accept George Bernard Shaw's canard about the concept of a "Catholic university" being a contradiction in terms. Their increasing presence has led to occasional expressions of concern from administrators about "the long-term maintenance of the Catholic identity of the university" but not to workable answers to the question of how to recruit committed faculty across the whole range of disciplines who will embody and express the fundamental purposes of the institution.

It is understandable that little serious attention has been paid to these questions of faculty hiring and commitment. These days even to raise it—and here I speak from experience—invites criticism that one is intolerant, divisive, narrow, sectarian, unconcerned with academic quality, or other labels which carry limited cachet in university circles. Yet the issue must be raised and discussed openly if the atrophy in the distinctive character of Catholic universities is to be arrested and reversed.

Let me address briefly, for illustrative purposes, just two areas which demand attention if a great Catholic university is to be anything but an unfulfilled promise. These are the immediate concern regarding initial recruitment and hiring of faculty and the more long-term concern regarding the provision of a pool of candidates for Catholic universities to draw from in their future hiring.

Despite the occasional public fretting and private hand-wringing by university administrators about the results of current hiring practices, hiring procedures in most Catholic universities differ little from those at secular schools. Advertisements are placed, dossiers are examined, judgments are made about the candidates' research and scholarly prospects, interviews are conducted, limited assessments of teaching ability are reached, and an appointment is made. There is little sustained effort to inform prospective faculty members about what the university is committed to and what is expected of a faculty member in that light. At interviews, the issue of Catholic identity, if raised at all, is likely to be done so defensively: "Oh, Notre Dame is a Catholic university—will that bother you?" My contention is that at many steps along the way the issue must be raised explicitly. For example, in advertising positions, Notre Dame's Catholic identity should be noted and some indication given that the university seeks to employ scholars who support its mission and who can contribute to its distinctive intellectual community; at the interview, the prospective candidate should be asked to discuss how he or she would contribute to the university's mission; the assessment of the candidate's likely contribution to the broad mission of the university should have weight in the final appointment decision.

Such procedures do not exclude faculty appointments for non-Catholics who are willing to respect and in varying ways contribute to the university's mission. (Here I must mention my gratitude to such non-Catholic scholars and colleagues as Alvin Plantinga and George Marsden, whose work and witness have influenced my thinking and strengthened my resolve on this question.) In fact, it is likely that given the present intellectual landscape, a great Catholic university will contribute effectively to ecumenism by providing Christian scholars of all traditions as well as non-Christian scholars an opportunity to study in an environment in which serious moral and religious questions are asked. In this circumstance, there might be an enhanced sense of what unites our traditions and some bridging of what divides them. And, a place like Notre Dame might prove an important place for training a new generation of non-Catholic Christian scholars who might serve in the remaining colleges and universities of their own denominations.

Concern for training the next generation of Catholic scholars and teachers, the candidate pool for the next decade, should be a primary concern of those who guide Catholic institutions today. Notre Dame should play its part in this endeavor. But the reality is that the vast majority of faculty who will serve in the Catholic universities of the future will be trained in secular research universities. Will those trained there be irredeemably branded with disdain for religion and have a narrow concern for the highly specialized professional demands of their particular discipline? Some undoubtedly will, and they should be unlikely candidates for recruitment by Catholic schools. But there are others who see their callings as engineer and artist, as scientist and humanist, as their vocation, as a way of being leaven in the world. These others must be identified and encouraged. Some interesting new initiatives have been undertaken recently to just this end: the Collegium project, which sponsors summer institutes aimed at recruiting and developing faculty "who can articulate and enrich the spiritual and intellectual life of their campuses"; and the Lilly Fellows Program, located at Valparaiso University, which firstly seeks to generate discussion of "Christian understandings of the nature of the academic vocation," and secondly provides postdoctoral fellowships aimed at preparing young scholars for "permanent employment within church-related institutions of higher learning." Worthy and welcome as these two ventures are, they highlight the appalling limits of the efforts of Catholic universities in this area to date.

Much more needs to be done. At a minimum, good Catholic universities should fund postdoctoral programs modeled on the Lilly Fellows Program as a way of identifying and encouraging young Catholic scholars. Notre Dame should go further. It needs to accept fully the responsibility which its prominence in American Catholic higher education places upon it and should handsomely fund an institute charged with grappling with the array of theoretical and practical questions faced by Catholic universities. Sustained and systematic thought and action must replace the ad hoc and limited efforts which occasionally sprout on Catholic campuses. Such an institute—let us christen it the Notre Dame Institute for Catholic Higher Education—might, among other things, foster reflection and discussion within and beyond the university on significant issues such as the role of theology and its relation to other disciplines in the arts and sciences; initiate and fund research unlocking neglected areas of the Catholic tradition; and organize symposia bringing together intellectuals prepared to wrestle with the Catholic university question. On the practical level, it should be a clearinghouse both for young Catholic scholars seeking positions and for Catholic colleges and universities seeking to make appointments to their faculties. It should encourage able Catholic undergraduates to consider the academic apostolate and should track interested Catholic graduate students and provide funding opportunities (dissertation fellowships, research and travel grants) to assist them to excel in their chosen fields. Such an institute might even arrange for training programs and internships for faculty and administrators of Catholic colleges and universities to better prepare them to undertake their important responsibilities.

The matter of faculty hiring is, of course, not a subject easily expressed in felicitous phrasing or beautiful conception, but if it is not addressed effectively and urgently, sublime evocations of the University of Paris in the thirteenth century or formulations of a Catholic university as elegant as Newman's will come to naught. Concerns about the moral development of students, the curriculum, the research agenda, and the sacredness of teaching will be moot. It is a matter that must be faced and now. What is needed is the will to act. Without it the "beacon," the "bridge," and the "crossroads" of Fr. Hesburgh's sturdy vision will be a pipedream supplanted by a one-way street to secularization.

### An Exciting Prospect

For some of us who love Notre Dame—both what it is and what it can and must become—hyperbole is a constant danger when we speak and write of it. This having been said, whatever the obstacles that confront us, the prospect for our venture is exhilarating if Notre Dame has the courage to stay on its distinct and professed course. This institution can develop further as a university in the conventional sense of a place of teaching, research, and publication, if its dedicated supporters provide the substantial resources required. But here and at other Catholic universities, this development must take a more distinct, yet expansive, form. Catholic universities must seek to understand the *whole* of reality. All the world is God's creation and all learning both about God and about the world must be welcomed. The Christian perspective holding to the unity of truth, because it is rooted in God, allows scholars in a Catholic university to seek the truth responsibly as part of their own search for God. This perspective holds the prospect of creating a genuine intellectual community linking the sciences, the professions, the humanities, and the arts.

We have a faith that seeks understanding and no area need be ignored, but a Catholic university has a special responsibility to pursue certain areas. Reflection upon and development of the Catholic intellectual and artistic tradition is essential.[13] In the present circumstances where many of the gods of modern thought (postmodernism with its attendant cultural nihilism, Marxism with its terrible consequences, latter-day liberalism with its inability to provide a coherent and grounded conception of good) have failed, the need for Catholic thought is more pressing than ever and has major implications for American and western culture generally.[14] If they fulfill their true vocations, Catholic universities will play their part in contributing to the needed renewal of social and political life of which John Paul II speaks in *Veritatis Splendor*.[15] In the current climate, Catholic views on matters such as moral truth, respect for human life, the dignity of persons, concern for the common good, the value of natural law, responsibilities as well as individual rights, the

13  For helpful insights on this matter, see Andrew M. Greeley, "The Catholic Imagination and the Catholic University," *America* 164, no. 10 (March 16, 1991): 285–88.

14  This point cannot be developed here, but see Richard John Neuhaus, *The Catholic Moment: The Paradox of the Church in the Modern World* (San Francisco: Harper and Row, 1987); and the comments of Michael Lacey in "The Backwardness of American Catholicism," CTSA Proceedings 46 (1991): 4–5.

15  John Paul II, *The Splendor of Truth*, encyclical letter, August 6, 1993. Note especially the section on "morality and the renewal of social and political life."

utility of the principle of subsidiarity, and the importance of family and community clearly have much to offer.

Catholic universities must manifest a different model of teaching and learning where both the intellectual and moral virtues are witnessed to and valued, where questions of ethics and character are not ignored. Those who graduate from these schools should have an informed view of what is good and seek to live a good life—a life in which faith is not sequestered in some private domain. In a Catholic university, neither students nor faculty should separate their religious beliefs from their lives as scientists, engineers, artists, lawyers, psychologists, or philosophers.[16] If we acknowledge the lordship of Jesus Christ and accept Him as the way, the truth, and the life, our lives can hardly be otherwise.

One should not underestimate the difficulty of the challenge that lies before a Catholic university like Notre Dame. Yet the Lord's ringing counsel to "be not afraid" and the recognition that fear and lack of vision are truly the principle obstacles in this venture should call committed women and men forward. Let us be about the work.

## The Heart of the Matter: The Role of Faculty—Catholics and Non-Catholics—in the Catholic University
### 1996

*My engagement on the issues of the role of faculty and the importance of hiring Catholics led to a number of invitations to address this matter at institutions beyond Notre Dame. In 1996, I received an invitation from Professor Don Briel at the University of St. Thomas to address this broad question. Don Briel had already established his innovative and important Center for Catholic Studies at St. Thomas. I am grateful to him for providing an opportunity for me to reflect on this crucial subject. I broadened the discussion and addressed the role of*

16 On this, see Etienne Gilson's celebrated essay, "The Intelligence in the Service of Christ the King," in his *Christianity and Philosophy* (New York and London: Sheed and Ward, 1939), 103–25.

*both Catholic and non-Catholic faculty in a Catholic university. This is a matter that retains its relevance to this day.*

Tonight I want to offer some brief reflections on the subject of the role of the faculty, both Catholic and non-Catholic, in a Catholic university. As a prelude I shall offer some hurried remarks on why it is that we are talking about this matter—a quick perusal, if you will, of what might be termed the "Catholic identity problem." Having gotten those of you who worry about this problem a little depressed, I shall move on to argue the central importance of the issue that concerns us here and the closely related issue of faculty hiring. Thereafter, I shall attempt to outline the special responsibilities that fall to those who teach at Catholic universities because of their distinctive mission and character. I shall conclude with an appeal for faculty to see our callings as scholars and teachers as a true vocation; indeed, to see ourselves as co-workers in the vineyard of Catholic higher education.

## Catholic Universities and Their Identity Problem

The issue of "the Catholic identity" of colleges and universities has been the subject for seemingly endless conversations, conferences, papers, studies, and reports.[1] A note of real urgency, however, has entered the conversation of late. Indeed, no less an observer than Archbishop Rembert Weakland of Milwaukee, a church leader who can hardly be derided as a "conservative" or as a "restorationist," has observed that "all Catholic institutions are in crisis." He suggests persuasively that "when the history of the last quarter of this century is written, it will emphasize how Catholics in the United States struggled with the question of the Catholic identity of the many institutions that were its glory in the early part of the century."[2] Margaret O'Brien Steinfels, the liberal editor of *Commonweal*,

1   A good summary of some of the literature on the topic is provided by Dr. John W. Healey in "The Catholic Identity of Colleges and Universities: An Interim Report," a paper he presented at Fordham University, April 19, 1996.
2   Rembert Weakland, "Foreword" to David O'Brien's *From the Heart of*

asserted at the 1995 meeting of the Association of Catholic Colleges and Universities (held right here at St. Thomas) that "we have a decade—ten years—in which this question of identity must be honestly addressed and definitely taken on as a commitment and core project of institutions *that hope to remain Catholic.*"[3]

Of course, as many of you know only too well, the "identity" issue emerged in the 1960's with the sudden collapse of the neoscholastic synthesis, which had provided the source for intellectual coherence for Catholic universities. Associated with this was the drive for academic "excellence" (as articulated in the 1967 Land O'Lakes statement) aimed at bringing Catholic education into the supposed mainstream of American higher education. The identity issue persists, as tonight's discussion demonstrates.

Notre Dame historian Philip Gleason, my colleague and former teacher, in the conclusion to his brilliant study of Catholic higher education in this [twentieth] century, has defined the enduring identity problem as "not institutional or organizational, but ideological." He explains: "It consists in a lack of consensus as to the substantive content of the ensemble of religious beliefs, moral commitments, and academic assumptions that supposedly constitute Catholic identity, and the consequent inability to specify what that identity entails for the practical functioning of Catholic colleges and universities." Not surprisingly, in light of this analysis, Gleason presents as an essential task for Catholic academics today the forging of "a vision that will provide what Neoscholasticism did for so many years—a theoretical rationale for the existence of Catholic colleges and universities as a distinctive element in American higher education."[4]

    *the American Church:Catholic Higher Education and American Culture,* (Maryknoll, N.Y.: Orbis Books, 1994), p. xi. [Archbishop Weakland subsequently resigned because of financial and sexual impropriety.]

3    Margaret O'Brien Steinfels, "The Catholic Intellectual Tradition," *Occasional Papers on Catholic Higher Education* Vol. 1, No. 1 (November, 1995), p. 5.

4    Philip Gleason, *Contending with Modernity: Catholic Higher Education in the Twentieth Century* (New York, 1995), pp. 320–22.

Diagnosing the problem has proved easier than prescribing an acceptable resolution for it. Although many Catholic colleges and universities have striven during the past decade to refocus their efforts by preparing mission statements, there is little evidence that these efforts have addressed the central issue effectively. Hence the warnings from Archbishop Weakland and Peggy Steinfels. Hence the continuing concern that Catholic institutions are advancing, although not by any clear and conscious decision, along a path to secularization similar to that trod by the Protestant universities and which George Marsden described so astutely in his *The Soul of the American University: From Protestant Establishment to Established Non-Belief.* Vestiges of Catholic identity might remain in campus ministry, or in residential life, or in the supposed influence of a religious order's tradition, but the central intellectual project largely replicates those of secular institutions. Increasingly, faculties are populated by scholars who have no noticeable allegiance to the institution's mission and no interest in a distinctive Catholic intellectual tradition.

## The Central Importance of Faculty

One might think that in these circumstances the essential task should be to address the issue which Philip Gleason raised—that is, the ideological question. I certainly don't deny the importance of work in this area, and I encourage those of you who contribute there to continue your investigations. However, I want to argue tonight that, somewhat contradictorily, the most urgent and central issue that needs to be addressed is more on the institutional/organizational side of things—that is, in the composition of the faculty. Indeed, it is in that area that the possibility of framing and implementing any new synthesis rests.

In a notable sermon at the opening Mass for the 1972 academic year, just five years after the Land O'Lakes statement, the Provost of Notre Dame, James T. Burtchaell, C.S.C., said:

"Let us for the moment, then, leave aside asking what might be the definition of a Catholic university and pose a more practical question: In the unpredictable and surely surprise-laden future of belief and higher learning, no matter what a Catholic university turns out to be, how can we best assure ourselves that Notre Dame will be one? Before all else," he continued, "by preserving a faculty which sustains our commitment. The key to the character of a university lies in a consciously dedicated company of teachers."[5]

Similarly the mission statement which leads off the report of the Colloquy for the Year 2000 submitted in May 1993 by Notre Dame's president, Edward A. Malloy, C.S.C., asserts, "The Catholic identity of the University depends upon, and is nurtured by, the continuing presence of a predominant number of Catholic intellectuals." It is hard to dispute the point—although I should add quickly that many do. The faculty is located at the heart of a university and only with true faculty commitment will a university fulfill its mission.

Unfortunately little serious and sustained attention has been paid recently to questions of faculty composition and commitment. In fact, these days even to raise it invites criticism. Peter Steinfels, referring to the issue of faculty hiring, declared in his talk at the ACCU meeting at St. Thomas in 1995 that it was until recently "the great unmentionable." Now, however, he discerns that "there is consensus . . . that the hiring question, no matter how explosive, must be faced." I suspect that he has overstated the "consensus" and certainly the willingness of Catholic institutions to act upon it. Yet the issue must be raised, discussed openly, and acted upon if the atrophy in the distinctive character of Catholic universities is to be arrested and reversed. Let me try to do so here in ways that are for the most part familiar, but which may lay the basis for some profitable discussion.

5    James T. Burtchaell, C.S.C., "Notre Dame and the Christian Teacher," *ND Journal of Education*, Vol. 4, No. 3 (Fall, 1973), p. 239.

## *Special Expectations and Responsibilities of Faculty in a Catholic University*

**Support for the Mission:** The essential components of a faculty member's contribution are usually seen as teaching and research, along with a third, more nebulous area known usually as "university service." I don't want to question these basic components but to argue that faculty at Catholic institutions have additional and special responsibilities. Prior to attending to teaching and research, teacher-scholars in Catholic universities should have a familiarity with, an understanding of, and a real support for the distinctive nature and mission of the university in which they will teach and research. Understanding this mission should influence the kind of teachers they will be and also might have some impact on their approach to research.

Faculty—Catholic and non-Catholics and indeed non-Christians and those of no religion—should appreciate and value the fact that in the words of Pope John Paul II's 1990 apostolic constitution on Catholic higher education, *Ex Corde Ecclesiae*, "besides the teaching, research and services common to all universities, a Catholic university, by institutional commitment, brings to its task the inspiration and light of the Christian message. In a Catholic university, therefore, Catholic ideals, attitudes and principles penetrate and inform university activities in accordance with the proper nature and autonomy of these activities. In a word, being both a university and Catholic, it must be both a community of scholars representing various branches of human knowledge and an academic institution in which Catholicism is vitally present and operative."[6]

It is extraordinary (or perhaps simply a sad commentary on hiring practices over the past two decades) that some faculty members presently teaching in Catholic universities either resent the distinctive mission of their school or don't want it to have any meaning—certainly not for them. Such a circumstance cannot

6    *Ex Corde Ecclesiae*, Section 14.

prevail. Faculty in a Catholic university should appreciate and support the mission of the institution, and they should seek out new colleagues to join their ranks who will do likewise. Fr. Richard John Neuhaus has expressed a somewhat similar view in his "Eleven Theses" address at Baylor University where he argued the importance that "all the faculty respect, or at least not actively oppose, the idea of a Christian university." He went on to argue that "the institution-defining decisions must be made by those who understand and support the institution's purpose" and that "discrimination is necessary in hiring and promotion— not necessarily discrimination on the basis of religious belief but discrimination on the basis of belief in the great good of being a Christian university."[7] Similarly, Notre Dame's mission statement notes: "What the University asks of all its scholars and students, however, is not a particular creedal affiliation, but a respect for the objectives of Notre Dame and a willingness to enter into the conversation that gives it life and character."

**Participation in a Catholic Community of Learning:** If faculty genuinely support the mission of a Catholic university they will see a clear obligation to participate in and to build up a distinctive learning community. *Ex Corde Ecclesiae* suggests that "a Catholic university pursues its objectives through its formation of an authentic human community animated by the spirit of Christ. The source of its unity springs from a common dedication to the truth, a common vision of the dignity of the human person and ultimately the person and message of Christ which gives the institution its distinctive character."[8]

A "learning community" is an overworked term and is hard to define in practice. Certainly it is hard to discern institutional examples on the current academic landscape. Now, regrettably,

7    Richard John Neuhaus, "The Christian University: Eleven Theses," *First Things*, No. 59 (January, 1996), p. 21. Neuhaus went on to say: "The university is better served by an agnostic who wants the university to be Christian than by a devout believer who does not."

8    *Ex Corde Ecclesiae*, Section 21.

universities are for the most part fragmented entities. But faculty in a Catholic university should see it as their challenge and obligation to overcome this debilitating intellectual fragmentation. They should welcome the chance to cooperate with colleagues across departmental lines and to contribute effectively to the institution as a whole. A shared commitment to "weave their faith into the full fabric of their intellectual life" and a collective desire to fashion an institution in which the most important of human concerns have not been banished should provide the basis for such collaboration.[9]

But who in their right minds will hire or tenure people solely because of their commitment to the mission of the institution or their willingness to build an authentic community of learning? Faculty obviously must make the grade at teaching and at research. But while commitment to the mission and a willingness to contribute to a learning community may not be sufficient for faculty in a Catholic university I want to argue strongly that they are essential.

Now, we should not pretend that such qualities are found in all faculty or all faculty prospects. Indeed they cut somewhat across the grain of academic culture. Generally speaking, faculty today are less loyal to institutions than to their particular scholarly disciplines and professions. The emphasis on disciplinary–based research and the reward structure which enforces it serve to dilute institutional loyalty and commitment. In many institutions that particular genie will be hard to put back into the bottle. In Catholic universities, however, the "genie" of faculty commitment to the institution's mission is central to the well-being and authenticity of the school.

**The Trivialization and Privatization of Religious Belief:** Faculty commitment to the mission of a Catholic university, however, is made even more problematic by the tendencies in our society to privatize or to trivialize religion. A Catholic uni-

9    Burtchaell, "Notre Dame and the Christian Teacher," p. 241.

versity cannot ordinarily expect a friendly reception because its very existence, if authentic, represents an implicit critique of the intellectual presuppositions of a highly secularized, elite culture. But Catholic institutions cannot and will not survive in any meaningful sense as Catholic if they are staffed by those who share the dominant elite attitude to religion. That said, my own sense is that the present danger for faculty in Catholic institutions is not primarily the trivialization of religious belief but the privatization of it. The former mocks religion conviction but the other sequesters it off in some personal space where it has little impact on other aspects of life and thought.

Tonight I don't wish to begin a full discussion of the complex issue of how faith relates to learning. As a historian of the U.S. foreign policy in the Cold War, I am still seeking greater clarity for myself in this area. And yet, this issue needs our close attention. Indeed, it is crucial that faculty in a Catholic university reject the "privatization of religion" model, and that they bring religious perspectives to bear in teaching and research.

**Faith-Filled Scholars**: Here we come to the real nub of the issue. *Catholic* faculty—who should be the predominant presence—in a Catholic university should be committed to both the profession of learning and the life of faith and willing to relate the two. How this might be done will vary considerably if one is a theologian rather than a chemical engineer, of course. But no one's professional commitment excludes them from the call to be faith-filled scholars. We simply wouldn't want to start making sacred-profane distinctions about academic disciplines which the fundamentally incarnational and sacramental nature of Catholicism would reject. "Any movement towards meaning and truth," to quote Michael Buckley, s.j., "is inchoatively religious."[10] Clearly, however, there are certain subjects which more appropriately lend themselves to religious perspectives and to

10  Buckley quoted in Leo O'Donovan, s.j., "The Analogy of a Catholic University," *Issues in Catholic Higher Education* (Winter, 1995).

direct engagement with the long and varied traditions of Catholic intellectual life. But scholars in all disciplines should be committed to the pursuit of truth and "to the larger intellectual conversation animated by the teachings found in Christian learning generally and in the Catholic tradition more particularly" which characterizes a true Catholic community of learning.[11] Naturally certain scholars bear a particular responsibility to nourish and to pass on the Catholic tradition and, we pray, to extend it and to explore its many facets—as I assume do those here associated with your Center for Catholic Studies. All faculty should support such work which rests at the core of a Catholic university.

I have set forth here as an important responsibility of Catholic faculty in a Catholic university the integration of faith and learning, although this will have quite different calibrations depending on the particular discipline involved. Let me introduce another calibration: the responsibility and role of faculty who are not Catholics in a Catholic university. This is an important and very delicate issue. One is almost destined to give offense. But what I find more offensive is the effort to tip-toe somewhat disingenuously around this question out of fear of being deemed somehow "not inclusive" enough.

I have already suggested that all faculty should support the mission of the university and contribute to its life as an intellectual community. In my experience at Notre Dame, some of those scholars who have been most concerned to maintain and to enhance its Christian-Catholic character have been faith-filled non-Catholics, among whom I number our new provost, Nathan Hatch, and valued colleagues like the philosopher Alvin Plantinga and the historians George Marsden and John Van Engen. So let me make clear the obvious point that by no means need only Catholics or Christians teach in a Catholic university. In fact, I think it likely that given the present American

11  I borrow here from the report of the Committee on Academic Life to the Colloquy for the Year 2000 (Christmas, 1992), p. 3.

academic landscape, genuine Catholic universities can contribute effectively to an ecumenism by providing Christian scholars of all traditions, and also non-Christians scholars, with an environment where faith and learning can be integrated and in which serious religious and moral questions can be asked. All such scholars may not ask these questions but they should support their being asked. Non-Catholic scholars should play their individual parts in making their universities better Catholic universities.

All this I hope suggests that professors in a Catholic university—especially the Catholic scholars—should not see their role as one in which they undertake only highly specialized research and in which they convey information in their area of technical competence to their students. I suggest that professors should profess much more and reveal to their students the faith that gives their lives meaning and purpose. Scholars who profess in this way will truly see their work not as a career but as a calling or vocation.

**The Vocation of Teacher**: Those who profess in this way surely will have a quite different approach to the "calling" of teacher. It is clear that the modern university has evolved in such a way that teaching has been downgraded. The emphasis and rewards have been placed on research, on the creation of knowledge—or what sometimes passes as knowledge! Detachment is the ruling mode for many teachers with classes structured so that faculty and students will remain largely strangers.[12] Students are much less "bother" that way! Mark Schwehn, dean of Christ College at Valparaiso University, has written persuasively of the need for a redefinition of a professor's responsibilities. Schwehn wants "to restore teaching to the premier place of dignity and honor that it once had . . ."[13] He naturally asks for

12  See William H. Willmon, "Reaching and Teaching the Abandoned Generation," *Christian Century*, October 20, 1993, p. 1017.

13  Mark Schwehn, *Exiles from Eden: Religion and the Academic Vocation in America* (New York: Oxford University Press, 1993), p. 75.

increased attention to the transmittal of ideas and skills, but he goes further and suggests that teachers must attend to shaping the moral character of their students. Perhaps one might go further and suggest even the shaping of students' souls.

Catholic faculty living out their vocation in a Catholic university will recognize that beyond transmitting knowledge and developing skills lies a crucial responsibility on their part to guide students in how to live in accord with the Gospel. *Ex Corde Ecclesiae,* when discussing university teachers, suggests that "Christians among the teachers are called to be witnesses and educators of authentic Christian life, which evidences attained integration between faith and life, and between professional competence and Christian wisdom."[14] Furthermore, all teachers are to be inspired by academic ideals and by the principles of an authentically human life. Christian-Catholic teachers have a marvelous opportunity here. This is clearly an invitation for them to be "leaven in the world." Recently it has been suggested that "a Catholic university should be a place in which the cultivation of [a] particular ethos is taking place, an ethos which involves, for example, compassion, humility, honesty, gratitude, critical reflection, spiritual discernment, and a generous concern for people who are suffering, or poor, or oppressed or excluded—a place where faith, hope, and an intelligent love are somehow operative and discussible."[15]

Surely teachers across the disciplines can play their part in forging and fashioning such an ethos. This is not a "task" to be shunted off to campus ministry. Students must see faculty who are not merely intellectuals, but women and men of character and conviction who engage their students and, dare one say it, truly serve them. This would be a key form of "university service." Faculty should join students at worship, respect their students' faith commitments, and encourage them to deepen their

14 *Ex Corde Ecclesiae,* Section 22.
15 Robert J. Egan, s.j. "Can Universities be Catholic: Some Reflections, Comments, Worries, and Suggestions" *Commonweal* (April 5, 1996), p. 14.

understanding of their beliefs. To teach in this way is essential if Catholic universities are to live up to their true potential. Let me also suggest that teaching in this way assures faculty a more authentic experience of their own Christian call.

### To the True Heart of the Matter

Let me bring these remarks to a close. I have tried to illuminate the central importance of faculty in fulfilling the mission of a Catholic university and the ways in which they might accomplish this. Through their explicit support of the mission, through full participation in the life of the university community, through willingness to relate faith and scholarship, and through pursuing teaching as a true vocation, the teacher witnesses Christian living. Some might see this as a difficult role to fulfill, and yet I know faculty who have fulfilled these roles as teachers. I'm sure you know some as well. We need more of them—men and women who are genuinely committed to this crucial enterprise of Catholic higher education.

In the end, the distinctive Catholic mission and character of Catholic universities will not be guaranteed by their charter, statues, or by-laws. Not by trustees, important though they are; not even by administrators, no matter how crucial their leadership and direction on this issue. Certainly the words of administrators won't suffice unless supported by actions. Such unsupported words might serve as a palliative to governing boards, alumni, parents, or benefactors but they don't honestly face the crucial issue.

In the end, faculty will determine the essential nature of their institution over the long haul. The "heart" and the "soul" occasionally surface as metaphors in the discussion over contemporary higher education. I titled my talk "The Heart of the Matter" in an attempt not only to emphasize the central importance of the faculty contribution in a Catholic university, but also as a genuflection in the direction of *Ex Corde Ecclesiae* (*From the Heart of the Church*). My colleague George Marsden, as you know, titled his book *The Soul of the American University*. Let me combine the metaphors to suggest that I want to ensure that no book is written relatively early in the new century entitled "The Lost Heart and Soul of the Catholic University." Faculty in Catholic universities over the next decade must respond to the challenge identified by Archbishop Weakland and Peggy Steinfels. One should not underestimate either the difficulty or the necessity of this challenge. I trust that faculty here at the University of St. Thomas, both Catholic and non-Catholic, will respond to it. I wish you well in the undertaking and promise my prayers for your endeavors.

# Section II: Matters Pastoral

## Senior Class Fellow Address
### 1992

*The class of 1992 at the University of Notre Dame elected me their senior class fellow. During the week of graduation activities, I gave a short address in Sacred Heart Basilica and offered some words of thanks and farewell. That now seems a long time ago. I'm older (and perhaps even wiser!) now, but I offer a modified section of my talk here. It reflects my effort to encourage the graduates as they journeyed forth.*

I want to talk about faith, and to help guide my thoughts I borrow from three "texts." The first is a modification of an Australian beer advertisement. The second is some counsel from my mum. The last is a horrendous greeting card-type platitude.

Faith is best lived and proclaimed in community, as you have demonstrated during your time here. As you leave, I pray that you will assume the role of community builders. Be folk who call forth the gifts of others, who reconcile differences, and who inject vitality and life into the communities you will join. When I was growing up, there was a line from an advertising jingle for my now favorite beer, Fourex (which I enjoy in moderation whenever I visit Down Under). The line went like this: "You need a big, big beer for a big, big thirst." Variations on this line became commonplace. An old nun who taught me used to say, "I've got a big, big stick for a bad, bad boy"; predictably, she threatened to use it a lot! No surprise, I have my own variation: "We have a big, big God for a big, big church," and there is room within it for us all. Whatever our interests and talents, we need to do our part to be the Church, to help shape it—to enflesh "the body of Christ" (1 Cor 13:27).

One childhood day, I was rambling on to my mum, who was doing some ironing at the time, as I recall. I was sharing with her my ambitions to play rugby for Australia and to serve as prime minister of the country, perhaps simultaneously! She cut me short by refusing to endorse my ambitions. She said simply, "All I want you to be is a good boy." Her tone conveyed that this was more than an effort to get me to behave there and then. The old girl was on to something, and she has worked the theme ever since.

We live in a culture and society that hyper-focuses on achievement and accomplishment. My hope, however, is that as you venture forth from this place you have a profound sense of yourself as a daughter or son of God—each of you precious in God's sight and each of you called personally to live a life inspired by the Gospel rather than simply conforming to the dictates of our time. I pray you will live a life, in short, that is *good*; a life in which your faith will not be sequestered into some private domain but will guide all your commitments and actions. Be aware that this may mean that you won't be "in" with a certain crowd. But persevere in what you believe to be right and true.

Some time ago I was over at Holy Cross House (my order's retirement home). On the notice board I saw a little poster which read, "You need both rain and sunshine to have a rainbow!" Frankly, I didn't know whether to laugh or to barf, but in the end I chuckled in a superior sort of way and thought: "O, God, I hope they don't subject me to this fuzzy stuff when I'm over here." However embarrassing it may be to admit it, those darn words stuck in my head. In the end, I took them as a sign that the Lord thought I should make an ass of myself and use them. Let me do so now. We know from our own experience that life is not all sunshine. I suspect that your years as a student have probably made that clear in various ways. I hope your experience has deepened your capacity to persevere in faith whatever rain may fall. Such perseverance in faith brings joy.

My friends, our religion, our faith, does not take us out of life but energizes and gives meaning to everyday life. It links us in solidarity to a community that stretches back two thousand years. This community has gone through history, ever changing and adapting, in one century never the same as before, its doors always open to the world. It has been sustained by men and women such as yourselves—the merciful, the single-hearted, the peacemakers. In all that time the hungry have been fed, the sick have been comforted, the strangers have been welcomed, and prisoners visited. And, deep in their hearts, men and women have discovered what makes life truly worthwhile. Dear friends, members of the class of 1992, keep the faith! Keep the faith, and in so doing, live it and share it.

## Charge to the Graduating Seniors on Last Visit to the Grotto 1995

*On the Thursday night leading into graduation weekend, the senior class visits the grotto dedicated to Our Lady of Lourdes at Notre Dame. It is a holy place. I delivered a charge to the class before their graduation and challenged them to be Christian disciples in the world. It is still the essential challenge I try to place before my treasured students as they complete their studies at the university.*

I am very grateful for the chance to speak with you here tonight at the grotto—this special place, this holy place. It gives me the chance to thank you for your contribution to Notre Dame during your time here. Notre Dame is a better place for your having been part of it. I thank you for your readiness to learn, your capacity for friendship, your willingness to serve others, and for your witness of faith. It is with real sadness that I think of you leaving this university, which, despite its limitations, we love. You will be missed.

These are special days for you as you move toward your

graduation—a week at Notre Dame with all your friends and nothing to do but enjoy each other's company and so forth. (There is a lot included in that "and so forth"!) But I suspect that they are days of mixed emotions for all of you. Certainly it is a time of happiness and excitement, a time during which you can celebrate the fact that you have earned something here and experienced something here that can never be taken from you. But it also is a time for saying farewell, a time to spend with close friends reflecting upon experiences you have shared—not just the great times but also the tough and difficult moments out of which deep friendships are mostly formed and in which our true characters are revealed. These are the last few days before you scatter to all parts of the country and the world and move on, as you must, to a different stage of your life.

Commencement on Sunday marks not only the fact that you have earned your Notre Dame degree but also, in a formal sense, the end of one phase of your life and the beginning of another. It is the beginning of a new, exciting, perhaps uncertain phase.

I am supposed to say something to you as you journey forward—to provide a charge to the senior class. I thought of trying to pass on some helpful counsel and advice, but in the next few days, I suspect that you will receive plenty of advice on what you must do in the future. You will hear about the challenges that await you and how you must work to make the world a better place, using well the knowledge you have gained here. Pay heed to it all, as I know you will. Our dear but troubled world needs the full contribution of each of you.

Rather than that, however, I want to focus not on what you should do but on who you must *be*; to speak of what I know in my heart makes life truly worthwhile.

I pray that in whatever you do, you will be Christian disciples—men and women of faith whose center of being manifests both a profound sense of being loved by God and a willingness to follow in the path of Jesus who has shown us the way. I hope that as you venture forth from this place each of you senses that you are precious in God's sight and called to live a life inspired by the Gospel rather than simply conforming to the dictates of contemporary culture and society.

I trust that as you leave Notre Dame you possess a moral core that makes you more than clever people but wise and good and courageous people. You must be the ones who refuse to be disinterested bystanders. You must be the ones willing to commit to a just cause. You must be the ones unafraid to stand for and to defend what is right. You must be the ones prepared to take the less traveled paths in which fidelity, sacrifice, duty, integrity, commitment, and compassion are not avoided but embraced.

My charge consists of these hopes and prayers. But I am not charging you to forge off in some big new direction. I'm asking you instead to be faithful to the call which Christians have sought to respond to for two thousand years. I'm asking you to join prior generations of Notre Dame graduates, perhaps including your parents, who came here to this special place of higher learning so that their hearts and souls as well as their minds might be nourished; who came here seeking not simply training for a career but an education for a life of meaning and purpose, and who discovered that it is faith which energizes and gives meaning to everyday life.

It is now time for you to leave Notre Dame and to venture forth to pursue your different vocations. We hope that your bonds to Our Lady's university will be strong and bring you back to visit often—not only for the inevitable game in the fall but also for times of celebration and joy and for moments of prayer and reflection in Sacred Heart and on this holy ground. Go forth with gratitude in your hearts for all that has been and with a deep trust that the Lord will guide you to live, as he did, in such a way that when you die, your love will survive and continue to grow.

Men and women of Notre Dame—members of the class of 1995—keep the faith, and may the risen Lord and Our Lady, Notre Dame, bless you always.

# Part II
# The Past Decade:
# Engaging the Issues and Taking Stands

# Section I: Teaching, Learning, and Research

## Teaching, Learning and What Really Matters: Reflections on Receiving the Rev. Charles E. Sheedy, C.S.C., Award for Outstanding Teaching in the College of Arts and Letters
### 2001

*I have been fortunate enough to win a number of teaching awards at Notre Dame. I appreciated them all but was most deeply touched when I received the Sheedy Award for Excellence in Teaching. I shared the award with my colleague from the Program of Liberal Studies, Stephen Fallon. By the time I gave this address, I had assumed my responsibilities as rector and superior of Moreau Seminary at Notre Dame and was engaged in a different manner of teaching than that which had so occupied my energies over the previous decade and a half. I trust the address reflects something of my passion for and commitment to teaching undergraduates at Notre Dame.*

I am grateful to receive this award named for Fr. Charlie Sheedy, a distinguished predecessor as a priest-teacher in the Congregation of Holy Cross at Notre Dame. I feel honored to join the company of the wonderful teachers who previously received this award—women and men who have seen teaching not as a job or career but as a vocation and calling. And I feel particularly honored to share the award this year with Steve Fallon. The best of teaching is, of course, done not by what we say or write but by how we live, and Steve has taught us much in that regard in these past years.

I feel especially glad to be here with Steve because his presence guarantees that you will hear at least one thoughtful reflection on teaching! I have a special connection to Steve because I had the privilege of baptizing his son Daniel. Daniel is now approaching his eleventh birthday—just about at the age when he should receive some vocation literature from me.

Permit me to extend some words of thanks:

I give thanks to God for my membership in and calling as a priest of Holy Cross. I would not be teaching at Notre Dame were I not a member of this order, and I am grateful that I have had the chance to serve here in the company of other devoted Holy Cross religious. We think of ourselves in the words of our constitutions as "educators in the faith," and this is what I have tried to be.

I want to thank two people in particular, both former teachers, not only for their kindness to me over the quarter century since I came here as a graduate student in 1976 but also for their witness as committed teachers.

First I want to thank my treasured mentor and friend, Vincent De Santis, for his unfailing encouragement and for his example as a person who simply loves to teach. Long may he continue to do so! And I must thank my dear elder brother in Holy Cross, Fr. Thomas Blantz, C.S.C., himself a Sheedy Award winner, for both his great support and his witness of dedication and concern for students. I was his teaching assistant here twenty-five years ago and he has been a guide and model for me ever since. I would be a better priest, teacher, and man if I had followed his example a bit more closely!

Needless to say I want to thank all my faculty and staff colleagues and friends, especially those in my own department where good teaching is appreciated. And, last but not least, I want to thank my dear students both past and present for their graciousness to me. One of my past students, Laura Holland Hoey, is here as a member of the College of Arts and Letters Advisory Board along with her husband Doug. I had the privilege of presiding at their wedding this past summer. If any of my present students are here and perplexed as to how I ever won a "teaching award" in light of what I have subjected you to this semester—well, let me offer to request funds from the advisory council to get a rebate for you!

Dean Mark Roche's generous invitation to Steve and myself to say some words asked us to address "some aspect of teaching." On first thought I considered trying to say something about good teaching—to pass along some lessons learned during my time as a teacher here, even (dare one be so immodest to say it) to share the notable or signature features of my teaching in hopes that they might benefit other teachers here. But, sad to say, I had some difficulty clarifying what my signature features are.

I don't have the wonderful gift of storytelling like my colleague Jim Smyth. I'm not fast enough on my feet to engage my students brilliantly in focused discussion as does my colleague Doris Bergen. I lack the endless patience and powerful analytic skill to work so ably with multiple students on their research and writing projects like my colleague Laura Crago. I know well that it is not my well-honed facility with new teaching techniques and computer technology, for I occasionally still need help to work a VCR and the mere thought of my having to give one of the now ubiquitous "power point presentations" is enough to have me calling for a stiff whiskey.

Of course some folk have offered suggestions for my supposed success as a teacher. When the Sheedy Award was announced last spring my insightful colleague Bob Schmuhl kindly noted that it came at a time when I wasn't teaching and asked if there was a connection there! Some have suggested that my accent helps; students are not too concerned with what I say but they enjoy listening to how I say it! Others suppose that my distinctive gestures and slightly manic physical presence in the classroom, which led an early student of mine named Paul Wasinger to compare me rather favorably to the John Cleese character in *Fawlty Towers*, have something to do it with it! Still others have suggested that the endless digressions on matters large and small but seemingly unrelated to the topic at hand have contributed. No one has suggested that my debonair appearance, my animal magnetism, or my gentle, retiring manner might be the explanation and, frankly, I'm a bit surprised by that!

Needless to say I hope that certain other factors contributed to whatever accomplishments I have attained in teaching. At my best, I sought to engage my students, to get to know them, to convey some sense of my passion for my subject and its importance such that students were transformed into fellow learners and, indeed, into friends.

This process of engagement was and is time-consuming, but it is most beneficial in terms of both good pedagogy and my own joy in teaching. I asked my students to work as hard as I did myself, and they responded. I have always treasured a note sent by which a former student, Carol Dominguez, passing along a brief quotation from *Great Expectations* in which Pip writes of his tutor Mr. Pocket: "If he had shown indifference as a master, I have no doubt I should have returned the compliment as a pupil; he gave me no such excuse, and each of us did the other justice." I like to think that many of my students might join me in saying of our courses together, "Each of us did the other justice."

In the end, however, it is pretty obvious what my signature feature is and I have already referred to it. I am a priest in the Holy Cross order and teaching for me is an apostolic work, a ministry. Please indulge me as I reflect in a rather personal way on that reality. I know this matter might seem a bit divorced from the experience of many of you here but it really isn't. Those of you who appreciate Fr. John Cavanaugh's observation that "good teaching is really a sort of sacramental action, a communication of spirit," will understand.

From the outset I began my teaching here with a strong sense that I was engaged upon a spiritual undertaking, that teaching was an important part of my priestly ministry. I knew that my task was not only about improving minds but shaping souls; that I was called to nurture not only the intellectual lives of my students but also their religious and moral lives, and to aid them in integrating the two. The founder of my order, Fr. Basil

Moreau, had outlined in his reflections on Christian pedagogy that the mind could not "be cultivated at the expense of the heart." The tradition of my religious community as educators in the faith and the best teacher-exemplars certainly had conveyed that to me. Nicholas Ayo, Steve Fallon's colleague in the Program of Liberal Studies and my confrere in Holy Cross, once referred to teachers as "living books." In a similar way Mark Schwehn, the dean of Christ College at Valparaiso University, speaks of "teachers in the classroom as texts." They allude, of course, to the fact that teachers convey as much by what they do and who they are as by what they say. My good teachers have modeled for me integrity, honesty, perseverance, intellectual and moral courage, and a profound commitment to the truth. I can only hope and pray that in some ways I have modeled such virtues for my students. More explicitly I hope I have also conveyed that I seek to follow in the path of Jesus and so to serve them; to awaken and deepen each person's sense of his or her own capacities and gifts; and to challenge them to use their gifts well and in the service of others. I wish I had done and could do this better.

I have tried in ways obvious and not-so-obvious to help my students uncover what really matters in life. As a teacher of history I have tried to clarify some of those great lessons of history that are often painfully learned—that things don't always turn out right, nor the way we expect, and certainly not the way we want. I have tried to convey by word and deed the need to respect the dignity of each human person and life, and have tried to emphasize our need to take responsibility for each other and for the common good. I have endeavored to explain that in the end a truly good life is about faith and family and friendship and that, especially in our privileged circumstances, we must lean into life from a disposition of gratitude rather than of resentment. I fear many of my students might have missed some of these aspects of my teaching endeavors by being overly concerned with getting the question on the Marshall Plan or the Cuban Missile Crisis or whatever correct on the final exam. Perhaps in the future I might be able to do this better.

In July of 1999 I had the opportunity to make a retreat in Assisi, the home of my favorite saint, holy Francis, who has always helped clarify for me what are the most important aspects of life and how I must allow God to dwell more fully within me. One hot day I hiked up the slopes of Mount Subasio to the Carceri Hermitage, a place where Francis and his companions often came to meditate and pray. I took with me the constitutions of my order and read them there and experienced the presence and call of the Lord in a powerful way. I sensed the Lord's call to me as a priest in Holy Cross to bring renewed commitment and energy to my teaching and scholarship, and to interact more charitably with others without surrendering my honest convictions and beliefs. This is what I returned to do and enjoyed a good year in which I actually taught new classes, including one on the history of my own country, Australia, that place which has such a hold on my heart and gut.

It was during the course of that year, however, that my provincial conveyed to me that he had not experienced the Lord's call for me in quite the same way I had. He asked me instead to serve as rector and superior of Moreau Seminary. Being a moderately headstrong person and having the additional backing of a mountainside spiritual experience, I was a bit surprised that he did not see my future exactly as I saw it. But, after prayer and reflection my head and my heart told me that God was calling me to accept this appointment and to give my best to it. Contributing to the good training of Holy Cross seminarians struck me as simply the most important and challenging ministry I could undertake. I now play some part in educating a new generation of Holy Cross "educators in the faith" so that they might follow in the footsteps of forebears like Charlie Sheedy by preaching the good news and by extending the reign of Jesus Christ in the hearts of men and women. I truly know it is by far the most important teaching assignment given to me, although it is a different form of "teaching" than most of what I have previously done. I have the privilege of working with men who know that their best selves will be discovered only when they pass beyond self–centeredness and selfishness and truly follow Christ in giving of themselves to others. I have always learned from my students, from their insights and goodness, but in this case I am very much a learner from and with my younger brothers in Holy Cross. We are wayfarers and pilgrims on the same journey and we guide each other by living the life as best we can, aided by God's abundant grace.

My own specific journey has taken me quite a distance from my homeland and given me the graced opportunity to serve here. I am fortunate to have had good companions with me at each stage along the way: my Moreau community, my dear students, my faith-filled collaborators in the higher education apostolate of Holy Cross, and so many able and committed teachers and learners with whom I have been able to work. I give thanks to God for all of them and ask his continued blessing as we pursue the "work" of teaching, learning, and keeping clear what really matters.

## John Zahm's Challenge
## to the Modern Catholic University
## 2003

*I served on the board of the University of Portland, which the Holy Cross order sponsors, for a number of terms and developed a real attachment to this fine school. I was honored to be invited there to deliver the Zahm lecture at an academic convocation which brought faculty and students together on the fabled Bluff. I took the opportunity to use John Zahm's debate with Andrew Morrissey as a departure point for reflections on how a Catholic university might engage the broad culture.*

It is a pleasure and an honor to be with you at the University of Portland to deliver the John A. Zahm Lecture. I welcome each and every opportunity to visit this special place.

When I was invited to deliver this lecture I first thought of sharing some thoughts on what might be called the "Australian experiment"—that is, the remarkable and ongoing exercise in nation-building Down Under. I wanted to do this as a way of marking your university's participation in a foreign study program in my homeland. Despite the encouragement of Brian Doyle—who actually suggested that I focus on rugby stories from Brisbane—the charter of the Zahm lecture to address some aspect of Catholic education in America began to weigh on me. So it is that today I want instead to speak about two matters that interest me and, hopefully, might interest you: firstly, John Zahm's vision for a Catholic university and, secondly, the responsibility of the Catholic university to engage the culture that surrounds it.

John Augustine Zahm is rightly honored here on the Bluff for his decision as U.S. provincial of Holy Cross to accept the invitation of Archbishop Alexander Christie for the order to assume responsibility for the fledgling Columbia University. This was in 1902. Were he to visit this campus today I am sure he would express deep pride at what has been accomplished. He would take a special pleasure in wandering the laboratories of Swindells Hall and in observing the vibrant scientific effort pursued at this Catholic university.

I suspect that many of you are very familiar with the essential details of Zahm's life. Indeed perhaps Ralph Weber's solid biography is required reading at UP. But on the off chance that there are a few here who have yet to peruse that worthy work, let me supply an overview of his life while trying to illustrate some crucial aspects of his approach to higher education. Zahm was born in 1851 and entered Notre Dame in 1867. After completing his initial studies he entered the Congregation of Holy Cross and was ordained a priest in 1875. Zahm was assigned to teach at Notre Dame where he served as professor of physics. He was a brilliant scholar and a most capable teacher and, according to the legends of the order, proudly intellectual, quite strong-willed, and also rather cold, even a bit "stand-offish." However that may be, Zahm was without a doubt one of the great contributors to the slow transformation of his institution from a college preparatory school to something approaching a genuine college. His own research in the physical sciences, when added to his notable achievements in securing proper facilities for serious scientific teaching, would warrant him an honored place among Holy Cross educators even should his life have been cut short in, say, 1890.

But his life was not cut short. He lived three more decades until his death in Munich in 1921. In the late 1880's and early 1890's Zahm gradually shifted focus from his scientific research to engage one of the great issues of his day—the relationship of science with religious faith. In an age when Darwinism and skepticism rocked the foundations of worldviews founded on fundamentalist and literalist interpretations of the Bible, Zahm brought his impressive intellectual powers to bear on the central issues. Culminating in his classic work *Evolution and Dogma* (1896), Zahm's argument for a version of theistic evolution expounded the theme that no conflict should exist between science and Catholicism. Zahm's intellectual efforts reflected a certain Americanist confidence and comfort in contemporary society and a vigorous willingness to engage the principal issues of his day. Sadly, given the largely well-grounded basis of his thinking, Zahm's work ran afoul of the Sacred Congregation of the Index (or the Holy Office as it was known after 1917) in the midst of the developing "Americanist crisis," and he was forced to retreat from his engagement on the matter.

While Zahm's personal efforts to engage important intellectual/cultural issues of the day were blocked, his surprising appointment as U.S. provincial of the order in 1898 provided him with an avenue to lay the groundwork for a more corporate effort by his order and ,by extension, Catholic colleges and universities to engage the broader culture. He committed his order to the proper training of a generation of Holy Cross priests who might contribute to serious scholarship. He wished to see our congregation seize the opportunity to be a "powerful and vital intellectual force." Behind Zahm's efforts to form Holy Cross religious into specialized scholars lay his tough-minded criticism of the limits of the Holy Cross institutions of his day and his clear recognition that they were insignificant contributors to the shaping of American society and culture. Zahm understood the developing modern university and its importance for the nation's intellectual life and he wanted to fashion Holy Cross institutions in light of that understanding.

The issue is seen at its sharpest in the debate over the future of Notre Dame. I think it fair to say that Zahm had a quite different vision of Notre Dame than its erstwhile founder, Edward Sorin, and most of Sorin's successors, including Zahm's contemporary and rival, Andrew Morrissey. (Morrissey, by the way, served as president of Notre Dame from 1893 until 1905.) Sorin, Morrissey, and company had, to be blunt, a narrower vision of Notre Dame than did Zahm. In his centennial history of the university Fr. Arthur Hope even dared to suggest that the revered founder "countenanced no moves that might make Notre Dame a real university." Zahm never directly criticized Sorin, with whom he related well, but after the founder's death he savagely criticized the institution which Sorin had built and over which Morrissey now presided. His undiluted sentiments are revealed in a forceful letter he wrote in 1897 to his brother Albert from Rome, where he had been dispatched to get him away from Notre Dame and the controversy over his views on evolution. Listen to these pointed remarks delivered with undisguised bitterness:

> "It would indeed be a trial for me to return to the dull, humdrum, unintellectual, dwarfing environment where I spent, or rather, wasted the best years of my life. What a pity it is that our people do not realize the necessity of a higher culture for their members, especially those who are to devote their lives to the ennobling work of education." With few exceptions, he declared, "not one at Notre Dame has the faintest conception of the wants of a university and the demands of the age in which we live. Notre Dame ought to be one of the first educational institutions in the

land, whereas it is in reality nothing more than a large boarding house for elementary students."

Despite his subsequent efforts as U.S. Provincial of Holy Cross, Zahm's vision lost out to the more cautious and parochial approach of Morrissey. Morrissey was by most accounts likable, genial, and practical. Morrissey was also politically astute and he maneuvered to replace Zahm as provincial in 1906, just a year after Zahm had forced his resignation as Notre Dame's president. Thereafter the more limited Morrissey approach prevailed—a result perhaps understandable given the immigrant background of much of the Catholic population and the virulent strain of anti-Catholicism that afflicted the host society. Indeed for a complex of reasons the Morrissey approach (if it might be termed that) prevailed not only at Notre Dame but also, and even more so, here at the infant Columbia University, as the careful histories by Professor Covert and Fr. Connelly record.

Thereafter poor Zahm, either from fatigue or in defeat and disgust, moved away and began a long period of traveling exile which took him on lengthy trips to Latin America and Europe, and which led to the publication of a series of entertaining travelogues. Now, I accept the maxim that "to travel is to learn" and I want to encourage all students present to avail yourselves of the wonderful range of possibilities Fr. Arthur Wheeler oversees. Nevertheless, there seems something sad about Zahm's endless wanderings in the final decade and a half of his life in that he was deprived of involvement in the central educational enterprise of Holy Cross that had been his life's work.

Perhaps the sadness regarding Zahm's "exile" is compounded by the sense of wasted opportunities in the Holy Cross schools we love, and also in Catholic institutions more generally. Now I won't waste a lot of time uttering those sad words "what might have been." We should be grateful that our institutions survived and that they did so in some way genuinely fulfilling the goals of the order's founder, Basil Moreau, to educate both the mind and the heart, to prepare not only "useful citizens for society" but also future "citizens of heaven." Their goal remained, as Professor James Covert put it in his *Point of Pride*, "to produce Christian humanists for the active life." Zahm assuredly would have endorsed this goal as a starting point, but he wanted to move beyond the more defensive position of an institution wherein vocational training was provided and Catholic doctrine and practice imbued in the students to equip them to withstand the rather unfriendly culture into which they would enter upon graduation. Instead, he favored a more ambitious and open approach. Both through his own personal scholarly efforts and through his labors to develop Holy Cross institutions Zahm clearly intended to engage the culture and to transform it. He wanted, as one observer put it, "to make Christian truths shine more brightly so that souls may be attracted to that which is Truth itself." He surely thought that the "Christian humanists" trained in Catholic colleges would be about this endeavor—that they might emerge equipped and ready to serve as instruments in Catholicism's shaping of the main elements of American culture and society.

Those familiar with American Catholic higher education in the twentieth century know that the open and engaging Zahm vision was not pursued. In the first half of the century, Catholic thinking and institutions developed on a rather separate track from their secular peer institutions. They stood over and against the dominant culture in most areas. While the Notre Dame football team might sally forth to engage all comers, Catholic universities marched to the beat of their own drummer. By the 1950's strong criticism was aimed at the universities, not only for their supposed "ghetto" status and siege mentality but also because of the failure of Catholic scholarship to influence the broad culture.

In his influential 1955 essay, "American Catholics and the Intellectual Life," Monsignor John Tracy Ellis quoted and endorsed the view of a British observer of American affairs, Denis Brogan, that "in no Western society is the intellectual prestige of Catholicism lower" than in the United States. Ellis's essay set off a firestorm of self-criticism among Catholic educators. By the 1960's things certainly were "a changing." Acting under the impulse of the Second Vatican Council, a new generation of Catholic university administrators eagerly sought to shed the defensive mentality. Catholic institutions now would be thought of, in the words of a noted university leader, as a crossroads "where all the intellectual and moral currents of our time meet and are thoroughly considered." The broad culture was to be seriously engaged. John Zahm must have been cheering from his grave.

Engaging the culture, however, proved a more complicated and challenging task than many of the leaders of Catholic universities of the 1960's expected—and also, dare we say it in a lecture devoted to his name—than John A. Zahm appreciated. Sadly, from the perspective provided by the last quarter century, we can see that some schools simply adopted what the legal scholar Mary Ann Glendon has termed in a somewhat different context "the way of the chameleon." They aimed to blend in with the "established patterns of secular culture" and did it so successfully that they became virtually unrecognizable as Catholic universities. They lost any capacity to engage thoughtfully and influence the culture. And this at a time when modern cultures, including those of the "advanced" societies of the contemporary West, increasingly discarded any transcendent sense, and as Pope John Paul II has argued, largely lost their capacity to provide a convincing account of freedom, truth, and the human good. In the United States a marginalization of religion took hold among the cultural elite which dominated the national media, policy making, the courts, the entertainment industry and, let us add, the universities. Religion might be tolerated for the masses so long as it was kept suitably privatized and sequestered from the broad political, social, and intellectual realms.

The lack of receptivity to religious perspectives on the part of cultural elites, however, in *no* way removes the obligation of the Church, its institutions, and its members to enter into a critical dialogue with contemporary cultures and to attempt to influence them in constructive ways. Given not only the fundamentally incarnational and sacramental nature of the Catholic worldview, but also the inescapable influence of culture upon the Church, it seems to me wrong-headed to suggest that the Church, and especially Church-sponsored educational institutions, might simply adopt an attitude of hostility to the culture and work only from a disposition of opposition to it. On the other hand, there is no justification for a passive acceptance of the culture, because an indiscriminate embrace of whatever cultural forces prevail at the moment may lead to the endorsement of values antithetical to the Gospel. Surely the aim should be to attempt, through dialogue, forceful advocacy, and patient witness, to shape a culture that is more favorable to Christian faith and practice. The pressing, indeed urgent, need for this dialogue and transforming action in the American context hardly bears comment. But how is it to be done and by whom?

Such questions are more easily posed than answered. Clearly all Christians are called forth to witness in the world and in so doing to influence the world around them. Yet, the history of the Catholic Church and its members in the United States is not a narrative of their transforming power within the culture and society. Rather it is more a story of assimilation, in which Catholics suitably accommodated themselves to the prevailing economic and political orders of market capitalism, liberal democracy, and the increasingly dominant secular culture. For the most part, and especially since Vatican II, Catholics as an identifiable group have rarely found themselves in great tension with the American environment, nor have they noticeably influenced this environment despite persuasive pleas that the time is right and the need great for them to do so.

In reflecting on how the Church might engage and influence American culture, attention has centered, not surprisingly, on the role that might be played by the substantial network of Catholic colleges and universities in the United States. Pope John Paul II's 1990 apostolic constitution *On Catholic Universities* (*Ex Corde Ecclesiae—From the Heart of the Church*) envisions the important contribution that Catholic universities have to make to the Church's work of evangelization and to its engagement with culture. The apostolic constitution clarifies that:

> All the basic academic activities of a Catholic university are connected with and in harmony with the evangelizing mission of the church: research carried out in the light of the Christian message which puts discoveries at the service of individuals and society; education offered in a faith context that forms men and women capable of rational and critical judgment and conscious of the transcendent dignity of the human person; professional training that incorporates ethical values and a sense of service to individuals and to society; the dialogue with culture that makes the faith better understood and the theological research that translates faith into contemporary language.

*Ex Corde Ecclesiae* evokes well the potential of Catholic universities in this broad domain. There should be no illusions, however, about the difficult challenge which lies before those institutions still aiming to fulfill their promise to contribute constructively to the culture.

Any honest examination would reveal that Catholic universities of late have more often been followers rather than leaders in determining their academic futures. As the Jesuit sociologist John Coleman has argued, Catholic institutions have "mirrored rather than challenged a consumerist, technological and individualistic view of education which is the regnant paradigm in American higher education." The trail for them, and in fact for the whole American academy, has been blazed by the great secular research universities. During the post-World War II era the great achievements of American science and technology won notable prestige for such institutions. At the same time such institutions also became the locale for much of the nation's intellectual life and the source of many of the ideas and proposals—both good and ill—that influenced the society and culture. These major institutions exercised a significant control over the definition of knowledge and the generation of knowledge. They largely provided the context in which Catholic institutions operated, especially from the 1960's onwards. As the Catholic schools passed through a quarter century of debate over their own mission and in many cases some attenuation of their identity, they were hardly fit to influence others. Far from being agents for change or significant contributors on the academic scene and in the broader culture, Catholic universities too often were simply the object of the very forces at work in the secular universities.

This situation must change if Catholic universities are to engage the broad culture in a genuine dialogue—in the kind of dialogue that John Zahm aimed to pursue over a century ago. Only vibrant Catholic institutions hold any promise of fulfilling the promise of *Ex Corde Ecclesiae* and exerting even some influence on contemporary American culture. If they are but pale imitations of their secular counterparts, they will surrender any ability to engage the culture and will merely reflect it: ultimately, they will be subject to it. While Catholic universities unavoidably and necessarily are part of and influenced by the academy as a whole, they need unwavering conviction to work towards a different vision of what a university must be.

The essential challenge for the contemporary Catholic university is to be faithful in pursuing its mission and in maintaining and enhancing its fundamental identity. Such a university will seek to provide a coherent model of the integration of religion and academic life and, in so doing, will accord theology a place of central importance. It will aim to validate the age-old Catholic presupposition that faith and reason are not mutually exclusive. It will be built upon the deep belief, which Zahm assuredly held, that the dedicated search for truth in its various aspects can be pursued appropriately in light of its "essential connection to the supreme Truth, who is God." The survival and development of institutions which are guided by this vision and which maintain high academic standards will certainly contribute to the culture, not least by demonstrating that first-rate academic institutions need not inexorably succumb to the dynamics of secularization. They can do much more.

Authentic Catholic institutions will transmit to the broad culture the intellectual and artistic heritage of Catholic Christianity and will foster creative developments in Catholic intellectual life across the whole range of inquiry from the humanities to the sciences to the professions. If true to their mission, Catholic institutions will challenge and influence parts of the prevailing culture of academe by renewing their treasured emphasis on community, and by successfully demonstrating their religiously–motivated concern for students, something which still seems to be highly valued here at the University of Portland. Surely genuine Catholic universities should manifest a distinct model of teaching and learning where both the intellectual and moral virtues are witnessed and valued, where questions of ethics and character are not ignored. They will dare to be scholarly institutions unafraid to form consciences. Those who graduate from such schools will have an informed view of what is good and will have been encouraged and challenged to live a good life, a life in which faith is not sequestered in some private domain. It is through such graduates that the Catholic university should expect to influence the culture and society around it.

As *Ex Corde Ecclesiae* makes clear, Catholic universities potentially have a more direct role to play through the scholarship generated within them. In Catholic universities scholars must engage in research which analyzes and critiques contemporary political, economic, and social developments from a Catholic perspective. Such scholars must be unafraid to undertake thoughtful social criticism in an effort to forge a more just and moral order. One must operate within the culture yet seek to transform it or, as John Coleman has put it, "to go against the grain by working within the culture to subvert it and deflect it." There is much that needs to be deflected!

Speaking about the potential of Catholic universities is relatively easy. Meeting that potential is much more difficult. Many nominally Catholic institutions have largely given up the effort, influenced by factors like the quest for prestige, acceptance by secular counterparts, and the desire to assert institutional autonomy from any Church authority. Fortunately, some Catholic institutions—among them I rejoice to say the University of Portland—have emerged from the turmoil of the post-Vatican II identity crisis still aiming to live up to their true potential. Their success in doing so will be largely determined by the inspired effort of committed faculty members, administrators and students like those of you gathered here. You are the on-site builders who must work to fulfill the ambitious plan of a visionary like John Zahm fully aware of the challenges and difficulties involved. You are the ones to make Christian truths shine more brightly so that souls may be attracted to that which is Truth itself. As a distinct tribute to Zahm, your own impressive scholarly community might continue to bring about the needed rapprochement between religion and science, building upon your existing and notable efforts.

May the Lord bless you in your important work.

## Comment on "Notre Dame's Vision for Undergraduate Education" 2008

*Notre Dame administrators like to engage in formulating statements that they think will capture a "vision" for undergraduate education. These are normally filled with academic jargon designed to please constituencies like accrediting agencies. I wrote a brief response to a circulated draft of such a statement.*

April 22, 2008

Dear Committee,

I read this draft last evening and was rather disappointed. It reads like a somewhat watered-down effort, the type of "product" of a committee which tries to touch the various bases but ends up with something that has a certain "public relations" boilerplate feel to it. The present mission statement of the university is superior.

Might I suggest that the committee carefully read Pope Benedict's recent address to Catholic educators and draw some inspiration from the following: "First and foremost every Catholic educational institution is a place to encounter the living God who in Jesus Christ reveals his transforming love and truth. This relationship elicits a desire to grow in the knowledge and understanding of Christ and his teaching. In this way those who meet him are drawn by the very power of the Gospel to lead a new life characterized by all that is beautiful, good and true; a life of Christian witness nurtured and strengthened within the community of the Lord's disciples, the Church." The present draft seems reluctant to mention Jesus Christ—how sad!

On a specific point—the draft suggests that Notre Dame nurture in its students "a keenly developed ethical sense." What does this mean in practice? Peter Singer at Princeton has a "keenly developed ethical sense" which apparently allows for the killing of babies. Would this "ethical sense" be what we encourage in our students?

I am not convinced that there is the need for a specific "vision statement" for undergraduate education, but if there is such a need we must have a superior effort to the present draft.

Bill Miscamble, C.S.C.
History Department

## Discerning One's Call in the Contemporary University: One Priest's Rambling Reflections on Happiness, Mission, and Meaning
### 2011

*The Edith Stein Project originated in response to the annual production of the* Vagina Monologues *at Notre Dame. The wonderful young women who began the project organized an initial series of conferences with a focus on women and Pope John Paul II's new feminism. They hoped to provide a vision of men and women as both equal in dignity and complementary. Since then, the Edith Stein conference has broadened its focus and makes a significant contribution to discussion of crucial issues on campus. I was glad to speak at the conference which reflected on the theme of vocation.*

## Introduction

My thoughts focus on the subject of vocation and how I, as a faculty member, have engaged students on this crucial question during my now quarter-century of teaching undergraduates at Notre Dame, and indeed how the university has engaged folk in thinking of their calling in life.

Can you believe that I began teaching here in 1986—that is, before most of you were born! I was completing my seminary studies at the time and the rector at Moreau Seminary graciously allowed me to put my history training to use and to teach one undergraduate course each semester. I subsequently joined the permanent faculty of the history department after my ordination in 1988 and have been working away in this part of the Lord's vineyard ever since.

I have had the good fortune to get to know a good number of my students—not as many as I would wish, but still a good number—and I stay in touch with some of them. Indeed I have presided at their weddings and baptized their children.

Some of those children, dare I say, are now selecting colleges. Some will soon be coming to Notre Dame. What is the situation that they will face? How have things changed since the time their parents studied here?

## Situation for College Students Today

Let me offer just a few comments on some of the challenges facing today's students that their parents may not have confronted, or at least not to the same degree. Perhaps we might have a discussion later on whether such factors as those I mention are really significant. Have they really handicapped those seeking to discern their calling?

Before doing so, however, let me note that students of this generation have to face similar challenges with regard to abusing alcohol, having sex without love or commitment, doing drugs etc. that have bedeviled college life especially since the 1960's. For too many students there is still a "booze to books and then back to booze," or is it "books to booze and then back to books" shift that seems to take place on Sundays as folk gear up for study and that goes into reverse on Thursday nights. But let me also note that college students today, especially in elite colleges like Notre Dame, are rather privileged and much more affluent. They have more "stuff" and there are more opportunities and possibilities provided.

**Technology and Communications:** We have witnessed an amazing revolution in communication and information since I began teaching here. Students today are wired for information of all sorts—the ubiquitous Facebook, Twitter, blogs, email, text messaging, television, smart phones, iPods and iPads, and so forth. There is a lot of "incoming."

I read a recent piece that complained that young people are inundated with information. But it suggested that the ability for deep contemplative thought is being lost. Of course, the complaint is that all this information covers over and even distorts a real quest for true wisdom. Could this be true?

**Seemingly Endless Choice:** We live in a world of endless choice. "Choice" is put forth "to seduce the consumer at every turn," said the *Economist* in a recent issue. Choice in what one eats, what one drinks, how one looks, what one studies, how one is entertained, what one does with one's money, what "lifestyle" one chooses.

And yet in what one writer calls "the paradox of choice," this is not all good. Too much choice can debilitate folk and lead to indecision—and even to a failure to choose at all. Choice can cause anxiety, confusion, and regret. People worry about making the wrong choice. Some suggest that young people are not well-equipped to make a long-term choice and then to stick with it. They fear that they might get it wrong—and so choose to defer. Could this possibly be true?

**Personal Autonomy and American Catholic Culture:** I think it fair to say that many Catholics of the baby boom generation, those born from 1946 through 1964 (perhaps your parents), largely moved beyond the religious subculture that aided Catholics in living out their faith way back in that last century. As a result, your parents raised you in the mainstream of American society. You have enjoyed affluence and, in your young lives, an emphasis has been placed on achievement and personal autonomy. Americans have become ever more accustomed to living more individualized lives. People here are driven by the temptations to get ahead, to consume more and to be entertained. In this age the overlapping communities of family, parish, and neighborhood have lost their significance and the role they played in your parents or grandparents' time.

Today the emphasis is on autonomy, and notions of community and solidarity just seem a little strange. We still talk here of the Notre Dame community and the Notre Dame family, but deep down isn't it primarily about the individual? About you? And yet with all this supposed autonomy and personal freedom students feel "an ill-defined restlessness," a "vague unease," as they ask, "Is this what I am supposed to be doing?" Has anyone ever asked this?

**Values and Tolerance:** It is said that this generation of young people is the most tolerant of any before it. They supposedly ask, "Who am I to say what someone else should think or do or believe?"

But tolerance has an ugly side. Writing in a 2009 Notre Dame magazine article, Colleen Moore, an alumnus who works at Notre Dame, suggested that "such high tolerance can also make them so afraid of offending or judging others that they become even more isolated from one another and from what they themselves believe. For many of these Catholic students—good, kind, and smart students—all religions are pretty much the same, Jesus is more a good example to follow than the Savior, stealing from the dining hall doesn't count but getting a good job, being 'nice' and happy do."

May I ask if Ms. Moore is right? Is tolerance the highest value? Do young people sense that they live in an increasingly relativistic world where no one should really say what is right or wrong either for them or others? Is it just about getting a good job, being "nice" and happy, whatever that may mean?

Now I could point to other signposts, such as the students' willingness to serve others through various volunteer programs that suggest that today's college folk are indeed concerned with more than themselves. They are generous and good and want to make a positive contribution. Some have clear goals as to what they should do with their lives.

But perhaps you might concede to me that there is a good deal of uncertainty and questioning that besets college students and young adults today. Just a week or so back a young woman came to see me and essentially said, "I spent all of high school with the big goal of getting into Notre Dame, but now that I'm here I am much less clear about what it is I should be doing." Is she just an isolated case? Shouldn't she have come to the university and found precisely the place where she could have her questions answered? Isn't that what the university is supposed to do?

### *The Contemporary University and the Meaning of Life*

Dear friends, I have some difficult news to report to you. Contemporary universities apparently are not that interested either in addressing questions of real meaning or in addressing crucial questions about life. In his provocative book *Excellence Without a Soul,* the former dean of Harvard College, Harry R. Lewis, observes that the "role of moral education has withered" in contemporary universities. He argues that "universities have forgotten their larger educational role for college students. . . . To help them grow up, to learn who they are, to search for a larger purpose in their lives, and to leave colleges better human beings." He argues that faculty members have given up for the most part on guiding students to seek a "larger purpose for their lives."

Harry Lewis is hardly some crank or outsider. In another telling comment, former Harvard president Derek Bok laments that students are not prepared to be good citizens on earth (he's not particularly worried about preparation for citizenship in heaven!). The distinguished literary scholar Andrew Delbanco of Columbia University regrets that students are not aided to confront the "ethical issues posed by modern life." Other examples could be given.

Of course the philosophers and intellectual historians among us could explain that this circumstance was rather likely given the triumph of secularization and the Enlightenment. Latter-day liberalism has failed to provide a coherent and well-grounded conception of the good and postmodernist thought has devolved into a kind of cultural nihilism. Intellect has been detached from morality. In this increasingly utilitarian world, the drift is toward asking "Will it work?" rather than "Is it right?" The former question, it seems, can be answered—at least in the sciences and engineering. But who can provide a basis for answering the latter question?

These are important issues but do they really apply at Catholic colleges and universities? Surely our schools are places where there is a deep concern for the formation of the whole person? Surely we are not limiting ourselves to providing a certain pre-professional or vocational training so that students can pursue some mere "career"? Surely we are places that want students to embrace the truth and not to content themselves with far less. One of my valued colleagues, Prof. Brad Gregory, remonstrates against students "absorbing the self-centered ideologies of the wider society just so that you can go out and live for yourself, make a bunch of money, buy a nice house, and get your Lexus." Surely it is here at places like Notre Dame that, again in the words of Brad Gregory, "We want you to become who God meant you to be, precisely and paradoxically by learning how to love and serve others."

Of course, Notre Dame proclaims that it is indeed educating the "whole person." It wants to say that here there is no "strong bifurcation between classroom education and the rest of your life." While the secular university's purpose is merely "to encourage critical thinking, expand your horizons, and help you gain sufficient knowledge to serve your vocational goals," at Notre Dame we claim to provide more. We say that we don't want to exclude from consideration your moral and religious views, your values and actions outside the classroom, the kind of person you want to be. In the ideal of Notre Dame we claim to provide an education for the whole person, an education that offers a coherent set of values and beliefs. Dare I say, we claim to provide training for folks to fulfill their vocation in life. We want to guide them to be Christian men and women.

### Do We Succeed?

Here we must get to the nub of the issue and ask: how well are we doing? Do we really deliver on this promise? Do we really aid our students to discern their vocations, their distinct callings? Where are the various elements brought together?

Let me speak a little to my own experience serving as a priest-teacher here at Notre Dame over this past quarter century. I have always seen myself as part of a much larger enterprise. Others are doing their part, and our collective effort will fulfill the promise. The broad curriculum, especially those required theology and philosophy courses, the encouragement to participate in the liturgy and to receive the sacraments, and the opportunities to serve especially encouraged by the Center for Social Concerns all play an integral role.

Nonetheless, I have hoped that my approach to teaching would reflect the Christian pedagogy outlined by the founder of my Holy Cross order, Blessed Fr. Basil Moreau, C.S.C., who instructed that "the mind could not be cultivated at the expense of the heart." Of course, the best teachers convey as much by what they do and who they are as by what they say. My good teachers have modeled for me integrity, honesty, perseverance, intellectual and moral courage, and a profound commitment to the truth. I can only pray that in some ways I have modeled such virtues for my students. More explicitly, I hope I have also conveyed my own desire to follow in the path of Jesus so as to serve them; to awaken and deepen each one's sense of his or her own giftedness; and to challenge them to use their gifts well in the service of others. But, friends, I wish I had done and could do this better!

I teach my courses on U.S. foreign policy, postwar presidents, and now Australian history (perhaps the latter should be a required course!), et cetera, and they are reasonably successful in the narrow sense of being decent "history courses," but I am increasingly troubled by my own failure to help my students discern what really matters in life. I hope that as a teacher of history I can clarify that some important lessons of the past are painfully learned: that things don't always turn out right, nor the way we expect, and certainly not the way we want.

But as I look honestly at my effort I am unsure whether I go further, whether I convey by word and deed such crucial values as respect for the dignity of every human person and life. Do I emphasize sufficiently a need to take responsibility for each other and for the common good? Do I reveal with conviction that in the end a truly good life is about faith and family and friendship? Do my students emerge from my classes with a clear sense that we must lean into life from the disposition of gratitude for our blessings rather than of resentment? Do they gain a more profound appreciation that they must pursue their calling as students in response to a deeper call to follow Christ?

I raise these questions regarding the limitations of my own courses because I don't want to be a person throwing stones from a glass house. I realize full well that I need to reflect on how I can better assist my students in this whole area.

That said, let me speculate that a lot of the education that occurs at Notre Dame reflects the bifurcation of which I spoke earlier. Is the education you receive here all that different from one you would receive at any other good school? Is the whole person really educated at Notre Dame?

Sadly, I fear that Notre Dame has been overly influenced by the general norms of the contemporary university. The "reward structure" of the contemporary university is not designed to support those faculty members who want to commit to educating the whole person, and ND is no different.

There are terrific faculty here at Notre Dame and wonderful operations like the Center for Ethics and Culture, but I'm afraid that much of what occurs here is but a replica of the bifurcated approach to education that is now criticized elsewhere; an approach that begs off providing an education that helps students discern a larger purpose in their lives.

In this circumstance, identifying good faculty and choosing courses wisely becomes very important. I still believe a rich and valuable Catholic education is available here if students are diligent in shaping that education. If one manages to take courses with the likes of Professors Solomon and Freddoso, Mary Keys and Brad Gregory, David Fagerberg and John Cavadini, then I suspect you will experience an education that, in the words of the university's mission statement, will aid " you to live morally worthy lives . . . guided by the Gospel and the Catholic tradition." These folk are reliable guides for you. Students will have to take the initiative and look for an education that moves far beyond mere vocational or professional training. You will be the better for it if you do.

*Happiness, Mission, Meaning, and What Really Matters*
Well, I promised "rambling reflections" in my title, and I trust I have delivered on that promise. I did also mention that they would be on "Happiness, Mission, Meaning, and What Really Matters," and I trust you might see that in a certain implicit way my remarks have touched on these crucial matters.

They also reveal how necessary gatherings like this conference are. I hope you will take full advantage of the many wonderful offerings available over these two days.

But let me make some more explicit comments. Some of you are probably aware that "happiness research" is a growing field in the academy right now. Researchers want to discover what it is that makes people happy and so forth. They have come to some working conclusions that might be of interest. They have determined that wealth doesn't make us that much happier, at least after a certain level of basic needs have been met; level of education and a high I.Q. doesn't guarantee happiness; youth doesn't guarantee it either.

On the positive side, this research indicates that religion, family, and friendship seemed to contribute. A book titled *Authentic Happiness,* by Martin Seligman (apparently a very big name in the happiness research field), concluded that the three main components of happiness are (1) pleasure, that is, doing things we like; (2) engagement, that is, involvement with one's family, work, relationships; (3) meaning, that is, using personal strengths and talents to serve some larger end. Of these three components, pleasure is the least consequential; engagement and meaning matter most.

Is this a surprise to us? Of course not! We know it from our own lives—we are more satisfied when we have the deep sense that our lives are meaningful and that what we do matters in the lives of others. The pursuit of pleasure can provide a temporary lift but it tends not to last. St. Ignatius of Loyola discerned this quite some time ago in a very experiential way.

In the end it seems, for religious and for secular folks, even the cerebral virtues like intellectual curiosity, love of learning, and discovery are less strongly tied to a satisfied life than the interpersonal virtues like kindness, gratitude, and the capacity for love. Now if I were a psychologist I would start telling you to try to be more generous and to deepen your relationships with folk around you—and that would be fine.

But I want to speak at a deeper level as a priest, a minister of the gospel, and as a disciple of Jesus Christ. Authentic happiness will only come when one's sense of meaning is derived from pursuing the mission God asks of you and allowing God's life to enter you.

Students of whatever time and place have to confront this challenging call—your parents' generation, your own generation, and your children's generation. They must discern God's call and do it. (It will change in certain details as you move from being students, but the fundamental call remains.) I think this is what Dr. Martin Luther King, Jr., was conveying in a 1956 sermon when he said, "I still believe that standing up for the truth of God is the greatest thing in the world. This is the end of life. The end of life is not to be happy. The end of life is not to achieve pleasure and avoid pain. The end of life is to do the will of God, come what may."

In a sense happiness will take care of itself if one has truly clarified what matters most. On his recent visit to Britain for the beatification of Blessed John Henry Newman, Pope Benedict spoke to a gathering of students and invited them to become saints. He said to them, "I am asking you not to be content with second best. I am asking you not to pursue one limited goal and ignore all the others." He then continued, "Happiness is something we all want, but one of the great tragedies in this world is that so many people never find it, because they look for in the wrong places. The key to it is very simple—true happiness is to be found in God." The Pope then explained we need to have the courage to place our deepest hopes in God alone . . . [for] only He can satisfy the deepest needs of our hearts."

We must strengthen and encourage each other as we seek to discover and live out our vocations. I hope and pray that Catholic universities like Notre Dame might, in the future, assist you better in this quest. I pray that each of you will have the courage to look to God and to do his will. Then, as good men and women have discovered over the centuries, you will find deep in your hearts what makes life truly worthwhile.

# Section II: The Faculty Issue—Again

## The Faculty "Problem":
## How Can Catholic Identity Be Preserved?
## 2007

*The statutes of the University of Notre Dame declare that "the essential character of the University as a Catholic institution of higher learning shall at all times be maintained." The mission statement of Notre Dame specifies what this requires by holding that "the Catholic identity of the University depends upon, and is nurtured by, the continuing presence of a predominant number of Catholic intellectuals." Fr. Edward A. Malloy clarified, at the time that the mission statement was adopted, that more than "a mere majority" of Catholic faculty would be required to meet this goal.*

*Determining who will teach in a Catholic university and take responsibility for its Catholic mission and character is the crucial issue that confronts Notre Dame. I reengaged this issue in the following essay, which was published in* America *magazine. The article drew a lively response.*

Catholic universities in the United States possess a certain Potemkin Village quality. While their buildings are quite real, what goes on within them has increasingly lost its distinctive content and come to resemble what occurs in secular institutions of higher learning. Students emerge from Catholic schools rather unfamiliar with the riches of the Catholic intellectual tradition and with their imaginations untouched by a religious sensibility. This reality is painstakingly revealed in *Catholic Higher Education* (Oxford University Press, 2006) by Melanie Morey and John Piderit, s.j., who predict that "a crisis is looming within American Catholic higher education." It will be increasingly difficult to maintain even a Catholic facade in the academic life of these institutions.

Morey, Piderit, and other thoughtful commentators argue that if Catholic universities are to navigate successfully through the difficult challenges of the moment, they must confront the fundamental issue of faculty composition and address the need to recruit a committed Catholic faculty. Is this possible? Or is the day too far past when an institution might renew its religious-ly–based mission by hiring faculty members who will support and sustain it?

## At the Tipping Point?

An examination of the present situation at the University of Notre Dame suggests that the tipping point is at hand—a parlous situation that assuredly is replicated in all the major Catholic universities. Dramatic action will be required to secure the school's Catholic identity. If Notre Dame, with its abundant resources and its storied role in Catholic education, fails in this effort, one must wonder who can succeed. Some specific details illustrate the nature of the crisis as it exists at Notre Dame.

Notre Dame's mission statement draws upon *Ex Corde Ecclesiae* and rightly declares that the "Catholic identity of the University depends upon . . . the continuing presence of a pre-dominant number of Catholic intellectuals" on the faculty. Nonetheless, the last three decades have seen a dramatic decline in the number of Catholic faculty members. The figure as of 2006 was 53%, which is somewhat inflated by those who answered "Catholic" on the faculty questionnaire but for whom the practice of the faith appears nominal at best.

The prospects for the immediate future clearly worry senior administrators. Notre Dame's provost, Thomas Burish, has explained: "When the prospective rate of Catholic retirements is plotted against the contemporary rate of Catholic hires as a constant, it is clear that soon Notre Dame will no longer have the predominant number of Catholic faculty members whom we require."

In Catholic universities, as in their secular counterparts, the academic department constitutes the key entity where hiring decisions are made. Today at Notre Dame, however, few departments conscientiously and enthusiastically support the mission statement's call for a predominant number of Catholic faculty: the theology department and the law school are notable and honorable exceptions.

In some departments, a person who tries to raise the issue in a serious way risks being marginalized. Professor Kevin Hart, a brilliant Catholic intellectual and the editor of the journal *Religion and Literature*, dared to do this in the English department. Hart objected to a candidate appointment he thought incompatible with the Catholic mission of the university and found himself roundly criticized for his intervention.

The issue can still be raised in the department I know best, the History department, yet that guarantees little, as is evident from the results of its recent hirings. There are now 32 members of the history department; only 12 are Catholic. This past year we hired three additional faculty members, only one of whom is Catholic. This is hardly the way to maintain a predominant number of Catholic intellectuals. In fact, we hired in exactly the reverse proportion needed. As it moves into the future, Notre Dame must hire at least two-thirds Catholic faculty simply to arrest the decline that ultimately puts at risk its identity as a Catholic school.

One sometimes hears that the root of the problem is not in the departmental hiring process, but rather that it is a "supply" problem: there just are not enough really good Catholic scholars out there. A corollary is that all the really smart Catholics have gone into law or medicine or business. But should we accept the supply-side argument? Forgive me for being a little skeptical. The Rev. Andrew Greeley's careful research since the 1960's put to rest the canards that Catholics were anti-intellectual, overly materialistic, academically inferior, and not well represented in graduate schools. He demonstrated that plenty of Catholics have pursued academic careers across a wide range of disciplines. Catholic scholars there are aplenty.

Implicitly the further claim is made that these scholars just are not good enough, given the present aspirations of universities like Notre Dame. Not enough of these scholars have the right academic pedigree: they have not received the imprimatur of an elite graduate school (the Ivy League, Chicago, Berkeley or Stanford, with an occasional stoop down to Michigan); they have not won the prominent fellowships or published with the prestigious presses. Perhaps there is something to this argument. Certainly a focus on the criteria of academic pedigree and prestige narrows the available pool. Forgive my skepticism, but I am familiar with too many cases in which an able Catholic did not obtain a position here.

### The Cambridge Cases

My skepticism was especially heightened from a particular episode in 1999–2000, when the history department investigated the possibility of appointing the distinguished British Catholic intellectual Eamon Duffy. Duffy, who teaches at the University of Cambridge, is the author of a landmark book, *The Stripping of the Altars*, which reframed how scholars have viewed the English Reformation. He is a historian of the first rank, well-known on both sides of the Atlantic. His appointment would have done much to raise the reputation of Notre Dame's history department.

Yet no offer was made to Eamon Duffy, so we do not know whether he would have come to northern Indiana. Colleagues worried about the "fit" (always a useful concern if you want to block something) and about the conditions of his employment, given that he would have done some significant teaching in Notre Dame's London program. But strikingly, there was concern that Eamon Duffy was too much of a "Catholic apologist" and that he engaged in discussion of contemporary church issues, notably in the pages of the British liberal Catholic magazine, *The Tablet*. His tone was deemed rather on the "polemical side" (Duffy dared to think that Queen Elizabeth I has a few things to answer for). The depth of Duffy's faith commitment, the impact of it on his scholarly work, and his intellectual commitments bothered certain people. So Eamon Duffy continues his teaching at Cambridge today, much to Notre Dame's loss.

Just a year or so before Eamon Duffy's appointment was considered, an appointment was made at Notre Dame of another Cambridge academic, this one in the English department. Professor Jill Mann was appointed for a five-year term to occupy an endowed chair each spring semester. Mann, a distinguished scholar and Chaucer specialist, served as president of the New Chaucer Society, where she gave a presidential address entitled "Chaucer and Atheism." As she blithely revealed in the opening paragraph of her address, the "atheism" to which she referred was her own. Notably, she appeared to want her atheism to have a major impact on her scholarly work.

Professor Mann recognized the importance of religion (both in medieval times and our own), but her intellectual suppositions were quite at odds with a Catholic worldview. Toward the conclusion of her address she said: "If you believe, as I do, that 'there's nobody here but us chickens,' then you also believe that there is no predetermined or transcendental truth. I agree with Richard Rorty and Stanley Fish that truth is not something we discover but something we make." For her, "the dangerous people . . . are not those who say that there is no absolute truth, but those who say there is, and that they know what it is." Perhaps she was unfamiliar with John Paul II's *Veritatis Splendor*; and presumably she might have found amusing—or even dangerous—the declaration in *Ex Corde Ecclesiae* that "it is the honor and responsibility of a Catholic university to consecrate itself without reserve to the cause of truth."

Professor Mann's views may have troubled some of those who approved her hire, just as they did a few hardy souls in the English department who were overwhelmingly outvoted. But the chance to make a notable appointment that would increase Notre Dame's visibility among its secular peers won out. Hiring an individual who might in certain ways undermine the school's true mission took a back seat to the payoffs in terms of academic prestige and reputation. Appointments like Mann's suggest that prestige trumps Catholic mission in the hiring process.

### Needed Action

Occasionally, of course, fine appointments are made. A recent press release proudly announced the appointment of Professor William Evans, a noted economist from the University of Maryland. But no press release advised that the aforementioned Kevin Hart of the English department had decided to leave Notre Dame for the University of Virginia. Notre Dame will need many more appointments like that of Evans, while still retaining scholars like Hart, if it is to forge a faculty truly supportive of its identity as a Catholic university.

The matter of hiring Catholic faculty has been of concern at Notre Dame for some time. The Rev. Robert Sullivan, of the history department and the Erasmus Institute, now heads an effort to identify able Catholic scholars. He also heads an ad hoc committee, whose members are appointed by Provost Thomas Burish, on recruiting outstanding Catholic faculty members. One of the charges for this committee is to identify "the best practices for hiring Catholic faculty members." One can only hope and pray for the success of these endeavors.

It must be understood, however, that this is not a matter that can be massaged by minor measures. The temptation for administrators is to hope that a little adjustment here and a bit of tinkering there might improve the situation without stirring faculty opposition. Settling for minor measures in the present circumstances, however, indicates a complicity in the secularization process. A major change in the hiring process is required, and the need for it must be approved at the level of the board of trustees and implemented with courageous leadership, whatever faculty resistance it generates.

If the seemingly inevitable downward trend in the Catholic percentage of the faculty is to be arrested and reversed, a major board decision calling for two-thirds of all future appointments to be committed Catholic scholars is essential. This would require very different ways of hiring from the department-based procedures of today. The university would need to engage in what might be termed strategic hiring or hiring for mission. A recognition that this approach is crucial to its identity could drive the endeavor. It would require Notre Dame (and other schools that want to preserve their Catholic mission and character) to be truly different from their secular "preferred peer" schools. Failure to take such action, however, will lead schools like Notre Dame to merely replicate such secular institutions and to surrender what remains of their distinctiveness. This is surely a sad prospect for those who hoped, with *Ex Corde Ecclesiae*, that a Catholic university might constitute "an authentic human community animated by the spirit of Christ."

## Are There Any (Really Good) Catholic Scholars Out There? Further Thoughts on the Faculty "Problem" 2007

*My article in* America *provoked reactions from a range of commentators. The very specificity of the article attracted attention—especially the references to the Cambridge scholars Eamon Duffy and Jill Mann.* America *magazine ran a special section of responses in a subsequent issue. A particularly notable response came from my history department colleague John McGreevy, who then served as chair of the history department and now serves as dean of the College of Arts and Letters at Notre Dame. (I had overseen John's own appointment at Notre Dame during my own term as chair of the history department.) McGreevy replied to me in the pages of* America's *sister publication* Commonweal, *and he took issue with some of my arguments. I responded quickly to him on the Mirror of Justice website, and I include my pointed response here.*

Raising questions concerning faculty hiring and commitment in Catholic universities is a somewhat risky business. To address the matter in a forthright manner invites criticism that one is either divisive or unconcerned with academic quality—labels which carry limited cachet in university circles. It is hardly surprising, then, that this crucial issue—the elephant in the room when considering the character and identity of Catholic universities and colleges—receives such little direct public discussion and attention.

Yet the overall reaction to my recent article in *America* made clear to me that serious participants in and observers of Catholic higher education know that this is an issue that must be faced if the atrophy in the distinctive character of Catholic universities is to be arrested and reversed. I am grateful to all those who took the opportunity to offer comments on my essay either in the letters gathered in a recent "State of the Question" compilation in *America* or in discussions on various blogs—most notably those of *Commonweal, America*, and "Mirror of Justice." I am especially appreciative of the response of my department chair John McGreevy that appeared in *America's* sister publication *Commonweal* under the title "Catholic Enough? Religious Identity at Notre Dame." His article provides my point of departure for some further comments. I will also address observations raised by other respondents.

Here I explore three crucial issues: (1) what number of committed Catholic faculty is needed to assure fulfillment of mission in a Catholic school; (2) the available supply of such dedicated scholars; and (3) the intellectual needs of Catholic students. But I must first emphasize that nothing in my piece should be read as showing a lack of appreciation for non-Catholic faculty who support the mission of a Catholic university. I have the utmost appreciation of the wonderful efforts of colleagues like David Solomon and George Marsden who contribute so effectively to the fulfillment of Notre Dame's mission as a Catholic university. Dare I say some of my best personal and professional friends are non-Catholics, and I am grateful to non-Catholic scholars who respect and, in multiple ways, contribute to the university's mission. Not surprisingly, then, I take exception to McGreevy's suggestion that on my "abacus" such faculty "do not count," with its implication that I dismiss the contribution of such folk. I do not. I value the contribution of my non-Catholic colleagues, but I hold that a Catholic university can be securely maintained and effectively developed only if there is a predominance of committed Catholics on its faculty. My most thoughtful non-Catholic colleagues hold the same position.

### The Question of Numbers

This leads to the questions of numbers. McGreevy accuses me of avoiding facts "less congenial" to my thesis and offers a litany of worthy developments which would form a fine basis for one of those reassuring presentations that administrators are so skilled at presenting to boards of trustees and advisory councils. Of course good things happen at Notre Dame. But in his effort to paint an upbeat picture of the current situation at Notre Dame, McGreevy neglects to address directly my concern that a "tipping point" is at hand. Nor does he indicate his agreement with the university mission statement's declaration that the "Catholic identity of the University depends upon . . . the continuing presence of a predominant number of Catholic intellectuals" on the faculty. These omissions are telling and perhaps point to a significant disagreement between us.

I hold that Notre Dame's integrity as a Catholic university and the furtherance of its mission will be secured only with a solid majority of committed Catholic faculty. I infer that McGreevy, while not objecting to this as a goal and while undoubtedly working hard to attract strong Catholic faculty to Notre Dame, likely could live with a smaller proportion of Catholics—let us term it a "critical mass" of, say, forty percent. But having a "critical number of Catholic faculty" is the strategy that a number of other Catholic colleges and universities adopted in the recent past, and the path they have trod is hardly reassuring. It leads inevitably to attenuation of mission as the "critical mass" percentage regularly gets revised downwards. It is a course Notre Dame cannot take if it wants to preserve its treasured heritage and build upon it.

Now I readily concede that numbers are not everything and have to be treated with a certain wariness. I suspect McGreevy would agree with me that it is numbers of committed Catholic faculty who embody the fundamental purposes of the institution that matter. Having a majority of folk who answer "Catholic" on the faculty questionnaire but who are either ambivalent or even hostile to the fundamental mission of the school hardly suffices. There are doubtless departments that score high in those numbers but fall short in commitment to mission. But the remedy, however, is certainly not to let the numbers slip still further, but rather to evaluate carefully the role prospective faculty members can play in fulfilling the mission.

### Are There Catholic Scholars Out There?

Are there sufficient numbers of such committed and capable Catholic scholars available to constitute a solid majority of the faculty at Notre Dame and other Catholic institutions? This is a central question. John McGreevy is rather pessimistic. He notes that "only 6 percent" of faculty at the top fifty research universities "self-identify as Catholic." That figure may seem relatively low and might prompt a curious person to wonder why Catholics, and religious believers in general, are so under-represented at the supposed top schools—but it actually represents a substantial raw number of faculty who are possible recruits to Notre Dame. Moreover, McGreevy critically limits the recruiting pool by referencing only these major research schools. First-rate Catholic scholars also ply their trade at fine liberal arts colleges and at so-called second-tier research institutions, a group which includes Notre Dame itself. Furthermore, the community of Catholic intellectuals is hardly limited to the United States. Notre Dame has a valued tradition, extending back for decades, of recruiting non-American Catholic scholars like Waldemar Gurian and Stephen Kertesz. This tradition surely must be continued. In short, the recruitment pool is significantly larger than McGreevy implies.

I am not suggesting that hiring Catholic faculty is easy—and this is especially the case in certain branches of science and engineering—but that it is feasible and essential. It requires enhanced efforts to identify Catholic scholars and to recruit them, and a deepened appreciation on the part of all who serve on hiring committees of the necessity for this. Without such faculty Catholic institutions inevitably will short-change their students and lose their fundamental purpose.

### The Intellectual Needs of Students

I wrote my initial article partly out of a concern that "students emerge from Catholic schools rather unfamiliar with the riches of the Catholic intellectual tradition and with their imaginations untouched by a religious sensibility." So I was rather surprised to read McGreevy's suggestion that my "preoccupation" with hiring Catholic faculty somehow or other meant I didn't take the "intellectual formation" of students seriously. This is a canard but let me brush by it to make a larger point. Professor McGreevy seems to think that "campus ministers" have a responsibility "to nurture the spiritual lives of students grappling with existential questions and decisions about their life trajectory," and that "social service centers inculcate a sense of responsibility for the poor as gospel obligation, not as noblesse oblige." Then comes "intellectual formation," as exemplified in a Catholic school, it seems, by lots of courses *about* religion. This is an extraordinary division of responsibilities and one which I doubt McGreevy would defend on mature reflection. Intellectual formation in a Catholic university is not to be detached or separated from faith questions or issues of morality and justice. A Catholic university exists in large part to allow for the integration of intellectual, moral, and religious thinking and faculty should engage students in reflection on such matters.

Additionally, this thinking, contra John McGreevy, does have a distinct confessional dimension to it. Lots of decent secular schools teach various courses about religion. Yet in adopting the "religious studies" model they affirm little as true about religion. This should not be the approach favored at Notre Dame or at any Catholic school. In such places deeply–held faith convictions should be in evidence, and faculty across the disciplines should encourage students to gain a deeper knowledge of Catholic thought and teaching to aid them to confront "matters of ultimate concern." Committed Catholic scholars serving as teachers, mentors, and models must each undertake this work in their own ways. An electrical engineer or a chemist might contribute in less direct ways than a theologian, but all would respect and appreciate the intellectual relevance of faith. By words and deeds they should convey to their students that faith is not to be sequestered off in some private domain, but should guide how they live in and engage our world.

### A Distinctive Approach?

There is some irony in the fact that Catholic institutions of higher learning increasingly have given up on a distinctive religious and moral approach to education and have come to resemble secular institutions of higher learning right at the time when thoughtful faculty in the most elite of such institutions note the barrenness of their own educational programs. Former Harvard president Derek Bok laments that students are not even prepared to be good citizens on earth—he doesn't worry about preparation for citizenship in heaven! Columbia's Andrew Delbanco regrets that students are not aided to confront the "ethical issues posed by modern life." The former dean of Harvard College, Harry R. Lewis, who titled his recent book *Excellence Without a Soul: How a Great University Forgot Education*, acknowledges that "moral education has withered" and that faculty have given up for the most part in guiding students to seek "a larger purpose for their lives."

Catholic universities should neither follow the lead of such schools nor use them as the measuring rod for "academic excellence." They should learn from them but have the courage and self-confidence to stay on their own distinct and professed courses. If they do so, what though the odds, they might contribute effectively by their witness to a renewal in American higher education. To play this role Catholic colleges and universities will require faculty truly committed to their mission. The crucial priority today is to identify, recruit, and hire them. Let me say again this will not be accomplished by minor measures but will require vigorous action by those entrusted with leadership in Catholic higher education.

# Section III: Notre Dame: Corporation or Community?

## The Corporate University: A Catholic Response
## 2006

*While the issue of faculty composition is the most important question that faces Notre Dame, because it is so integrally connected to Catholic mission and identity, we should not ignore the impact here of developing corporate trends in American universities. Notre Dame likes to present itself as a family, and this presentation is borne out in times of crisis. Sadly, however, Notre Dame has also developed in such a way that notions of community are overwhelmed by the dictates of a mere commercial enterprise. In the following essay, I argue that a Catholic institution like Notre Dame must be "mission driven" rather than "market driven." The essay was meant to raise concerns and to prompt further conversation.*

The commercialization or "corporatization" of American higher education has dramatically changed the character and conduct of colleges and universities over the past quarter century. The literature on this subject is large and growing. A mere sampling of recent works includes: *Universities in the Marketplace*, by Derek Bok (2003); *University Inc.*, by Jennifer Washburn (2005); *Academic Capitalism*, by Sheila Slaughter and Gary Rhoades (2004); *Knowledge and Money*, by Robert Geiger (2004); and the wonderfully titled work by David L. Kirp, *Shakespeare, Einstein, and the Bottom Line: The Marketing of Higher Education* (2003).

The process these observers describe has taken place within

the context of extraordinary developments in the American economic system. Over recent decades the United States has been on what the popular economist Robert Samuelson has aptly called a long "consumption binge," during which Americans have been able "to indulge their self-indulgence." The spectacular economic stimulus provided by the supercharged American consumer has guaranteed growth not only in the American economy but in other parts of the world, which work to satisfy the voracious American appetite for all sorts of goods and services. Whatever the economic consequences, the mentality of consumption is deeply rooted in the American psyche. The powerful advertising industry and the skillful work of the marketers plant the desire for things within us, and we find it hard to resist.

In the contemporary economic system the corporation dominates. The negative press resulting from the greed and criminal activity pervasive in onetime corporate giants like Enron and Tyco has not led to a reining in of corporate influence. Organized labor is weak and the public sector deemed suspect. The techniques of the successful corporation are to be admired and emulated. Market share must be maintained and increased or a market niche defined. Profit must be maximized. To serve the bottom line, cost-cutting, downsizing and outsourcing become the norm. The point hardly needs to be belabored.

## Changing Institutions

The nation's colleges and universities naturally sought to benefit from the climate of heightened business dominance. Derek Bok, former president of Harvard University, has argued that ever since the late 1970s "universities have been much more aggressive than they previously were in trying to make money from their research and education activities," as they launched "vigorous patent licensing programs, for-profit ventures in Internet education, and a wide variety of other commercial initiatives." The pace of such activities has only quickened in the past decade. As Bok notes, entrepreneurship is no longer the province of the athletic departments and development offices.

Commercialization now spreads through science and engineering faculties, business schools, and far beyond.

Critics of the commercialization trend in higher education present the development as a result of the effort to "commodify" education. In their more fevered descriptions, this effort is promoted by businessmen and corporate lawyers on university boards of trustees and aims to reduce the faculty to the status of employees and to make the universities simply serve the interests of corporate America. The ever-sober Bok places the blame elsewhere. In his portrayal universities, especially the elite research institutions, simply could not resist the temptation of "the rapid growth of money-making opportunities provided by a more technologically sophisticated, knowledge-based economy." The heightened competition among institutions to secure their reputations and rankings demanded ever greater resources. In such circumstances schools could not pass up the chance to make money that could make them "bigger and better." It surely would have been un-American for them to do so.

Indeed, American universities always have had a well-developed readiness to obtain money and resources wherever they might be found, whether the source was public or private. The 19th-century land-grant schools and the great private institutions built upon the huge benefactions of one-time robber barons-turned–philanthropists illustrate this well. Funds from the G.I. Bill aided many colleges and universities after World War II and set a trend that made the federal government a preferred source for funding. In the Cold War era, schools like M.I.T., Cal Berkeley, and Stanford raked in millions of federal dollars for science and engineering research. At the same time, the universities sought out foundation support and were untiring and increasingly sophisticated in their efforts to obtain gifts from wealthy alumni and other major donors. (Most Catholic colleges and universities were slower in these efforts than their private and public peers, but it is fair to say that they have caught up in their eagerness to raise funds.)

While the aggressive effort to raise money is hardly new, the most recent approach to doing so through the commercialization of higher education has raised significant questions about its consequences for American colleges and universities. The impact of this process has been widespread, touching on most of the key elements that constitute the contemporary university, even influencing the very language used by academic administrators to define what they do.

Jennifer Washburn in *University Inc.* noted that academic administrators increasingly tend to refer to parents as customers, to students as consumers, and to education and research as products. They talk about branding and marketing and place great emphasis on advertising. Schools seek to convey an image and to appeal to a certain market. Some of this is surely necessary—one must recruit students, after all—but in institutions dedicated to the search for truth, irony intrudes in the development of public relations strategies modeled on the corporate sector. The language of the corporate sector has entered the lexicon of university administrators. Such terms as performance assessment, quality control, competitive edge, pricing structure, multiskilling, and (the current favorite) metrics are now well lodged in the academic *lingua franca*.

The presence of corporate operations on campus provides visuals, so to speak, to confirm the commercialization trend. At my university we have "outsourced" the selling of books and apparel, copying, fast-food service, and coffee-making to Folletts, Kinko's, Burger King, Subway, and Starbucks. But it does not stop there. For strategic planning we call in McKinsey and Company. For hiring academic administrators, we enlist the services of outside head-hunters. We contract with Adidas and, as college football fans know well, with NBC. These arrangements—with the exception of the NBC contract—are mirrored on most campuses and when assessed on their own terms are, for the most part, defensible. Yet unquestionably they contribute to a pervasive business atmosphere on campus.

Few of the major groups that form the contemporary

university remain untouched by the commercialization emphasis. Governing boards at most American universities tend to be dominated by business executives and corporate lawyers. Understandably, given their backgrounds, they look at universities and find "inefficiencies" in lots of areas. They favor the introduction of "proper" management techniques and welcome the use of corporate language. They bring the corporate mentality to campus.

According to Washburn, today's university administrators appear little troubled by the commercialization/corporatization process because, increasingly, *they* are selected not for their educational expertise but for their corporate know-how. In a rather shocked (and somewhat naïve) tone she reveals that even university presidents "are chosen on the basis of their ability to raise money and [for] their close ties to the corporate sector." Some presidents of major American universities now sit on the boards of directors of large corporations and, not uncommonly as Washburn notes, "they earn executive-level salaries." In such circumstances should it surprise anyone that contemporary university leaders are willing to adopt a more corporate style of management?

One might have expected the faculty to provide some brake on the commercialization process, given their survey-substantiated liberal political leanings. This, with notable exceptions, has not happened. Faculty in the elite and trend-setting institutions adjusted easily to the notion that they were academic entrepreneurs who had to look out for themselves. In 1991 Henry Rosovsky, dean of Harvard's School of Arts and Sciences, observed that the faculty had "become a society largely without rules, or to put it differently, the tenured members of the faculty—frequently as individuals—make their own rules" regarding such matters as teaching loads, outside business ventures, consulting time versus teaching time, and so on. In Rosovsky's portrayal, a me-first ethos was destroying what was left of an older civic attitude, according to which "a professor's primary obligation is to the institution—essentially to her or his students and colleagues and that all else is secondary."

It is hardly surprising that students, for the most part, adapt to the prevailing ethos on campuses. Even at the best campuses, the idea of learning for its own sake or as an avenue to wisdom seems outdated and naïve. Ross Gregory Douthat suggested in his memoir *Privilege: Harvard and the Education of the Ruling Class* (2005) that "the *real* business" of a Harvard education should be understood as "the pursuit of success and the personal connections from which such success has always flowed." Seen from his close-up vantage point, Harvard students emerged as "corner-cutting careerists," whose sense of worth was tied up with the future wealth and power they would accumulate. Of course, careerist tendencies are hardly limited to the banks of the Charles River. Students at most institutions increasingly see themselves as preparing for a place in corporate America so as to earn a good income to allow for appropriate levels of consumption (and to allow them to repay their college loans).

Predictably, the business emphasis on campuses has implications for what is taught there. In a world where consumer demand guides the curriculum, the humanities are on the defensive. Computing and information technology, along with biotechnology, are the rage. When the norms of what Bok calls our practical and profit-driven culture prevail, it is likely that certain disciplines will be dispatched to the intellectual burial ground.

### A Catholic Response

Catholic colleges and universities have been less affected by the mixing of educational activities and commercial ventures than many of the major research institutions. Their continued commitment to some kind of core curriculum, the place of undergraduate education at the center of their activities, and the communal spirit evident on many campuses help in this regard. But the current experience of larger schools (including Notre Dame) with the business paradigm, and the changing focus in many places on what is taught, suggests that this broad development should be of concern to all involved in Catholic higher education. Dangers loom along with opportunities.

If Catholic colleges and universities are to be faithful to their mission, as set forth so beautifully in *Ex Corde Ecclesiae* (1990), they must certainly resist any temptation to pursue a path that might lead them to become mere training centers for those who staff the existing economic system and/or research engines for American corporations. Here Catholic universities and colleges have a distinct advantage over so many of their secular peers, whose missions have become vague. The clarity of purpose of Catholic universities consecrated to "the cause of truth" and to serving "both the dignity of man and the good of the church" provides a real counterweight to the lure of money that drives the commercialization impulse.

One might expect that Catholic institutions faithful to their mission will foster a vision of life and a moral compass within their students such that more than material success is used as a measure for a good life. Catholic institutions founded on the conviction that human persons are created in the image and likeness of God and called upon to follow the way of Christ can hardly acquiesce in a system that views men and women as mere economic units.

It is easy to suggest, of course, that Catholic institutions must be mission-driven rather than market-driven: implementing mission-driven programs will be much harder and will require the support of all the key elements in any institution. Governing boards must understand and support the distinct mission. Administrators must determine priorities in light of it. They must even accept that bigger does not always mean better. Faculty must resist the me-first ethos and sign on to the communal endeavor that characterizes any genuine Catholic university. Hiring for mission should involve selecting faculty who want to participate in an intellectual community rather than those who look for a temporary base to pursue their own academic entrepreneurship. Students who enroll must be open to reflecting on what matters most in life as contrasted with a desire simply to get a degree or ticket to a well-paying position.

Realists on Catholic campuses know full well that business pressures and commercial practices are not easily restrained. In fact, Catholic schools should employ such practices so long as they serve rather than determine the mission.

Might this be the right moment for the Association of Catholic Colleges and Universities to consider the commercialization of Catholic higher education and to take measures to assure that the corporate influence does not overwhelm its member schools? The ACCU has given much attention to the relationship of the institutional church to Catholic universities. They should give at least some careful attention to *this* growing concern.

In closing, let me offer two small but specific proposals. If these were implemented in concert by American Catholic colleges and universities, they would have a real impact and be a serious expression of the institutions' fidelity to their mission instead of to the market. These develop from the suggestion of the U.S. bishops made back in 1980, that "for the college or university to be an authentic teacher of [social] justice, it must conduct its own affairs in a just way." In light of this, Catholic schools, especially those with significant financial resources, should undertake to provide a "living wage" for their lowest paid employees. And as a matter of urgency, they should take the lead in American higher education in providing just compensation for adjunct faculty. The exploitation of such folk should end on Catholic campuses. Dare one say that this accomplishment might even be something "marketable" in American higher education?

In the end, if Catholic universities are serious about their mission, they will offer clear instruction in Catholic social teaching, with its foundational principles of the dignity of the human person and concern for the common good. If they do so with any rigor, they will go on to raise some sharp questions about the present distribution of wealth and about people enslaved to material possessions. In short, a Catholic university should be a place where a serious critique of the consumerism and corporate capitalism that so dominates our age is consistently aired. A Catholic university overwhelmed by the commercial/corporate model will be incapable of such an endeavor.

# Section IV: Controversies

## *The Vagina Monologues*

### Open Letter on *The Vagina Monologues*
### Controversy to Fr. Jenkins
### 2006

The Vagina Monologues *consists of a series of presentations that, to borrow the words of Fr. John Jenkins, include "graphic descriptions of homosexual, extramarital heterosexual, and auto-erotic experiences . . . [including] even a depiction of the seduction of a sixteen-year old girl by an adult woman." Strangely, this sad 'play' has become part of the standard dramatic repertoire in student productions on American college campuses. Prior to taking office, Fr. Jenkins indicated that he would not permit the production of this effort which undermines sound Catholic sexual ethics. Under faculty pressure he reversed his position and permitted the production of the play. I expressed my concern to him privately and then shared my opposition in this letter.*

Dear John,

I write to object to your decision to permit the continued regular production of *The Vagina Monologues* on our campus. I write in this public manner to alert our faculty colleagues and our treasured students that not all members of the Congregation of Holy Cross, to which we belong, endorse your decision. Speaking for myself, I find the decision deeply damaging to Notre Dame and its mission as a Catholic university. It is a decision that I beg you to reconsider and to reverse.

When you were appointed president of Notre Dame there was hope that you might address and reverse the attenuation and drift in our Catholic mission that characterized our recent past. My own hope was that you would urgently address such crucial issues as faculty hiring, the development of a curriculum that truly conveys the richness of the Catholic intellectual tradition to our students, and the insidious effects on teaching and learning of the increasing corporate ethos at Notre Dame. For whatever reasons, you chose to place your initial emphasis on the regular production and sponsorship by elements of the university of *The Vagina Monologues* and *The Queer Film Festival*. You put forth the position that "an event which has the implicit or explicit sponsorship of the university as a whole, or one of its units, or a university recognized organization, and which either is or appears to be in name or content clearly and egregiously contrary to or inconsistent with the fundamental values of a Catholic university, should not be allowed at Notre Dame." This was a position of such obvious good sense that I never considered that you would retreat from it. Sadly, you have done precisely that.

In asking why you would reverse a sound position, which you obviously had reached after much thought and prayer, one must conclude that you were influenced by those contributors to the debate who favored the continued production of *The Vagina Monologues*. Presumably, you were influenced by the young women who produce this play and somehow see it as a contribution to the prevention of violence against women. Undoubtedly, you were influenced by the convictions of certain senior Arts and Letters faculty that any restriction on this play would damage our academic "reputation," especially among those preferred peer schools whose regard we crave. Whatever the reasons, I must tell you that your decision is viewed as "backing down." Indeed, it is hard to understand it in any other terms.

You should know that in taking this decision you have brought the most joy to those who care least about Notre Dame's Catholic mission. You have won for yourself a certain short-term popularity with some students and certain faculty but have done real damage to our beloved school and its distinct place in American higher education. By your decision you move us further along the dangerous path where we ape our secular peers and take all our signals from them. Knowing you and having conversed with you on matters relating to Notre Dame's Catholic mission in the past, I suspect that you recognize this in your own heart. Yet you seemingly have allowed the possibility of some protest to cause you to change your own stated position. You were called to be courageous, and you settled for being popular. This is not your best self. This is not genuine leadership.

In your recent "Closing Statement" you reveal a level of naiveté about the process of a Catholic university engaging the broad culture that is striking and deeply harmful to our purpose as a Catholic university. We live at a time when the elite culture is programmed to trivialize religion. Furthermore, much of popular culture is deeply antithetical to religious conviction and practice. It offers a worldview completely at odds with any Catholic vision. It is a worldview from which none of us can be sequestered: indeed, many of our students arrive here far more deeply influenced by the reigning culture than by faith convictions.

Amidst this larger context you are ready to permit the continued production and promotion of a play which, as our colleague Paolo Carozza rightly put it, "seems to reduce the meaning and value of women's lives to their sexual experiences and organs, reinforcing a perspective on the human person that is itself fundamentally a form of violence." Dialogue with this point of view is ridiculous. It should be contested and resisted at Notre Dame, but never promoted. Notre Dame must hold to a higher view of the dignity of women and men. Might I ask, if this play does not meet your criteria of an "expression that is overt and insistent in its contempt for the values and sensibilities of this university," what would?

My concern is that you have been "spooked" by the fear of negative publicity if you were to "suppress speech on this campus." Here, it seems, you have a special opportunity to rethink your position. Know well that there is much hypocrisy abroad in the American academy on the issue of "academic freedom." Note that NYU had no difficulty recently in suppressing the "free speech" rights of the students who wanted to discuss and display the Danish cartoons. Note that folk at Brown University get by with a "speech code" that bans all "verbal behavior" that may cause "feelings of impotence, anger or disenfranchisement." In the American academy it is only certain kinds of speech that are protected. And, as Professor Gary Anderson pointed out in his constructive contribution to this debate, a rather narrow range of politically correct views tends to prevail in the faculties of many institutions which influences what that "speech" is. Notre Dame presently has a wider range of perspectives represented than most institutions who are forever prattling on about their diversity. (They are all "diverse" in the same predictable way!)

Please have the confidence to shape Notre Dame into a truly distinct institution. Take up the challenge to clarify for our secular peers that Notre Dame allows, as they do not, "classroom engagement with religious beliefs precisely as religious" as Brad Gregory put it so well. Reveal to them with the eloquence of which you are capable that the very values and convictions which allow us to consider a whole range of questions beyond their scope also necessitate us to restrict the repeated public performance and promotion of works which are deeply offensive to our values.

John, let me commend you for your admirable goal of seeking to find "ways to prevent violence against women." Over my years of teaching and pastoral service at Notre Dame I have sought to encourage my female students to appreciate their innate dignity and to respect themselves rightly. I have been blessed to come to know some amazing women whom I now count as dear friends. Drawing on conversations with such women about the circumstances they find at Notre Dame leads me to suggest that your rather elaborate committee formed to pursue this goal has the whiff of a public relations exercise about it. The painful reality is that much of the violence against women in our society results from a sick view that separates sex from love and genuine relationship. The fallout from this distorted view includes the commodification of sex, the portrayal of women as objects, and the blatant refusal of some men to treat women with dignity and respect. Yet how will the committee be able to address such issues when you have approved the continued production of a play that reduces women to body parts? Surely you see the contradiction here? I request that this contradiction be an early agenda item for consideration by this committee.

What I ask of you in this letter will require you to dig deep into your heart and soul and to reopen a matter of which I am sure you want to be well rid. I suspect you have had moments when you wished never to hear of *The Vagina Monologues* again, and we both know that there are many other important matters claiming your attention. But careful readers of works like George Marsden's *The Soul of the American University* know that decisions similar to yours, which conformed religious schools to their secular peers, inexorably led them down a dangerous path to the full surrender of their religious mission and identity. Regrettably, places like Georgetown University are well advanced on this course. Do not let us merely follow them: to do so would be a betrayal of our predecessors in Holy Cross. Instead, Notre Dame must lead the way in American Catholic higher education. Please go back to your best self and to your original instincts and position on this matter. Don't embarrass those of us who want to work with you to build a great Catholic university. Lead us!

Know of my prayers for you during this holiest of weeks.

Fraternally in Holy Cross,

Bill Miscamble, C.S.C.
Associate Professor of History

## Presentation on Fr. Jenkins' "Closing Statement on Academic Freedom and Catholic Character" 2006

*The production of* The Vagina Monologues *in 2006 prompted a significant debate regarding not simply the play itself but larger questions concerning academic freedom and the Catholic mission of Notre Dame. A number of alumni participated in this debate, and the issue attracted a sizable crowd to a panel at the annual alumni reunion. I accepted an invitation to contribute on this panel and took the opportunity to explore how a Catholic university could and should engage the broad culture.*

I thank the organizers of this panel for their initiative in bringing us together here. And I thank each one of you for coming. Whatever your perspective on *The Vagina Monologues* and on the broad question of academic freedom and Catholic character, your presence here testifies to your concern and interest in our university. (I gather you could be off at a session on how to develop the habits to be a more highly effective person but you have come here instead—surely a testament to your concern for the common good!)

I want to try to address a number of matters in a brief manner as a prompt to further discussion after our presentations. I assume that many of you have read the open letter I wrote to Fr. John Jenkins so I won't simply repeat what I said there. I want to encourage you to think broadly about what this particular controversy says about the direction of Notre Dame.

I want to address the following points: (1) the significance of this issue in light of Notre Dame's current situation; (2) the historical background regarding religious colleges and universities; (3) whether or not there should be any restrictions on speech and performances at a university like ours; (4) the way in which a special and distinctive university like Notre Dame should engage the culture; (5) the call for Notre Dame to be a leader rather than a follower in this broad area. And all this within the ten to twelve minutes the organizers have allocated to me!

First then to the significance of this issue: those who have read my letter know that I would have preferred Fr. Jenkins to have addressed as priorities such issues as faculty hiring, the content of the curriculum and the increasing corporate ethos at Notre Dame. He chose instead to focus on the regular production and sponsorship of *The Vagina Monologues* and *The Queer Film Festival.*

He framed the issue, incorrectly in my view, as an issue pitting Catholic character over and against academic freedom and asked the whole university community to reflect on this issue. In so doing he elevated the matter to one of real importance. He helped make this matter a defining one for the kind of school Notre Dame will be. Sadly, his closing statement for the most part clarified that Notre Dame will allow itself to be defined increasingly by other universities as we conform to their notion of what a university is.

Now some wonderful alumni have asked those of us who object to *The Vagina Monologues* and see its regular performance at Notre Dame as deleterious to our Catholic mission, if this play can really be that much of a problem. They usually couple the question with evidence of student religious practice—for example, Mass attendance, visits to the Grotto (even outside of exam times and football season), student commitment to service, et cetera—to argue that the Catholic character of Notre Dame remains strong. Why make a fuss?

The answer is quite simple. Much as I admire and work to encourage our students in their religious commitments, this is not what ultimately determines the religious character of the university. *That* is defined by what is taught and by who teaches it. John Jenkins' closing statement must be understood in light of a university whose faculty is increasingly distant from or even antithetical to its Catholic mission. In some ways the promotion of such events as *The Vagina Monologues* and the formerly named "Queer Film Festival" is a reflection of that changing faculty. I would argue that *The Vagina Monologues* are significant in themselves but even more so as a reflection of developing trends in the university that aim to eviscerate its Catholic mission.

This leads me to the matter of historical background. I am a historian and, while I wouldn't argue that history provides us with explicit lessons, it can provide us with examples of paths which one might choose to take or *not* take. For religious schools who want to retain their religious identity and commitments there are plenty of examples of paths *not* to take. Examples abound in my colleague George Marsden's insightful book, *The Soul of the American University*. *Marsden* details the process of secularization in many of the one-time Protestant schools and clarifies that it doesn't happen overnight or as a result of major debate and a firm resolution to change the nature of the school. It happens through myriads of decisions and appointments, none of which seem particularly significant, until the cumulative effect has been to alter the nature of the school beyond recognition. This is a path which Catholic schools have been on for some time. It is not a pretty picture. We shouldn't pretend that it can't happen to us. Indeed, I regret to inform you that it is happening to us. You may be familiar with George Santayana's dictum that "those who forget the past are condemned to repeat it." I'm not sure this is a lesson we have grasped. At least I saw no evidence of it in Fr. Jenkins' closing statement.

Let me turn to the issue of whether or not there should be any restrictions on speech and performances at a university like ours. It has been suggested by Don Wycliff, the university spokesman, that those of us who object to *The Vagina Monologues* want to turn Notre Dame into a "gated Catholic enclave." The implication was that supporters of the Jenkins closing statement would welcome presentations of every sort so long as they were followed by a panel discussion to state the "Catholic point of view."

This does not appear to be John Jenkins' point of view. In his opening address he gave examples of plays and conferences which he thought would be inappropriate at a Catholic university, for example, the older version of the Oberammergau Passion Play and the one-sided conference on "The Moral Legitimacy of Infanticide and Euthanasia." I don't think he has backed away from that position.

Let me suggest that all universities have "gates" of one sort or another. As I noted in my letter, NYU recently had no difficulty in suppressing the "free speech" rights of the students who wanted to discuss and display the Danish cartoons. Folk at Brown University get by with a "speech code" that bans all "verbal behavior" that may cause "feelings of impotence, anger or disenfranchisement." Ask Larry Summers is he feels free at Harvard to discuss whether there might be innate, genetically based gender differences in cognition that just might contribute to the fact that more men than women achieve the very highest scores in mathematics aptitude tests! Finally, as we know well, and as the ACLU enforces vigorously, classroom speech revelatory of faith convictions and religious beliefs is banned in all state-sponsored institutions.

The issue really is, if one can get by the cheap-shot "gated community" comments, what kind of gate will be enforced. I personally like the standard mentioned by John Jenkins in his closing statement as appropriate for Notre Dame, namely, "expression that is overt and insistent in its contempt for the values and sensibilities of this University."

My question: what would constitute such expression for Fr. Jenkins if not *The Vagina Monologues*? Let me probe further: would an art exhibit which featured, say, Andres Serrano's "Piss Christ," or the Chris Ofili dung-clotted "Holy Virgin Mary," be just fine and an opportunity to engage the culture, as long as there was a panel discussion at the end of it?

Should the university place any restriction on certain rap and hip-hop performances with their disgraceful lyrics and images that so degrade and exploit women? (I pose the latter question because Spelman, the historically black college for women in Atlanta, had the courage in 2004 to cancel an appearance on campus of the rapper Nelly, whose "Tip Drill" video had taken to a new and disgusting level the image of African-American women as 'rump-shaking' meat, apparently available for cash by passing a credit card through the cheeks of a woman's buttocks or by throwing money between her legs. Sorry for inflicting that upon you but it is necessary to make the point.) Let me say two things: I hope we might have the same courage as Spelman College, and I also would hope this would be an example of the contemporary culture that Notre Dame would prefer to "engage" at a distance. I put *The Vagina Monologues* in the same category as Nelly's video, with the former's "graphic descriptions of homosexual, extra-marital heterosexual, and auto-erotic experiences. . . . [and] with its depiction of the seduction of a sixteen year-old girl by an adult woman" and all staged with a rather "celebratory attitude." (I am quoting John Jenkins there but from his opening statement.)

This brings me to my fourth point, that is, the way in which Notre Dame should engage the culture. I assure you I am all for Notre Dame engaging the culture. I go further: Notre Dame has a responsibility to do this and indeed to seek to transform and renew a culture that is in many ways rather sick.

We must engage it but we need not *promote* those elements of it that are antithetical to our mission—as the regular production of *The Vagina Monologues* on our campus does. Here let me make clear that I don't want to eliminate discussion of ideas. The classroom is a place where ideas of all sorts must be considered. We should talk about the sad ideas that undergird *The Vagina Monologues* in our classrooms. If some professor wants to teach the "play" then so be it. (*Mein Kampf* is not restricted either.) But a Catholic university doesn't have to surrender all its standards. Engaging the culture cannot and should not mean, as Fr. Brian Shanley, O.P., president of Providence College noted in an address explaining his decision to ban the play, "the complete license to perform or display any work of art regardless of its intellectual or moral content." Notre Dame has the right and duty to maintain some legitimate standards as we engage the culture. This, in my view, is how John Jenkins should have framed the issue in the first place.

Lastly, to the call for Notre Dame to be a leader rather than a follower in this broad area: one of the saddest aspects of the "Closing Statement" was John Jenkins' refusal to forge a distinctive path for Notre Dame. In my letter I urged him not to let Notre Dame merely follow those Catholic schools that are conforming themselves to their secular peers. I suggested that to follow that course would be a betrayal of our predecessors in Holy Cross. You alumni should be well aware that Notre Dame can pursue this path and still be a "success" as a university measured in secular terms; it can be even more wealthy and famous and prestigious than it is today. But it will have surrendered its sacred responsibility to be a great Catholic university where profound learning and the quest for truth are not separated from moral behavior, the spiritual quest, and communal responsibility.

There is some irony in that close observers of the American academic scene regularly note the moral bankruptcy of much of higher education today. Harry Lewis states bluntly that Harvard, where he served as dean, "has lost, indeed willingly surrendered, its moral authority to shape the souls of its students. . . . Harvard articulates no ideals of what it means to be a good person."

Dear alumni, might I ask you to use your influence to prevent Notre Dame from going down the path that Harvard trod? Help keep us a place concerned for the souls as well as the minds and hearts of our students. Notre Dame must lead the way in American Catholic higher education.

# The Obama Commencement

## Open Letter by Holy Cross Priests on Obama Invitation 2009

*I knew well that I would have to express in public my opposition to the decision to honor President Obama at the 2009 commencement. I planned to write some kind of letter or op-ed in my own name, but I was approached by a number of the younger priests in the Holy Cross Order and they suggested that we compose a joint letter directed to the Notre Dame community. After drafting the letter, we approached some further Holy Cross religious whom we knew had expressed reservations about the Obama invitation. Some signed, and some did not. Some feared possible negative consequences for them at Notre Dame, and some worried that it would handicap their ability to minister effectively on campus. I remain forever grateful to the courageous priests who signed the letter. I include it here because it clearly reveals my position in the spring of 2009.*

We write as priests of the Congregation of Holy Cross and as proud graduates of the University of Notre Dame to voice our objection to the university's decision to honor President Barack Obama by inviting him to deliver this year's commencement address and by conferring on him an honorary Doctor of Law degree.

We wish to associate ourselves with and encourage those courageous students and treasured alumni who, while deeply loving Notre Dame, vigorously oppose this sad and regrettable decision of the university administration.

It is our deep conviction that Notre Dame should lead by word and deed in upholding the Church's fundamental teaching that human life must be respected and protected from the moment of conception. In so doing the university must take seriously the 2004 instruction of the U.S. Catholic bishops that "Catholic institutions should not honor those who act in defiance of our fundamental moral principles. They should not be given awards, honors, or platforms which would suggest support for their actions."

We especially regret the fissure that the invitation to President Obama has opened between Notre Dame and its local ordinary and many of his fellow bishops. We express our deep gratitude to Bishop John D'Arcy for his leadership and moral clarity. We ask that the university give renewed consideration to Bishop D'Arcy's thoughtful counsel which always has Notre Dame's best interests at heart.

The university pursues a dangerous course when it allows itself to decide for and by itself what part of being a Catholic institution it will choose to embrace. Although undoubtedly unintended, the university administration's decision portends a distancing of Notre Dame from the Church which is its lifeblood and the source of its identity and real strength. Such a distancing puts at risk the true soul of Notre Dame.

We regret that our position on this issue puts us at odds with our brother priest in Holy Cross, Fr. John Jenkins, C.S.C. Yet, in this instance, for the good of Notre Dame and the Congregation of Holy Cross, we cannot remain silent. Notre Dame's decision has caused moral confusion and given many reason to believe that the university's stance against the terrible evil of abortion is weak and easily trumped by other considerations.

We prayerfully request that Fr. Jenkins and the fellows of the university, who are entrusted with responsibility for maintaining its essential character as a Catholic institution of higher learning, revisit this matter immediately. Failure to do so will damage the integrity of the institution and detract from all the good work that occurs at Notre Dame and from the impressive labors of its many faithful students and professors.

We offer these views as we enter Holy Week, recalling the triumph of Christ's holy cross. As "men with hope to bring" we are confident that Notre Dame may yet give true honor to its patroness, and witness to her Son, through its commitment to the sanctity of life.

# Honoring Obama, Notre Dame, and American Catholic Life
## 2009

*President Barack Obama served as the principal speaker at Notre Dame's one hundred and sixty-fourth commencement ceremony on May 17, 2009. He also received an honorary doctorate from the university on this occasion. The invitation provoked enormous criticism, including public statements from numerous Catholic bishops, and it damaged Notre Dame's reputation among the American Catholic community. The university presented the occasion as an opportunity for "dialogue," but in reality the event was merely an occasion for President Obama to make a play for Catholic support. In the course of his address, he attracted applause by promising to "honor the conscience of those who disagree with abortion" and to "draft a sensible conscience clause"—promises that appear empty in light of the Department of Health and Human Services mandates requiring employers, including institutions like Notre Dame, to provide health insurance covering abortion-inducing drugs, contraceptives, and sterilizations.*

*On commencement day, President Obama was cheered wildly inside the Joyce Athletic and Convocation Center. The formal commencement, however, was not the only gathering of significance on that day. On the south quad of the university, three thousand devoted students, alumni, and friends of the university gathered together. Fr. Kevin Russeau presided at a beautiful and reverential Mass. A protest rally, organized by the students of NDResponse, took place after the mass. Six speakers addressed the gathering; I was deeply privileged to be one of them. It was a sad day at Notre Dame yet this remarkable rally revealed the university at its best.*

True friends of Notre Dame, I thank you for your presence.

I want to thank especially our treasured students in NDResponse for inviting me to be with you. It is a great privilege and honor. As I look out on the good and decent people gathered here, I know one thing: there is no place I would rather be.

I have been a teacher at Notre Dame for more than two decades. But today I come before you primarily as a Holy Cross priest, a member of the religious order that founded Notre Dame more than a century and half ago.

On November 26, 1842, an extraordinary French priest named Edward Sorin and a small band of Holy Cross brothers arrived at this site, a place where French missionaries had once ministered to the Potawatomi Indians. Fr. Sorin christened the place Notre Dame du Lac. He and his Holy Cross confreres began the work of building a college with a small log chapel as their point of departure. They aimed to serve Christ here, and to evangelize in His name under the patronage of the Blessed Mother.

When the young priest wrote home to his superior, Fr. Basil Moreau, the founder of the Holy Cross order, he put it this way: here in northern Indiana, he hoped to establish "one of the most powerful means for good in this country." Since then, the university has prospered.

But building this university was not an easy task. The tiny school faced horrendous tribulations during its initial years. Damaging fires, a terrible cholera outbreak, and a series of financial crises failed to halt the onward march of the school. Whatever the odds against them, Fr. Sorin and his collaborators never gave up.

Those of you familiar with Notre Dame's history would know that this tenacity had perhaps its finest moment on April 23, 1879. That was the day that the so-called "big fire" swept over the campus. In just three hours much of the work of the previous three decades lay in ashes. A few days later, Fr. Sorin trudged through the still-smoldering ruins of the venture to which he had devoted his life. Then he called the whole community into the campus church—which had miraculously survived the fierce blaze. With absolute faith and confidence, Fr. Sorin looked forward and told his anxious band of followers this: "If it were *all* gone I should not give up." The effect was electric. As one observer put it, after that "there was never a shadow of a doubt as to the future of Notre Dame."

Under God's providential care, our university did recover and grow. Fr. Sorin, his determined band, and the generations of Holy Cross religious and their lay collaborators who followed built something special. Their blood, sweat, and tears are in the bricks and mortar—and they are reflected in the lives that they touched.

They were "educators in the faith" who understood, in the words of Fr. Moreau, "that the mind could not be cultivated at the expense of the heart." These folk built Notre Dame into a distinctive place that nurtured its students' religious and moral development, as well as their intellectual lives. Notre Dame challenged them to serve God and neighbor. And, as it did so, it proudly proclaimed its Catholic identity and its loyal membership in a Church that was and is unafraid to speak of moral truths and foundational principles and beliefs. In the process, Notre Dame came to hold a special place in the hearts of Catholics all across America.

Now friends, jump ahead to today. The formal leadership of the University still proclaims its fidelity to this vision. University leaders assert that Notre Dame is and will be different, so that it can make a difference. University leaders assure the parents of incoming freshmen that Notre Dame won't be like those "other" schools that merely associate themselves with a Catholic or Jesuit "tradition." No, to the contrary: here at Notre Dame, their children will find an institution unashamedly Catholic and willing to embrace all the tenets of our faith. Notre Dame will instruct its students in the Church's moral truths, foundational beliefs, and principles.

Of late, that rhetoric seems to ring rather hollow. The words have not been matched by deeds. Instead of fostering the moral development of its students Notre Dame's leaders have planted the damaging seeds of moral confusion.

By honoring President Obama, the Notre Dame administration has let the students and their parents down. And it has betrayed the loyal and faith-filled alumni who rely on Notre Dame to stand firm on matters of fundamental Catholic teaching—and so to affirm the sanctity of life.

The honor extended to Barack Obama says very loudly that support for practically unlimited access to abortion as well as approval for the destruction of embryonic life to harvest stem cells, are not major problems for those charged with leading Notre Dame. Catholic teaching seems easily trumped by other issues, and by the opportunity to welcome the president to our campus. Bishop John D'Arcy, the great bishop of this diocese who so loves Notre Dame, said it well: Notre Dame chose "prestige over truth." How embarrassing for an institution dedicated to the pursuit of truth to settle for temporal attention over eternal honor.

Friends, just ask yourselves whether anyone, regardless of their other accomplishments, would be honored here at Notre Dame if they held racist or anti-Semitic sentiments. They would not—and rightly so! Yet at this commencement Notre Dame honors a politician who readily proclaims his support for the Freedom of Choice Act, and who is clearly the most radically pro-abortion president in this great nation's history.

As you know well, Notre Dame undertook this sad action in the face of the 2004 instruction of the U.S. Catholic bishops that "Catholic institutions should not honor those who act in defiance of our fundamental moral principles." In so doing, the administration has distanced the university from the Church that is its lifeblood and the ultimate source of its identity.

A number of my fellow Holy Cross priests and I believe that such a distancing puts at risk the true soul of Notre Dame. Regrettably, this distancing also puts Notre Dame in the service of those who seek to damage the teaching authority of our Bishops. What a sad circumstance for an institution that should stand at the very heart of the Church.

Now, we can be sure that today the president will offer a fine address, crafted by a talented speechwriting team to appeal to a "Catholic audience." No doubt too, President Obama will deliver it eloquently. There will surely be a tribute to Notre Dame's former president, Fr. Hesburgh, for his important work on civil rights. The president will claim that he is influenced by Catholic social teaching and will appeal for folk to work together in the areas where common ground can be found. Most of the crowd will cheer, the photos will be taken, and soon the event will be over. The president will board Air Force One and fly away.

But what matters for us here is less what President Obama says, but rather what the day will mean for Notre Dame and its place in American Catholic life. The truth is this: This painful episode has damaged the ethos and spirit of Notre Dame. But there is another truth that we must also remember: it is not the end of the story!

Some among the administration of Notre Dame will want the issue to go away quickly. It may even be likely that there are some among them who genuinely understand the evil of abortion, and who are inwardly troubled by these recent events whatever their outward bravado. They will have a chance to show through future deeds and in very practical ways Notre Dame's commitment to the pro-life cause. Let us hope and pray that they take up that opportunity. But we cannot rely on them. As we have seen, left on their own, their commitment will never be more than tepid.

Instead, let us link ourselves with those Holy Cross religious over the generations who never gave up—whatever the setbacks, whatever the trials, whatever the personal cost. In some ways, the task before us today is tougher than theirs. In those early days, the problems were clear; so too was the mission.

Now we are engaged in a more intellectual and spiritual struggle. Will we be true to the founding vision? Can we resist the subtle and not–so -subtle temptations to surrender our distinct religious identity, to conform to the reigning and rather barren secular paradigm of what a university should be?

The Obama visit suggests that the university's leadership has succumbed to this temptation. Yet when we look back on these days, I have a sense that what will stand out is how a group of dedicated pro-life students, wonderful alumni, and ordinary Catholics who cherish this place refused to acquiesce in the administration's willingness to wink at its most fundamental values in exchange for the public relations coup that attends a presidential visit.

The people who refuse to give up—and I speak especially of you students—have taken on the role of teachers here. While the administration and many of the faculty sold out easily for the photo-ops, et cetera, you and some of your alumni sisters and brothers showed the benefits of your Notre Dame education. You held firm to the foundational principles of respect for life and for the dignity of every person. You are the ones who have understood what really matters. You refused just to go along; you have made your voice heard.

You represent the very best of Notre Dame. You, along with your dedicated and truth-speaking professors and faithful alums, are the ones who can help Notre Dame recover from this painful and self-inflicted wound. You will not find it easy, and you will have moments where you will be discouraged. But you must remember there is so much that is good at Notre Dame that you can never relent in your efforts to call this place to be its best and true self, proud of its Catholic identity and its loyal membership in the Church.

When I think of our courageous NDResponse students my mind goes quickly to a marvelous passage in J.R.R. Tolkien's *The Two Towers*. *Lord of the Rings* aficionados will know the passage well. It is delivered as Frodo and Sam eat what may be their last meal together before going down into the nameless land. Sam says:

> And we shouldn't be here at all, if we had known more about it before we started. But I suppose it's often that way. The brave things in the old tales and songs, Mr. Frodo: adventures, I used to call them. I used to think that they were things the wonderful folk of the stories went out and looked for, because they wanted them, because they were exciting and life was a bit dull, a kind of sport, as you might say. But that's not the way of it with tales that really mattered, or the ones that   stay   in

the mind. Folk seem to have been just landed in them, usually their paths were laid that way, as you put it. But I suspect that they had lots of chances, like us, of turning back, only they didn't.

Friends, let us move forward together and let us never turn back. Let us take our instruction from the Lord, in the words that the great champion of life, John Paul II, used at the outset of his papacy: Be not afraid. Let us labor in this vineyard, so that Notre Dame might regain its true soul, be faithful in its mission as a Catholic university, and truly become the "powerful means for good" that Fr. Sorin dreamed about.

Thank you for having me. May Our Lady, Notre Dame du Lac, keep you close. And may she ever watch over the university that bears her name.

# The Appointment of Roxanne Martino, Pro-Life Efforts, and the Future of Notre Dame

## Life Matters, the Roxanne Martino Case, and the Catholic Character of Notre Dame
## 2011

*The Notre Dame Board of Fellows elected Roxanne Martino to the Notre Dame Board of Trustees in the spring of 2011. It was soon revealed that Martino, a Chicago businesswoman and Notre Dame alumna, had made sizeable contributions to the pro-abortion political action committee, EMILY's List. Both the university president, Fr. John Jenkins, and the chair of the board of trustees, Mr. Richard Notebaert, sought to defend Ms. Martino and to allow for her continued service as a Notre Dame trustee. I objected to her appointment and called publically for her resignation in two addresses in early June. The longer version included here was given to a meeting of the Sycamore Trust at Notre Dame. A shorter version of it was given on a panel entitled "The Catholic Identity, Character, and Mission of Notre Dame," held as part of the annual alumni reunion on June 4, 2011. In light of negative publicity and increasing opposition from a number of alumni, Ms. Martino decided to resign from the board on June 8.*

Thank you so much for the opportunity to be here today. I want to thank each one of you for coming to this breakfast, and more especially for your love and interest in Notre Dame and its future. I want to give special thanks to Bill Dempsey and Project Sycamore for hosting us this morning.

I'm not sure how many of you are regular subscribers to the Project Sycamore bulletins, but I'm sure that those of you who are would readily agree with me as to the important role which Bill Dempsey and his colleagues are playing in forcing serious discussion about the present course and future direction of the university we love. Indeed, Project Sycamore provides a greatly needed service by promoting the Catholic character and mission of Notre Dame. It provides a sustained and deeply thoughtful monitoring of developments, and works to influence Notre Dame for the good. Let me encourage any of you who may not have done so to subscribe to Project Sycamore and to receive its regular bulletins.

Friends, I want to offer a quick overview of some recent developments at Notre Dame and to give some evaluation of where we are as a Catholic university. My colleague and friend, Prof. David Solomon, will speak as well and plans to address primarily matters associated with the Center for Ethics and Culture, which he heads, and also matters concerning the curriculum. After we are both done I hope there will be plenty of time for questions and observations from you.

Let me make clear at the outset that there are many wonderful developments taking place at Notre Dame. Some good teaching occurs and good scholarship is undertaken. Some good hires are made. We benefit from such fine initiatives as the Alliance for Catholic Education. We are fortunate and privileged to have fine students attend and most benefit from their time here. The place looks great, and even some of our sports teams are pretty successful.

Now, you know that the Notre Dame public relations machine is excellent at producing expensive visual presentations, all kinds of engaging website material, and glossy brochures to propagate a highly positive view of things around the place. Some folk here seem to think it inappropriate if one does not simply join the PR cheerleading squad and read from the "frequently asked questions" sheet (known as the "UND Night FAQs") prepared for speakers who hit the road for Universal Notre Dame Night presentations.

But I see my responsibility differently. I first arrived here to begin graduate studies in 1976 and have been teaching here as a priest in Holy Cross for a quarter century. It is hard for me to imagine teaching anywhere else. I actually believe in the intelligence of Notre Dame alums and their spouses—and I don't think you should have to settle for canned answers. I have taught some great students over the years, and I am confident they can handle the reality of our situation. I feel the same about each of you.

I draw some inspiration for my remarks today from a story told about my favorite American president, Harry S. Truman. The story is told by Bill Moyers who served as an aide to Lyndon B. Johnson. It took place in Truman's home on Delaware Avenue in Independence, Missouri in 1965. Moyer describes the incident:

> L.B.J. brought a passel of his young aides, because he was insistent that we would meet Harry Truman. We were in a circle in what was the dining room of his house. And L.B.J. brought Harry Truman around and had every one of the aides shake his hand and introduced us each by name.
>
> As we were leaving, Harry Truman said: "Boys, you take care of the president." And somebody said, "He can take care of himself."
>
> Truman said, "Boys let me tell you what I mean. Since the president won the largest plurality in American political history last fall he's going to say, "Two plus two is five isn't it?'"
>
> And everyone in the room is going to say: "Yes, Mr. President, two plus two is five."
>
> And he's going to say, "The sun comes up in the west, right?" And everyone's going to say, "Yes, Mr. President, the sun comes up in the west."
>
> And he's going to say: 'I don't have to put my pants on one leg at a time do I?"
>
> And everyone in the room's going to say, "No, Mr. President, you don't have to put your pants on one leg at a time."
>
> And your job, boys, is to tell the president, "Two plus two is still four, the sun still comes up in the east, and we don't care how you put your pants on, but your fly is unzipped."

Let me try to talk to you plainly and directly about recent developments here. Forgive the brevity with which I pass over events—but our time is relatively short. It is just over two years ago since the May 2009 commencement at which Notre Dame honored President Barack Obama, a politician deeply committed to the abortion regime that prevails in the United States today. This was in many ways a sad event. As you may recall, the visit brought forth criticism of the country's leading Catholic university from over eighty bishops, from literally thousands of Notre Dame alumni, and from hundreds of thousands of committed Catholic folk who love Notre Dame and expected more from her.

My purpose here is not to rehash the Obama visit in any detail but to use it as my point of departure and to review what has happened subsequently at Notre Dame. The Obama visit was explained and defended by Fr. John Jenkins, the president, and by Richard Notebaert, the chair of the Board of Trustees, as an exercise in "dialogue." This was misleading, of course. There was no two-way exchange of views at any time. It is a sad exercise in obfuscation to suggest so, rather like saying that two plus two equals five. But it is not the only occasion they have engaged in such behavior, as we shall see.

On one level the visit of President Obama was a "success" for Notre Dame (great visuals, cheering crowds on the actual day), but the real picture is a more complicated one. The visit put Notre Dame at odds in a very direct way with the local ordinary, Bishop John D'Arcy. It strained the university's relationship with the institutional Church. It is fair to say that it was a source of scandal for many.

The Notre Dame administration was surprised by the extent of the negative reaction, however much they might deny that. They had given out a very mixed moral message on the life issue. Indeed, they had chosen "prestige over truth," to use the words of Bishop D'Arcy. Far from being able to celebrate the Obama visit, the administration was pushed into the work of damage limitation, at least to some degree.

## *Damage Limitation*

Perhaps we should take some heart from the fact that the Notre Dame administration was pushed into damage limitation mode. Sadly, the pressure to do so did not really come from within the university—certainly not from the faculty, not from the trustees, and not, I regret to say, from the Holy Cross community. No, it was Notre Dame alumni and friends who challenged the university, as well as the realization that ND's reputation and credibility as a Catholic university had been hurt and was in need of speedy repair.

Of course, there was no indication of regret. There was no apology to Bishop D'Arcy, who is now retired and been replaced by Bishop Kevin Rhoades. There is surprisingly little mention of the event in administration publicity: in fact, there is a certain downplaying of it. What received more attention were worthy initiatives to strengthen Notre Dame's pro-life credentials.

Curiously, there was enormous room for the Notre Dame administration to act in this area, for there was little of substance to demonstrate the reality of Fr. Jenkins' oft-given assurance that Notre Dame was "unambiguously prolife." Indeed, we might see it as a measure of the ongoing secularization of Catholic universities that they have clearly distanced themselves from pro-life endeavors. Instead of being institutional bastions of support and sustenance for the pro-life movement they often seem to be embarrassed to be associated with the most important moral cause of our time. (Such a pro-life course, my friends, is just not the way you impress the *New York Times* and your preferred peer institutions out there on the East Coast.)

Nonetheless, Fr. Jenkins took some actions. He set up the Notre Dame Task Force on Supporting the Choice for Life, which was chaired by John Cavadini (Theology) and Peg Brinig (Law). This group worked hard and produced two valuable statements: an Institutional Statement Supporting the Choice for Life, which indicated the university's commitment to the sanctity of human life from conception to natural death, and the University of

Notre Dame's Statement of Principles for Institutional Charitable Activity.

There were other positive developments. Fr. Jenkins and a considerably larger faculty group participated in the March for Life in both 2010 and 2011. Fr. Jenkins quietly resigned from the Millennium Promise Board. (One should note that Fr. Hesburgh had never resigned from the board of the Rockefeller Foundation despite its extensive support of population control measures throughout the Third World.) The Office of Life Initiatives was established and Mary Daly was appointed to staff it. The Alumni Association appointed a Life Initiatives Coordinator to liaise with clubs and assist and support their endeavors. I hope alums will benefit greatly from the efforts of Beth Bubik, said coordinator. Finally, a firm commitment was made not to engage in embryonic stem cell research. Let us be grateful for these measures. They are at least something but we should not overstate them.

The main pro-life efforts on campus continued to be those pushed by the students in Notre Dame Right to Life and by those faculty most closely associated with the Center for Ethics and Culture, certain terrific folk in the Law School, and the Faculty for Life group. The central administration did what they felt was required but little more. Certainly there was no generosity of spirit towards the ND 88—indeed, quite the opposite.

There could and must be a much stronger effort to support and sustain the pro-life cause at Notre Dame. We should proudly see ourselves as the institution that will train a new generation of pro-life leaders. There must be strong institutional support for Project Guadalupe, the effort led by Prof. David Solomon and the Notre Dame Fund to Protect Human Life to equip young folk to engage effectively in the pro-life struggle.

There are many other ways in which Notre Dame could further demonstrate its deep commitment to the pro-life cause. At a minimum we should assure that our students leave Notre Dame more likely to be pro-life than when they enter, which is not the case now. (Perhaps the institution could gift them with a copy of

John Paul II's *Evangelium Vitae* and encourage them to read and discuss it.) Most certainly the institution should do something more to support pregnant students in need—and not just ND students but young women from other colleges. Such work is being done successfully through the "Room at the Inn" organization associated with Belmont Abbey College in Charlotte, North Carolina.

Friends, we all know that there is much more that Notre Dame can do if there is the desire and commitment to do so. But is there that desire and commitment? Is there a real and deeply–felt need to demonstrate that Notre Dame is unambiguously pro-life? Recent events would suggest otherwise.

### The Roxanne Martino Case

Some of you are very familiar with the case from reading the informative Project Sycamore bulletins and the forceful pieces written by the *Wall Street Journal* columnist Bill McGurn. The basic details are these: the Fellows of Notre Dame have elected Roxanne Martino to the Board of Trustees. Ms. Martino is a Chicago businesswoman and ND alumna, who has given over $25,000 to the pro-abortion political action committee, EMILY's List. Her most recent donation was $5,000, made last December. (This is apparently the maximum amount permitted.)

Mr. Notebaert and Fr. Jenkins have sought to defend Ms. Martino. They assert that Ms. Martino (who, by the way, handles other people's investments) was simply unaware of the purposes of EMILY's List to which she donated over a ten-year period. They are seeking to mount an "ignorance defense" on behalf of Ms. Martino claiming that she did not know that EMILY's List took a pro-choice position. I suspect they must think that Notre Dame graduates are idiots who will simply accept this and move on to worrying about next football season.

Perhaps they think that saying "two plus two equals five" will really make it so. Their dissembling is an embarrassment to our university. That the leaders of Notre Dame are seeking to defend such an appointment is simply a disgrace, and it must be named as such. Clearly a mistake was made in vetting Ms. Martino. Certainly I know from a Holy Cross member of the Fellows that they had no knowledge of Ms. Martino's history of giving to EMILY's List when they voted in her favor.

But I ask you: would an "unambiguously pro-life" institution seek to defend this appointment? And that "defense" is becoming increasingly more difficult. Today [June 4, 2011], a report reveals that "Ms. Martino gave to *another* group solely dedicated to advancing abortion rights: the Illinois State Personal Pac. Like EMILY's List, this group makes no secret of its agenda, stating up front across the top of its home page: 'Vital to Electing a Pro-choice Illinois.'" As Bill McGurn noted, "This new information makes the official spin that Emily's List was an accident much harder to swallow." Surely, there should have been a quick and honest admission of a mistake and a request for Ms. Martino to stand down. Surely she herself should be genuinely troubled at having given substantial money to EMILY's List? (Hopefully, she might take some actions in subsequent years to demonstrate the depths of her acceptance of Catholic teaching on respect for every human life and compensate for her sad track record of generosity to an organization that promotes and defends one of the most liberal abortion regimes in the world.) Under any view, Ms. Martino should not set policies for and help determine the broad direction of Notre Dame!

In many ways this matter is more important than the Obama fiasco for what it means about the future direction of Notre Dame and for what it tells us about those who lead our university. Already the case has raised for me substantial questions about the suitability of Mr. Notebaert to lead our board. He has emerged as the main defender of Ms. Martino and seems to have supplanted Fr. Jenkins in determining university policy on the matter. If he can't understand the damage that an appointment like this does to Notre Dame's credibility and reputation as a Catholic university then his credentials and capabilities to lead the board are open to question.

Regrettably, the six Holy Cross fellows seem ready to acquiesce in Mr. Notebaert's decisions. This has not been in episode in which Holy Cross has sought to lead. I know this disappoints many of you who expect more of the order. (I can only say as someone who served as rector of Moreau Seminary some years ago that there are some among the younger Holy Cross priests who see the matter differently. They wish to be explicit in their loyalty to the Church and they understand that loyalty to Christ is integrally related to commitment to his Church. I hope and pray they will have the chance to exercise some influence in this place.)

### A Catholic University at its Heart

In the end, for Notre Dame to be unambiguously pro-life it will have to be very clear that it wants to be a Catholic university at its heart and not just at the periphery. Notre Dame must clarify what is the foundational document that guides its present course and its future direction.

Mr. Notebaert seems to think that the Land O'Lakes Statement with its strictures for complete institutional autonomy from the Church should serve this role. This is a disastrous course and one that pushes us further down the road to the marginalization of religion and ultimately to secularization. It is a course that asks us to ape and to mirror the secular schools that rank ahead of us in the *U.S. New and World Report* rankings.

The alternate course is the one offered by John Paul II' s *Ex Corde Ecclesiae*, and which is already incorporated into Notre Dame's mission statement. Our mission statement reads: "[A] Catholic university draws its a basic inspiration from Jesus Christ as the source of wisdom and from the conviction that in him all things can be brought to their completion. As a Catholic university, Notre Dame wishes to contribute to this educational mission."

The debate between these two versions is occurring right now. How this contest is resolved in practice will determine the long-term direction of Notre Dame. Will we merely settle for a

Catholic "gloss" on or around Notre Dame? This is what my colleague Fred Freddoso (Philosophy) was getting at when he suggested that Notre Dame might be willing to be "a public school in a Catholic neighborhood." There would still be the beautiful Basilica, perhaps even chapels in the dorms, touchdown Jesus, the Lady on the Dome, and even a couple of old priests drooling in their rocking chairs on the Corby Hall porch. But the central academic project would not be guided by Catholic principles or by the call of Christ.

Dear alumni friends, please don't allow the university to settle for this. There are enormous issues at stake. I ask you to keep track of two essential, related areas.

The first is what is taught and how. This is the whole area of curriculum. Will Notre Dame provide a distinct Catholic education which offers not only intellectual but moral and spiritual formation? Can Notre Dame provide an education that aids students to be not only smart but good? Can it be a place where, as Pope John Paul II wrote in *Veritatis Splendor*, young men and women of our day can come and ask: "Teacher, what must I do to have eternal life?" and not be laughed at and dismissed?

The second is who teaches here. Will we have faculty (Catholics and non-Catholics alike) who are supportive of the broad and distinct mission of Notre Dame? I will be glad to address these issues in our question and answer session. Faculty hiring and the content of the curriculum are essential matters.

Let me beseech you again to stay involved with Notre Dame. Some folk occasionally get so disappointed with the school that they want to break ties with it. This is a foolish course and a recipe for defeat for all that is best at Notre Dame. Stay and fight. Yet you must recognize that the pressures to simply conform to the reigning secular education model are strong. There are already plenty of schools where intellect has managed to detach itself from morality—places like Princeton, where Professor Peter Singer holds an endowed chair and yet thinks it is okay to kill babies. Is this the model we want to conform to and imitate?

Rather, would you not have Notre Dame be the place that unabashedly pursues the truth in these challenging times for the church and society? Shouldn't it strive to be "different"—to be a place where faith and reason, in the words of John Paul II, "are like two wings on which the human spirit rises to the contemplation of the truth"? Would you not rather that Notre Dame be the place that resisted the vain temptation to gain the whole world at the expense of its soul?

## Saving Notre Dame's Soul
## 2011

*Kathryn Jean Lopez is the current editor-at-large of the widely read* National Review Online, *where she has written and edited for more than a decade. She brings a most important Catholic perspective into the public square. She also writes frequently for a variety of Catholic publications, including the* National Catholic Register. *Kathryn approached me for an interview, and I was glad to respond to her questions. In this interview I drew attention to a significant number of matters including the efforts to remove David Solomon from the directorship of the Center for Ethics and Culture and the important endeavors of the Notre Dame Fund to Protect Human Life. I also spoke to my own love for Notre Dame and to the important role it can and must play in the Catholic Church in the United States. The interview was published on August 5, 2011, and it generated a lively response. An edited version is offered here which eliminates some repetition regarding the Roxanne Martino affair.*

*Has Notre Dame moved beyond the scandal of Barack Obama being honored there?*
It certainly has not. Notre Dame's honoring of a president who is deeply committed to the terrible abortion regime which prevails in the United States today damaged its reputation and credibility as a Catholic university. . . . Notre Dame is still struggling to overcome the harm done. While it has undertaken some

"damage limitation" measures, it certainly has not regained its previous treasured place in American Catholic life. Notre Dame's reputation as a Catholic university is still in need of repair.

*There have been some terrific developments since President Obama was on campus. There is the impressive Fund to Protect Human Life and you lead a chapter of University Faculty for Life. Notre Dame's participation in the March for Life has increased. And from the administration, too: there is now an Office of Life Initiatives and an alumni office for the same purpose, among other things. Are these just for show or real steps in the right direction?*

You are right to say that there have been some important developments on campus following the Obama visit. The ND administration's measures have been steps in the right direction. A firm commitment has been made not to engage in embryonic stem cell research. The Office of Life Initiatives and the alumni association's life initiatives coordinator are doing valuable work. Fr. Jenkins joined a considerably larger faculty group in the March for Life in both 2010 and 2011. Yet, while I commend these measures, it is clear that the major pro-life initiatives on campus still rest with groups that don't have serious administration support such as the Center for Ethics and Culture and the Notre Dame Fund to Protect Human Life, both of which are led by Professor David Solomon. We will know the administration is really serious about supporting the pro-life effort at Notre Dame when they offer such initiatives full support. This is not the case at the moment. Quite the opposite! In fact there is an effort afoot to force David Solomon from his directorship of the Center for Ethics and Culture just as he is getting Project Guadalupe firmly established. This makes no sense for an institution supposedly committed to supporting the pro-life cause.

*As you know, I just peeked in on this wonderful Project Guadalupe program run by the Fund to Protect Human Life. But its future is in jeopardy, isn't it? How could that be and how can there be a solution? Peace talks between the fund and the administration?*

I am so glad you came to Notre Dame to see just part of our overall Project Guadalupe. You came to the very successful Notre Dame Vita Institute which is an intensive two-week summer academic program dedicated to educating participants about fundamental human life issues. The twenty-five initial participants were terrific and we trust that what they gained at the Vita Institute will aid them in their respective and important work. The Vita Institute is a key stage of the overall project but it is linked to pro-life curriculum development and (we hope) an interdisciplinary master's program. These efforts aim to ensure that Notre Dame plays a crucial role in forming the next generation of pro-life leaders. This endeavor is off and running and yet the administration seems determined to choke it in infancy by forcing out the person who has designed it and brought it into being—namely David Solomon.

You ask, "How can there be a solution?" The answer is rather simple. There is no need for "peace talks." Instead, the administration should give this effort its enthusiastic support including allowing the employment of appropriate staff. That is what an "unambiguously pro-life institution" should and must do. How the administration acts on this matter over the coming year will reveal much about the kind of institution Notre Dame is and plans to be.

*Has David Solomon been the victim of retaliation? Can that be fixed?*
David Solomon had the courage to speak in opposition to Notre Dame's honoring of President Obama. This stance certainly seems to have led to recriminations against him. Already one effort was made to oust him from his directorship of the Center for Ethics and Culture (CEC) but this was foiled because of fear of bad publicity for Notre Dame. But the administration seems determined to move him on without any concern for the damage that would do to the important work of the CEC. In doing so the administration is removing the person whose great pro-life work

was recently recognized by the national University Faculty for Life organization with its annual Smith Award. The administration seems to want to neuter the person who has been the leader of our pro-life efforts at Notre Dame. It is little short of a disgrace.

We need a firm statement from the administration that David Solomon will continue in his duties until all stages of Project Guadalupe are up and running. Notre Dame should be a place that appreciates and celebrates all that he has done and is doing.

*Who are the ND 88 and what is their status? Did something go very wrong there?*
The ND 88 are the pro-life demonstrators arrested at the time of the Obama fiasco and charged with criminal trespass. The group included priests and nuns, notables like Norma McCovey (the "Roe" of *Roe v. Wade*), but mostly just ordinary folk. While in the past Notre Dame had not pressed to prosecute pro-gay and anti-military trespassers arrested in similar circumstances on campus, in this instance the university refused to request that the prosecutions be dropped. It was a strange and mean action and hardly that of an institution wanting to re-establish its pro-life credentials.

Fortunately, the ND 88 had excellent legal representation, and they indicated their intention to sue the university for discriminatory arrest. In this circumstance Notre Dame prudently agreed to ask the prosecutor to dismiss the trespass charges, which he promptly did. This is something that should have been done at the outset and a painful episode could have been avoided. That it wasn't reflects very poorly on Notre Dame and on the judgment of those who guided the university's decisions on this matter.

*Is "prestige over truth," as Bishop John D'Arcy put it, a deep-rooted problem there?*
Bishop John D'Arcy, the great bishop-emeritus of our diocese, who so loves Notre Dame, said it well when he noted that Notre Dame chose "prestige over truth" in inviting President Obama.

It was embarrassing for an institution dedicated to the pursuit of truth to settle for temporary attention over eternal honor. But the issue goes beyond the one case as your question correctly implies. It ties into the desire of some to have Notre Dame conform fully to the reigning secular education model and to impress the supposed elite institutions of American higher education with our accomplishments. . . . It is a dangerously misguided path.

*What's right with Notre Dame?*
Ah, this is a much more pleasant question to answer. There are many positive developments occurring at Notre Dame. Some good teaching occurs and good scholarship is undertaken. There are some terrific faculty members—Catholic and non-Catholic alike—who are deeply committed to Notre Dame's true mission, but we need more of them. We are home to some wonderful initiatives like the Alliance for Catholic Education, which can truly benefit the Church and society. We are fortunate to have fine students attend here and most of them benefit from their time with us. We have loyal alumni and friends who want Notre Dame to be its best self. Notre Dame also still has the continuing involvement and commitment of its founding religious community, the Congregation of Holy Cross. This is crucial, whatever the order's limitations in guiding the school in recent years. In a more general sense the university has the notable resources of the rich, if somewhat neglected, Catholic intellectual tradition to draw upon.

In the end there is surely enough right that Notre Dame can recover from the fraying of its Catholic identity. Sadly, not every major Catholic university can have that said of them, which, let me add, gives me no pleasure whatsoever. I want all major Catholic universities to work to restore their Catholic identities.

*What do you love most about Notre Dame?*
I will answer this in a personal way. I first arrived here to begin graduate studies in 1976. I studied for the priesthood here and was

ordained here in Sacred Heart Basilica. I have been teaching here
as a priest in Holy Cross for a quarter of a century. Occasionally
other possibilities have been put to me but I can't imagine teaching
anywhere else. I love the place—not just what it is but what it can
be. My blood, dare I say it, is in the bricks. I am very grateful that
at Notre Dame I have had the opportunity to serve as a priest-
teacher and scholar, to engage my students, and to search with
them for what really matters in life and beyond. I love saying Mass
on campus, especially in the chapels of the residence halls. I love
presiding at weddings of my former students and friends both on
campus and away from it. It's a great place to be a priest. Of course,
I love the beauty of the campus, although increasingly less so during the wintertime. I could go on—the basilica, the Lady on the
Dome, the Grotto, the crucifix in the Moreau Seminary Chapel. But
enough, will anyone still be reading this?

*You speak frankly about the identity of Notre Dame. Are you personal-
ly afraid of retaliation?*
I'm not afraid of retaliation in any serious way. I get an occasional cold shoulder but it is barely worth mentioning. Nonetheless, I
regret to say that retaliation cannot be ruled out for faculty and
staff at Notre Dame who raise their voice against the administration. One would be naïve to do so given the dismissal of Bill Kirk
last year after his twenty-plus years of devoted and exemplary
service to Notre Dame. To add insult to injury this dismissal was
carried out in a callous way (the "here is a cardboard box, please
clean out your desk" technique). It had a chilling impact on the
willingness of folk who labor without the benefit of tenure to
make public their deeply–held pro-life convictions and principles.

*You're a Holy Cross priest, living at Notre Dame. Given your protests
of some of what Fr. Jenkins has done as president, is it hard to live in
community there?*
I haven't found it hard to live in community but I was told my
presence in the university community would make life difficult
for others! I am very fortunate to live in the Moreau Seminary

community where the priests, brothers, and seminarians treat me as a true confrere, and I do my best to reciprocate.

*What should alumnae who love Notre Dame as a Catholic institution of higher learning and want it to truly be "unambiguously pro-life," be doing, saying, and supporting?*
This is a very important question. . . . Notre Dame alums must recognize the crucial issues involved and keep working and pressuring the university to adopt the *Ex Corde Ecclesiae* model. One of the truly beneficial things to come out of the Obama visit was that it revealed that dedicated alumni/alumnae would neither be cowed by the administration nor would they swallow the nonsensical "spin" about "dialogue" put out by Fr. Jenkins. Alums must continue to make their views known to the administration.

I especially encourage alums to keep informed about developments at Notre Dame by subscribing to the Sycamore Trust bulletins. Bill Dempsey and his colleagues at Sycamore have done a great job of promoting the Catholic character and mission of Notre Dame by providing a sustained and deeply thoughtful monitoring of events there.

Furthermore, alumni/alumnae should contribute financially to the university in areas that specifically support its Catholic identity and its pro-life mission.

*Is football too much of a priority at Notre Dame?*
I am an Australian. I like sport and I have grown to love Notre Dame football, although I confess I still have a deeper love for Rugby League! I was present at Notre Dame for the 1977 and 1988 National Championships, and I want to see us add to our list. I have no time at all for those who would like to see us "follow the Ivy League" and "downgrade" football. This is nonsense and reflects a total lack of understanding of the important place of football in Notre Dame's tradition. But we must be careful to do football right. We must have proper academic and personal standards for our players and ask our

coaches to act with integrity. We have to resist some of the corporate temptations that so beset college sport, especially football.

*Is Notre Dame important to the Catholic Church in America? Why?*
Notre Dame can be important for the Catholic Church in America, but it assuredly won't be if it simply conforms to the reigning secular education model. There are already plenty of schools where intellect has managed to detach itself from morality. Who will care about Notre Dame if it is merely a Duke or Northwestern "wannabee"?

It must distinguish itself by offering an education that aids its students (and faculty) to be not only smart but good. If Notre Dame lives out this vision it will surely play a part in the revitalization of the Church in the U.S. that is taking place right now. The university could truly serve the Church far beyond what it is doing. Let me ask your readers to pray for Notre Dame.


## Mr. Notebaert, *Ex Corde Ecclesiae*, and the Future of Notre Dame
### 2011

*Mr. Richard Notebaert's service as chair of the board of trustees has been less than stellar, to put it bluntly, Indeed, it is questionable whether Mr. Notebaert has a firm grasp on the identity and mission of Notre Dame as a Catholic university, as I outline in the following piece. He played important roles in the regrettable Obama and Martino affairs that have damaged Notre Dame's reputation. I sought to make the Notre Dame community aware of his failure in this op-ed piece published in the* Irish Rover *in December 2011. One can only hope that Mr. Notebaert's successor will be better equipped to serve Notre Dame as chair of its Board of Trustees.*

Richard C. Notebaert was elected to a three-year term as chair of the University of Notre Dame's Board of Trustees in 2007. He was elected to a further three-year term in 2010. First elected to the Board in 1997, Notebaert subsequently served as chair of its University Relations and Public Affairs and Communications Committee prior to succeeding Cleveland lawyer Patrick F. McCartan as chair of the full board. Sadly, there is good reason to believe that Notebaert is ill-suited to this important role.

On initial glance Notebaert's credentials to serve as board chair appear impeccable. He epitomizes the trustee blessed with notable corporate experience and credentials along with a generous capacity for giving. Born in Montréal in 1947, Notebaert grew up in Columbus, Ohio, and then attended the University of Wisconsin, after which he joined the marketing department of Wisconsin Bell. So began his distinguished business career which culminated in his leading three major American companies—Ameritech Corporation, Tellabs, and Qwest Communications International. He retired as CEO of Qwest in August 2007 soon after taking up his formal responsibilities as chair of Notre Dame's board.

Astute business observers credit Notebaert with Ameritech's notable growth and financial success during his leadership of the company in the 1990's. He is also credited with saving Tellabs from dissolution, and, most notably, with staving off bankruptcy for Qwest when the situation at the Denver-based communications giant seemed hopeless. Shareholders loved him. He proved capable of devising strategies to better meet customer needs and cutting costs, both by eliminating jobs and reducing benefits. During his time at Qwest, Notebaert was criticized for shaving retiree benefits while his own salary, bonuses, and stock options came in one year at over $20 million. Public complaints surfaced at Qwest's annual shareholders meeting in 2007 but Notebaert defended his performance, clarifying that he had donated to non-profits the proceeds of an $18 million stock options sale of the previous year.

During his tenure at Ameritech, Notebaert and his wife Peggy emerged as leading figures on the Chicago philanthropic scene. In 1998 they donated $5 million to help build the

Peggy Notebaert Natural History Museum, a wonderful Chicago institution specially noted for its "Butterfly Haven" exhibition. (Parenthetically, let me offer a word of advice—if you are at the museum for a wedding reception or the like please don't attempt to carry a glass of wine into the butterfly exhibition!)

Of course, Notre Dame has also been the beneficiary of Dick and Peggy Notebaert's notable generosity. In 2008 they made a $10 million gift to fund a new fellowship initiative in the university's graduate school. Notebaert Premier Fellowships are awarded to the top doctoral prospects admitted to Notre Dame each year.

Notebaert's personal example contributed to the success of the recently concluded "Spirit of Notre Dame" campaign. He also played an important role in steering the University of Notre Dame to make a generous contribution to the Holy Cross Order to fund the education of its younger members and to provide appropriate care for its elderly priests and brothers.

Notebaert is well-regarded on campus and is occasionally called upon to address groups ranging from undergraduate students in the Mendoza College of Business to participants in the newly initiated "ND Lead Program," which is designed to train the next generation of Notre Dame "leaders." In his talks he draws readily on his corporate experience and encourages his listeners to be "real." He speaks in a calm and measured manner and asks them to adopt the key elements that he believes drove him during his career—passion, setting hard objectives which can be measured, and adhering to a clear ethical framework. He emphasizes the need for a "moral rudder."

Given his record of business accomplishment and philanthropic generosity, what could lead to questions about such a man's competence to chair the board of trustees at Notre Dame? The answer, in short, arises from a recognition that Mr. Notebaert evidently does not possess a firm grasp on the identity and mission of Notre Dame as a Catholic university.

This painful reality became patently clear at the end of last academic year when the fellows of Notre Dame elected Roxanne Martino to the board of trustees. Ms. Martino, a Chicago businesswoman and an ND alumna, had given over $25,000 to the pro-abortion PAC, EMILY's List. She also donated to a group largely dedicated to advancing abortion rights, the Illinois State Personal PAC.

Clearly, a significant failure was made in the vetting of Ms. Martino. But instead of a quick and honest admission of a mistake and a request for her to stand down, Notebaert sought to defend Ms. Martino, claiming that she was simply unaware of the purposes of EMILY's list. That pathetic explanation could not withstand scrutiny, and, eventually, Ms. Martino decided to stand down.

Surprisingly, Notebaert appeared willing to allow a significant donor to "pro-choice" organizations to hold a seat on the board which sets the policies and broad direction for the university. He emerged as the main defender of Ms. Martino and seemed to supplant University President Fr. John Jenkins, CSC, in determining university policy on the matter. He appeared not to understand the damage that an appointment like this would do to Notre Dame's standing as a Catholic university.

Notebaert offered a quite misleading statement on the matter, and subsequently he offered no apology for either his apparent dissembling or for his failure to vet this appointment with appropriate diligence. He has yet to give any public assurance that contributing to explicitly "pro-choice" organizations is incompatible with service on the Notre Dame Board of Trustees.

The problem with Mr. Notebaert's leadership at Notre Dame, however, runs deeper than his serious mishandling of the Martino matter. It rests in his seemingly limited understanding of Notre Dame's mission and in his apparent lack of appreciation for the role that John Paul II's apostolic constitution, *Ex Corde Ecclesiae*, must play in guiding Notre Dame. Such deficiencies are perhaps unsurprising in light of the fact that he is neither a Notre Dame alumnus nor has he any significant prior experience in Catholic higher education.

His limitations in this regard were publicly displayed in the rather cavalier response he offered to Bishop John D'Arcy's pastoral reflection written in the aftermath of Notre Dame's honoring of President Obama at its 2009 commencement. In a superb article (published in *America*, August 31, 2009), Bishop D'Arcy noted his responsibility to call institutions like Notre Dame "to give public witness to the fullness of Catholic faith." He went on to note the silence and inaction of Notre Dame's Board of Trustees during the Obama episode, and he concluded by posing some "critical questions" regarding the relationship of Notre Dame to the Catholic Church. Most fundamentally he asked: "Where will the great Catholic universities search for a guiding light in the years ahead? Will it be the Land O'Lakes statement or *Ex Corde Ecclesiae?*"

In his response Notebaert embarrassingly stretched to defend Notre Dame's honoring of President Obama on the grounds that it provided an opening for dialogue. He paid no attention to the damage that the Obama invitation inflicted on Notre Dame's standing in the broad Catholic community, and he breezed past any serious consideration of the relationship between Notre Dame and the Catholic Church. He ended, however, with an apparent endorsement of the Land O'Lakes statement as the guiding charter for Notre Dame. Herein lies the problem and it is one that must be faced honestly by Mr. Notebaert and his fellow trustees.

Let me state the matter plainly as a question: Does Mr. Notebaert hold that the Land O'Lakes statement, with its strictures for institutional autonomy from the Church and the aping of our supposed secular peers, should guide Notre Dame into the future? Is this the vision he puts before the future leaders of Notre Dame?

Furthermore, it must be asked: Does he therefore reject *Ex Corde Ecclesiae* as the foundational document for Notre Dame's fulfilling its mission as a Catholic university? If so, does he also reject its clear guidance for a close pastoral relationship between the local ordinary and the university, its crucial requirement for a majority of committed Catholics to prevail in the faculty ranks, and its distinct recognition of the central importance of theology in the university?

The answers to these questions have important implications for the kind of university Notre Dame will be. They assuredly will help clarify whether Notre Dame will travel down a path which puts ratings over principles and prestige over truth. They will indicate whether Notre Dame should continue scurrying after such goals as an invitation to join the American Association of Universities, whatever the involvement of that organization with embryonic stem-cell research. They will help determine whether Notre Dame will provide a moral vision for its students grounded in such principles as the dignity of each human person and deep concern for the common good.

It has now become a "tradition" at Notre Dame for the Laetare Medal, the university's highest honor awarded annually to recognize outstanding service to the Catholic Church and society, to be conferred on the retiring chair of the board of trustees as a token of gratitude for services rendered. Dick Notebaert should be at short odds to receive the award in 2013. Yet, before the medal with its Latin inscription, "Magna est veritas et prevalebit" ("Truth is mighty, and it shall prevail") makes its way to the Notebaert family trophy room, perhaps the future recipient might take some clear actions to warrant it. He might begin with an unequivocal statement affirming *Ex Corde Ecclesiae* as the guiding light for Notre Dame in the years ahead.

# Bishop Jenky, Civility, and Conviction

## Defending Bishop Jenky
## 2012

*In early April 2012, Bishop Daniel Jenky, C.S.C., of the Peoria diocese, warned that the Obama administration's actions limiting the religious liberty of churches and church affiliated agencies could lead to persecution parallel to that which afflicted churches under Nazi Germany and Soviet Russia. He told a men's conference in Peoria that, "Hitler and Stalin, at their better moments, would just barely tolerate some churches remaining open, but would not tolerate any competition with the state in education, social services, and health care. In clear violation of our First Amendment rights, Barack Obama—with his radical, pro abortion and extreme secularist agenda—now seems intent on following a similar path."*

*In response, a number of Notre Dame professors denounced the bishop and alleged that his comments "demonstrate ignorance of history, insensitivity to victims of genocide and absence of judgment." I was contacted by John Burger of the* National Catholic Register *to offer a response, and my interview with him is included here.*

*Do you know Bishop Jenky?*
I do indeed. He's of course a member of the Congregation of Holy Cross, and I've known him since I came to the order as a seminarian 30 years ago. He's a terrific priest and a great bishop.

*Have you worked with him closely?*
He was the rector of Sacred Heart Basilica in my younger days as a priest here on campus and was the superior of the Holy

Cross community to which I belonged here during those years. But then he was taken away from us and made auxiliary bishop here in Fort Wayne-South Bend. And then he was made bishop of Peoria about 10 years ago. So for the last 15 years or so, I've seen him periodically. He comes back to visit and so on.

*What do you think of this brouhaha over his remarks?*
I have found the reaction of my faculty colleagues quite embarrassing—embarrassing because these academics disgracefully misused Bishop Jenky's words by taking them out of context. It has been a little disappointing, to say the least. Bishop Jenky was making remarks about the religious liberty issue, and some of my colleagues implied that the bishop was suggesting that President Obama was on his way to adopting the entire Hitler-Stalin agenda. It's a mischaracterization that is unworthy of supposedly serious scholars.

*You're a historian, albeit your specialty is American history.*
I am a historian, and I challenge the signatories to this letter criticizing Bishop Jenky to point to one part of his homily that is historically inaccurate.

*Is he historically accurate?*
Absolutely. By the way, Bishop Jenky was a history major when he was an undergraduate here at Notre Dame. He has read quite a bit of history in his day. And he is a good student of it.

*Why do you think they would take his remarks out of context?*
Well, this is to engage in speculation, and I probably shouldn't go down this path myself; one should be cautious. But I think this very poorly crafted letter says more about the rather predictable and ideological bias of the signatories than it does about Bishop Jenky's courageous homily.

*But do you feel that he might have overstepped any kind of line?*
No. His homily was a courageous homily that pointed to the

pattern of behavior of a number of regimes to limit religious freedom and to attack religious institutions.

*Is there any way you might characterize the professors who signed the letter—i.e., do they all have something in common?*
Most are concentrated in the College of Arts and Letters. I would say that there's a kind of a piling-on mentality at work here.

*Do you know of any who have allied themselves with the U.S. bishops on the religious liberty battle?*
None of the signatories on the list come to mind as having spoken out publicly on the religious liberty issue, nor can I say that any of the folks I saw on the list jump out at me—I'm not saying that there aren't any—but none jump out at me as being vocally pro-life.

*What do you know of Bishop Jenky's contributions as a member of the board of fellows at Notre Dame, particularly regarding the university's Catholic character?*
The board of fellows is the key decision-making group that selects the trustees at Notre Dame. It's comprised of six members of the Congregation of Holy Cross and six lay persons. I think Bishop Jenky has always been an engaged and active member of the board of fellows and also the board of trustees. (When you're a fellow, you're also a trustee.) He deeply loves Notre Dame and has sought to build up Notre Dame's Catholic mission and identity, has defended Notre Dame for the good things that go on here, and deeply wishes the best for Notre Dame. So he's been a valued contributor to the work of the board of fellows and board of trustees.

## Civility, Courage, and Conviction at Notre Dame
## 2012

*Universities like Notre Dame must be places that host vigorous exchanges of views about matters of importance. Significant and controversial issues should be debated with genuine civility. Regrettably, however, calls for civility can be misused to stifle serious discussion. I expressed concerns about this practice in this essay published in the* Irish Rover *in October of 2012. I also made clear that, in the present circumstances where religious liberty is under fire, Notre Dame must not hide behind a* faux *civility but rather must be ready to stand tall to defend the Church's institutional freedom and to articulate its own Catholic convictions.*

Civility is in vogue at Notre Dame these days. On campus we have had panel discussions exploring how to improve civic engagement with less partisan rhetoric. This year's university forum, "A More Perfect Union: The Future of America's Democracy," aims at fostering civil discussion of national political issues. And almost all of us have seen one of those ubiquitous posters of our university president asking students to "Take the Pledge"—that is the "Notre Dame Pledge for Virtuous Discourse," which encourages students to engage in respectful dialogue.

In this Notre Dame is by no means unique. Public appeals to civility have been voiced regularly throughout American history, including during periods when political discourse was far fiercer than anything experienced today. Nonetheless, in the wake of the eye-rolling, laughter, and dismissive interruptions that characterized Joe Biden's performance in the recent vice presidential debate, it is good to be reminded of the importance of civility for democratic dialogue.

True civility, however, is not to be mistaken for saccharine niceness. True civility assumes vigorous exchanges of views about matters of importance. A local example of what I mean was the robust debate over Truman's use of the atomic bomb held on campus last year in which I had the good fortune to engage two capable interlocutors, Professors David Solomon and Michael Baxter. Each put forth strong arguments that were often diametrically opposed to mine. (Some *Rover* readers might recall it.) We disagreed sharply, and our strong criticism reflected those disagreements. Yet we managed to do so in a civil fashion, which meant that none of us tried in any way to inhibit the others from expressing honestly held views.

Regrettably, not all advocates of "civility" follow this course. Some appear to use their advocacy for civility as a cover to stifle genuine debate, especially over important issues. This is false civility because it becomes not simply a vehicle to prevent serious discussion but also a weapon to use against one's political foes. Sometimes, too, civility serves as a refuge to disguise the fact that its advocates want to avoid taking tough public stands on difficult issues. Sadly, present day Notre Dame provides evidence of these practices.

Let me give one example. Late last spring, 154 Notre Dame faculty responded to a powerful homily given by Peoria Bishop Daniel Jenky in defense of religious freedom against various actions affecting the church at both the national and state levels. In his homily, Bishop Jenky quite accurately gave four instances of governments—those of Bismarck, Clemenceau, Hitler and Stalin—that "tried to force Christians to huddle and hide only within the confines of their churches." He suggested further, also rightly, certain parallels with recent actions by the Obama administration and an Illinois state government, which had imposed unacceptable terms on the workings of certain Catholic social service agencies. Did the offended faculty members react by writing a civil note to Bishop Jenky contesting his view? Hardly. Their ire up and their blood presumably boiling, they instead falsely and publicly accused Bishop Jenky of "ignorance of history, insensitivity to genocide, and absence of judgment." They further demanded that he resign as a fellow and trustee of the university. They in no way, however, addressed the substance of Bishop Jenky's legitimate concerns. So much for measured, careful, and respectful dialogue! The faculty petition was an effort to silence a church leader and expel him from the Notre Dame family. The irony here apparently is lost on some of the signatories who still present themselves as monitors of "civility" on campus.

In reality the threats to civility and genuine dialogue these days come mainly from those determined to limit and restrain the expression of views grounded in religious convictions or that defend the valuable work of religious institutions. Fr. Jenkins himself has said that dialogue with the Obama administration proved fruitless when seeking relief from the HHS mandates that require that employers and institutions provide health insurance covering abortifacients, sterilization and contraception even when the employers deem these to be morally wrong. Notre Dame's experience in this sad episode is but part of a larger, dangerous effort to restrict religious freedom and to assault conscience rights and protection.

Last month the cardinal archbishop of Washington, D.C., Donald Wuerl, pointed out that an "increasingly bold, ideologically driven and progressively intolerant secular humanism" is intent on driving religious voices out of the public square. The evidence abounds far beyond the HHS mandate issue and touches important matters like sexuality, marriage, discrimination laws, healthcare policy concerning abortion and end of life issues, and foreign aid. For example, one might ask the president of Chick-fil-A if he would like to articulate again (and in a civil manner!) the historical Christian view of marriage so that he could risk his business interests being threatened anew by the mayor of Boston and his cohort. Or the chief diversity officer at Gallaudet University, who noted the irony that she was suspended for having a diverse view—she signed a petition in support of traditional marriage.

Even views that are not religiously based but which might support traditional Christian views are targeted, including in universities where academic freedom supposedly prevails. For example one might ask the sociology professor at the University of Texas at Austin, Mark Regnerus, what his experience of civility has been after he had the audacity to conclude after careful research that "adult children of parents who had same-sex romantic relationships, including same-sex couples, had more emotional and social problems than do adult children of heterosexual parents with intact marriages." It has been reported by our distinguished faculty colleague Christian Smith that Regnerus was "smeared in the media and subjected to an inquiry by his university over allegations of scientific misconduct." Where were the civility-monitors who came to his aid or pleaded for respectful dialogue from those who tried to have him fired?

Especially in these circumstances of hostility toward traditional values, Notre Dame must demonstrate real leadership and exhibit courage in defending religious liberty and the rights of conscience. As the leading Catholic university, we have a special obligation to articulate fundamental church teaching on the dignity of each human person and the right to life of the unborn as well as on the sanctity of marriage. Notre Dame must avoid tepid engagement on these now controversial issues.

Father Jenkins deserves credit for launching a lawsuit in defense of religious liberty against a president on whom he bestowed an honorary degree. What concerns me, however, is his recent problematic statement that his "deepest conviction" is to find a "way to talk to one another in ways that are respectful and reasoned." This view seems grounded in the squishy notion of "epistemic humility," including even "about truths believed to be revealed," which he offered in a talk at the Aquinas Institute at Emory University in 2011. It certainly resonates with his commencement address at Wesley Theological Seminary in May of 2012, in which he elevated "respectful discourse" as a crucial end dependent upon deep convictions being expressed as "an effort to persuade." Yet, Notre Dame's recent experience of failed negotiations with the Obama administration surely suffices to reveal the limits of this rather unrealistic approach.

Whoever wins the presidential election in November, one thing is certain: the challenge to religious liberty, and especially to the freedom of religious institutions to pursue their appropriate missions, will continue. The temptation for Notre Dame will be to lay low in this conflict and perhaps confine itself to bland statements that debate be conducted with civility. Such a course puts a rather skewed tolerance as the highest good, ignores any claims to objective truths and neglects the moral obligation to stand up for those truths. Although it will be preferred by those who strangely crave the regard of some of the main vehicles of aggressive secularism in politics, the media and the academy, this wimpish option must be resisted fully if Notre Dame is to fulfill its fundamental calling as a Catholic university.

It is unclear if Notre Dame will stand tall to this challenge. Will we fight publicly for the Church's institutional freedom—or just leave it "to the courts" as the more tepid advocate? Will we raise our voice in defense of traditional Christian marriage? Are we prepared to fight more openly and vigorously for the lives of the unborn?

Of late Notre Dame has mounted a careful public relations effort to display the range of worthy causes for which it is willing to "fight." All are commendable, and it is inspiring to see publicized Notre Dame's efforts to combat natural disasters, to protect the health of children, and to rebuild war-torn communities. How much more commendable and inspiring it would be if Notre Dame placed its prestige and influence in support of other important causes that are less likely to attract universal approval. We will know that Notre Dame has moved to a new level of courage and conviction when it airs TV spots during its football games that testify to its willingness to fight for the lives of the unborn—and in defense of traditional marriage.

In the end, Notre Dame is confronted with a crucial decision: whether we wish at our very heart to be a Catholic university. Will we be a place that pursues the truth and is willing to defend it? Will we be a place that holds firmly that there are moral absolutes and that the defense of them trumps mere tolerance? Will we be a place where genuine civil dialogue occurs in the context of true courage and conviction?

We can and should debate these issues in civility. But we should never invoke civility as a way to avoid taking a stand.

# Section V: Student Life/Counsel for Students

## Fear and the Christian Life
### 2004

*Addressing students in less formal settings has always been part of my ministry at the university. I gave the first version of the talk below at a "Breaking Bread" dinner. This series continues still and has been the venue for some wonderful faculty-student exchanges. I have given my "fear" talk in other contexts, including most recently at the Edith Stein conference held at Notre Dame in February 2012. The talk, somewhat edited here, is directed to undergraduate students. I humbly suggest, however, that it can be read with profit by students of all ages.*

I want to thank you for coming tonight. I am very honored to be the first speaker of the "Breaking Bread" series sponsored by the Center for Ethics and Culture and organized by the amazing Jennie Bradley.

To be honest, I agreed to give this talk this evening primarily because it was a dear former student who asked me. I certainly didn't give it because I thought I had a lot to say on the topic which Jennie assigned, namely "FEAR and the Christian Life."

I deferred thinking seriously about the topic until quite recently, when a certain mild fear (let us say) began to overtake me that I didn't really have much of any consequence to say!

I regretted that I had succumbed to Jennie's request to speak on "fear" and wished I had persuaded her to let me inflict upon you a talk I gave for a Vocare retreat group a while back on "Christian Discipleship and What Really Matters." Not for the first time I felt just slightly that the adage "fools rush in where angels *fear* to tread" applied to me!

But overcoming that fear proved possible because I heard the ringing words of that well-known (at least to me) theologian-philosopher—namely my mother!—ringing in my ears: "Go on. Do this as best you can. It will be good for you." And to tell you the truth I also kept getting signs from the Holy Spirit on the matter (or, at least, I kept coming across references to "fear").

I'm on the email list of a chap who gave a workshop at Moreau Seminary some years ago. I have often thought of getting off the list but I have been afraid to hurt his feelings. Anyway, day in and day out his "thought for the day" comes through to greet me when I open up my email after morning prayer. Most of the time I send them straight to the trash but sometime back, right after receiving Jennie's assignment, the "thought for the day" was on "Thoughts for Life" and it included such proverbial wisdom as:

The greatest mistake      Giving Up
The most useless asset     Pride
The greatest knowledge   God

But leading off the list and what really caught my eye was this one:

The Greatest Handicap    FEAR!

I concluded that someone was trying to tell me something!

Now I got a further indication that "fear" was stalking me when, while reading the pages of the *New York Times* a month or so ago, I came upon an article entitled: "Is Fear Itself the Enemy? Or Perhaps the Lack of It?" The article reported a conference on "Fear: Its Uses and Abuses." Former Vice President Al Gore gave the keynote and talked—rather shrilly perhaps—of how the present American government "is preoccupied with instilling fear." The conference theme was that fear was being "encouraged by our government and exacerbated by our media," and I suspect that quite a bit of fear was generated among the conference participants! Nonetheless, they listened to talks on such worthy and less political topics as "fear in literature," "the social psychology of fear," and "the neuro-psychology of fear," which clarified that fear "tends to drive out reflective thought with its stimulus of the 'lateral nucleus of the amydala.'"

Anyway, at least in the *Times'* report on the conference, I found no suggestion that any of the participants had raised the suggestion that fear might be confronted in some way by living the Christian life. I suspect that had someone done so it might have generated a lot of fear, and perhaps a proponent of that notion might have been ridiculed by other participants. (But at least I knew that Jennie Bradley was up on what was rather fashionable in academic circles ; talking about fear is "au courant" and we are on the cutting edge here tonight. Aren't you reassured?)

I felt reassured that nobody else was talking about "Fear *and* the Christian Life" and began to assemble a few thoughts, which I trust I will get to before my 25 minutes runs out! I planned to make a couple of historical references, then to note a couple of scripture passages, and finally to mention a few models of those who have overcome fear in living out their discipleship in the hope that this would stimulate our various discussions over dinner.

I hadn't really put pen to paper but my talk was taking shape in my head when the ever helpful Jennie brought over to me last Thursday the powerful book by the great Anglican theologian and scripture scholar N.T. Wright, entitled *Following Jesus: Biblical Reflections on Discipleship,* which contains a truly insightful reflection on "Fear and Living by Faith." In addition she included copies of all these profound quotations from the Gospels and from good Pope John XXIII, Pope John Paul II, and Cardinal Newman.

I felt a little queasy: I succumbed to the awful practice of comparing and thought my ideas a little weak. Indeed, I confided to my friend, Fr. Paul Kollman that what came to my mind was the well-know "Peanuts" cartoon where Linus, Lucy, and Charlie Brown are lying on the grass, watching clouds.

Lucy says, "If you use your imagination, you can see lots of things in cloud formations. What do you see, Linus?"

He answers, "Well those clouds over there look like a map of

British Honduras on the Caribbean. That cloud up there looks a little like the profile of Thomas Eakins, the famous painter and sculptor. And that group of clouds there gives me the impression of the stoning of Stephen . . . . I can see the Apostle Paul standing there to one side."

"Uh-huh," Lucy says, "That's very good. What do you see in the clouds, Charlie Brown?"

"I was going to say I saw a ducky and a horsy," Charlie Brown replied, "but I changed my mind."

Look, I can't change my mind on what to say, but I have sought to incorporate some of Dr. Tom Wright's explication on the subject into this talk and I must encourage you to go home tonight and to read Chapter Seven: "The God who Raises the Dead. " Reading that will make you want to read the whole book!

### What is Fear?

Fear is actually a multi-faceted and complicated thing. It has attracted the interest of philosophers from the time of Plato and Aristotle, and the topic is the subject of intense study by modern psychologists. Some fear is quite legitimate. For example, if you come from Australia (or even if you have only read Bill Bryson's *In a Sunburned Country*) you know there are plenty of things of which to be afraid. Little kids in my homeland are trained to be afraid of snakes since so many of them are poisonous. I'm telling you that it is okay to be afraid if a twenty foot "great white" is swimmingly menacingly toward you. The point is that God made us in such a way that we can develop certain almost instinctive responses to dangerous situations and creatures. Certain fears are justified.

But fear is much more prevalent than those rather justifiable fears brought on by natural dangers. Some fear is clearly generated by the actions of men and women. Think of the fear of nuclear attack during the Cold War (little kids like Professor Solomon hiding under their desks in preparation for a possible nuclear strike in the 1950's). Think of the fear today of terrorist threats in certain parts of the world—it makes one glad to be in South Bend, doesn't it?!

If we could only settle the Middle East conflict, persuade the Al-Qaeda members to take up organic farming, settle all ethnic, religious, and political problems, would we be able to eliminate fear? It doesn't seem likely.

The answer is made brutally obvious by N.T. Wright who suggests that we live in a world "in which we eat, sleep, and breathe fear." Wright details the stages of human fear.

First, he writes, "We emerge from the warmth of the womb into the cold of the cosmos, and we're afraid of being alone, of being unloved, of being abandoned." Any of you experienced that? Then, "we mix with other children, other teenagers, other young adults, and we're afraid of looking stupid, of being left behind in some race that we all seem to be automatically entered for." Could this apply to you? After that "we contemplate jobs, and we're afraid both that we mightn't get the one we really want and that if we get it we mightn't be able to do it properly." Any seniors here right now? Don't worry: "that double fear lasts for many people all through their lives."

Work is not the only source of worry. As Wright clarifies, "We contemplate marriage and we're afraid both that we might never find the right person and that if we do marry it may turn out to be a disaster. We consider a career move, and are afraid both of stepping off the ladder and of missing the golden opportunity. We look ahead to retirement, and are afraid both of growing older and more feeble and, (of course) of dying suddenly." And, as Wright further explains, "these are just some of the big ones."

Aside from fears at every stage along the journey of life, we all experience our own particular fears. I suspect that each of you have your own special fears. Perhaps we could have a sharing on that; each table could report back on the weirdest fear or the most entertaining! Okay, we won't do that, but let us admit that we succumb to certain fears at some level. We can't avoid it. It seems a part of the human condition, if you will.

Now, I'm not suggesting that the younger people have it as tough as the dear faculty here. My guess is that most students don't "lie awake at night possessed by the terrible fear that life is impossible. [But] Sometimes when . . . [some older folk, although surely not this special group of faculty] least expect it they can wake up overwhelmed by a massive sense of loneliness, misery, chaos, death: appalled by the agony and futility of existence." The world seems dark to them and they are not sure which way to go. See what you have to look forward to!

But let's not focus on the older folk. What fears do our beloved Domers hold? Surely not fear of failure? Not among this group where everyone wants to be "above average" or better! Might it be fear of rejection? Fear of commitment? Okay, I'll stop. I see the guys getting nervous. Let me add just one more: the fear of doing something really unusual, like serving as sister, brother, or priest in the Church. (On the latter, have no fear, for it is a good life!)

### Finding Freedom from Fear

What can we do to address all this fear? Do we just grin and bear it and even try to joke about it (sort of like "whistling in the dark")? Do we acknowledge the fear and make regular appointments with a therapist? Ah, but surely politics might have the answer?

Some notable political figures from the past have sought to campaign against fear and to declare war upon it. Think of FDR in his first inaugural address (March 1933) trying to rouse the hope and courage of his people in the midst of the Great Depression with that powerful entreaty, "The only thing we have to fear is fear itself." Or his including "freedom from fear" in the war aims that he and Winston Churchill adopted in 1941. One might admire FDR's ambitious goal but also concede that it remains unfulfilled. As tempting as the idea may sometimes seem politics can't solve everything, and we should not expect it to do so.

Of course, we should always be on the lookout for those who

seek to generate and exploit fear in others as their tactic to obtain or retain power. We've all read *The Prince* and we all know Machiavelli's dictum that for a leader "it is far safer to be feared than loved." He obviously didn't take seriously the words of the First Letter of John (4:18): "There is no fear in love, but perfect love casts out fear."

By the way, I do think a little controlled fear comes in handy in certain stages of the parent-child relationship and the teacher-student relationship. For example, I've come to admire those old Irish Sisters of Mercy who scared me into learning how to read and write in my little Catholic school in Australia forty years ago!

But, to get back on track, if resignation, laughing in the face of fear, therapy, and politics do not provide long-term and lasting answers, then what does?

I thought you would never ask. I want to offer the following as an antidote to fear: faith, the Christian life, and the discipleship of the Lord Jesus Christ. Now certain cynics or critics of religion might laugh or sneer at this proposal. They might suggest that religion is the root cause of a lot of fear. They would imply that people have been scared into being Christians and scared into living by the commandments of the Lord.

Certainly, who can deny that in the pre-Vatican II period there was much more use of fear as a pastoral instrument. Great "old Monsignor McGillicuddy" types all over the world (they were usually Irish with a strong Jansenist streak) preached hell-fire and damnation sermons and their object was clear. They wanted to scare the hell out of people so as to keep them out of hell! The portrayals of the worms, maggots, and fiery furnace of "Gehenna" were used to good effect. One could literally feel the fires nipping at one's rear end—especially when those Redemptorist priests came to town to preach the parish mission.

Let me reveal how non-politically-correct I am by suggesting that this approach is not *all* bad. In the age of Enron and World.com we should be afraid to lie, cheat, slander, and so on because of the damage it does to others, to ourselves, and to our community and most of all because it separates us from God's way. But thanks to moral relativism we are able to explain away just about anything, indeed, even hideous things. We may fear many things but we have lost the fear of Satan, the fear of hell.

While fear of hell may not be a bad thing, Pope John Paul II has eloquently preached during his whole pontificate that faith cannot and should not be based on fear. One cannot live the Christian life well if motivated only by the desire to avoid divine punishment. If we try this we have missed the point. As one careful student of Pope John Paul (Cardinal Avery Dulles) has argued, in the pope's view, "[F]ear . . . diminishes the scope of freedom and makes only a poor Christian." John Paul II "holds up the perfect motives of hope, trust and love as grounds for joyful adherence to the Lord." The pope continues to stand by the theme of his inaugural homily: "Do not be afraid. . . . Open wide the doors to Christ. He alone has the words of life, yes, of eternal life." In very simple terms we must embrace the gift of faith that can sustain us and guide through "the many dangers, toils and snares" that abound in the world not out of a negative but out of a positive motive.

This is what Wright points to so effectively as he explains the most repeated command in the Bible: "Do not be afraid." He explains that positive belief in the Resurrection of the Lord Jesus is central, "because the God who made the world is the God who raised Jesus from the dead and who calls us to follow him." Faith in the Resurrection is central because, as Paul essentially told the Corinthians long ago, if Jesus didn't rise from the dead, "then the whole Christian thing is a waste of time."

But the Resurrection is true: ours is a God who raises the dead. As Wright beautifully points out: "The true God gives new life, deeper, richer life and helps us towards full mature humanness, by prizing open the clenched fists of our fears in order to give his own life and love into our empty waiting hands." This is the God who can be trusted, whatever the dangers that surround us, whatever the fears we hold. This is the God of whom the psalmist wrote:

"The Lord is my light and my salvation; whom shall I fear? The Lord is the strength of my life; of whom should I be afraid."

"Though a host should encamp against me, my heart shall not fear Though war should rise against me in this will I be confident" (Psalm 27, 1 & 3).

Oh, to be in the position of the psalmist! But let us be frank: "living by faith rather than by fear is so odd for us" as Wright puts it, "so scary for us, that it takes a lot of learning." Bit by bit, we must "open ourselves to the power of the resurrection God." Perhaps it is a lifelong task.

There is a kind of inverse relationship here, I think: as our trust and hope in the Lord increases our fears will decrease. When we have resolved to follow the Lord, we have fewer things to worry about. Some of the normal decisions of life are put into right perspective. We appreciate more powerfully that, as the Constitutions of the Congregation of Holy Cross put it, "[T]here is no failure the Lord's love cannot reverse, no humiliation he cannot dissolve, no routine he cannot transfigure. All is swallowed up in victory. He has nothing but gifts to offer." We focus with gratitude on what we have rather than seething with resentment on what we do not. We come to understand what really matters.

Now some of you may be in this position right now and can guide the rest of us. You may be able to give us some quick directions on how to live by faith rather than by fear. Bring that to your discussions. Let me also suggest that the scriptures provide us with some wonderful models of folk who had to overcome their fears to respond to God's call.

Two Sundays ago, we heard of the call of Moses from God to lead the Israelites from slavery in Egypt to the promised land. He probably felt secure tending his father-in-law's flocks and protested that he was not a good speaker but he overcame his hesitation and fear and accepted the Lord's call.

Or think of Peter being invited by the Lord to "put out into the deep." The Gospel of Luke records a fascinating episode when Jesus tells Simon Peter, who had been fishing all night and caught nothing, to lower his nets again. When he did, such was the catch that the boat was almost pulled under. Thereupon Simon Peter shouted out, "Leave me, Lord. I am a sinful man." He felt himself unworthy because it suddenly struck him that he was in the company of God. Peter is not alone in this kind of reaction; plenty of folk find it difficult to be near God. Perhaps we might be like Simon Peter and feel ourselves unworthy. We may even be fearful to let God come too close. But it is instructive to look at the response which greeted Simon. He was greeted not with criticism of his unworthiness but rather with a charge from God, with a call. Jesus greeted Simon tenderly and said, "Be not afraid, follow me, and you will catch men and women together with me."

Well, I select these two as examples because obviously their trials and tribulations didn't end with their call. Neither will ours. They are models for us in moving forward into an ever-deepening relationship with the Lord God. It takes time but one must begin. One must truly root one's life in responding to God's call. This must be the central reality of our life. We must answer our particular call—even when it involves "putting out into the deep" so as to follow the Lord. We are being called to live our lives in Christ with a new fearlessness and intensity.

We must not be afraid to live our faith openly and publicly here at Notre Dame—we must avoid carefully sequestering it into some private sphere as so many Christians do. We need to encourage and support each other in overcoming our fears to live the Christian life so that we can respond to a special call— perhaps even to lead others from slavery or entrapment in poverty, ignorance, addiction, or injustice.

Let me say in conclusion: Respond to the call of discipleship. Follow the Lord on the journey. There may be some fears along the way but trust in the Lord, and, whatever you do, don't turn back.

## Some Advice for Future Catholic Politicians
## 2011

*I am presently working on a volume exploring the contributions, both positive and negative, of Catholic politicians from John F. Kennedy through to the present. It is a subject that interests me greatly. I have given talks and published some popular pieces on this subject, includ-ing essays on Governors Mario Cuomo and Robert P. Casey in* Notre Dame magazine. *I encourage students to consider the political voca-tion. Never have strong and competent Catholic politicians been more needed than they are today. The brief essay that follows is an effort to encourage and to guide those who might pursue this crucial calling.*

In his first encyclical letter *Deus Caritas Est* (God Is Love), Pope Benedict XVI reminded us, "Building a just social and civil order, wherein each person receives what is his or her due, is an essential task which every generation must take up anew." This is essentially the work of lay women and men. My hope is that there are numbered among readers of *The Rover* able women and men who wish to take up the vocation of politics and so to engage in this crucial work. The Church aims to help inform her members in pursuing this vocation, and in this effort Catholic colleges and universities have a special role to play, for they have a treasured intellectual tradition and great wisdom to pass along to their students.

Students at schools such as Notre Dame should emerge with a clear understanding of Catholic moral teaching and social doc-trine and so be ready to play their part in shaping their society for the good. In the Pastoral Constitution on the Church in the Modern World (*Gaudium et Spes*), issued in December of 1965, the council fathers at Vatican II addressed the whole issue of Catholics' political participation. They honored the political vocation and conveyed that Christian politicians are called upon to engage the modern world in ways that promote the dignity of each person and the common good. They are to serve within their own domain as "leaven." They certainly are not to see their political activities as separate from their religious commitments. The council fathers emphasized that "there be no false opposition between professional and social activities on the one part, and religious life on the other." They firmly rejected any compartmentalization of faith and political engagement.

Sadly, the impact of the vision for Catholic politicians set forth in *Gaudium et Spes* has been minimal at best over the past decades. Many politicians who self–identified as Catholics hid behind the notion that religion was a private matter. They blended in and refrained from utilizing the moral and social teachings of their religion as an inspiration and guide for their actions. They did this despite the fact that some of the fundamental problems of the American polity and society—the assault on human life, the decline of family and community, unrestrained individualism at the expense of the common good, rampant relativism in values—presented a unique opportunity and challenge to Catholics to contribute in the public domain.

The privatized religion model largely triumphed despite both the efforts of those who pushed the "consistent ethic of life/seamless garment" approach in the 1980's and the courageous witness of some faithful Catholic politicians such as the pro-life governor of Pennsylvania, Robert P. Casey. The increasingly blunt pronouncements from official Church teaching regarding the responsibilities of Catholic politicians in encyclicals like *Evangelium Vitae* (1995) and in the "Doctrinal Note on Some Questions Regarding the Participation of Catholics in Political Life" went largely unheeded by many professedly Catholic politicians.

We can lament this sad story and even admit that prospects for any rapid change seem dim. Yet, perhaps we might see things in a longer-term perspective such that this last forty years has been a difficult period in which many Catholic politicians lost their way. They failed to benefit from the guidance of *Gaudium et Spes*. They failed to build upon the example of Governor Casey and other courageous politicians who understood well that politics and faith must meet. Surely, however, a crucial task is also to look forward and to see how a new generation might take up the challenge to live out the call to serve faithfully as Catholic politicians. Let me offer some brief counsel, drawn from a number of thoughtful commentators, on how this might be done better.

I borrow firstly from Mary Ann Glendon, the distinguished Harvard Law professor and former U.S. ambassador to the Vatican. In her 1996 commencement address at Notre Dame, she clarified that "religious participants in public debates will not be as effective unless they can speak in terms that are persuasive to men and women of good will—of all faiths, and of no faith. One will not get far if one preaches only to the converted." The key is to work for what is right and good by persuading others of the rightness and goodness of your objectives. In doing so one must utilize reason accessible to all to clarify the ethical foundations for one's political choices and actions. Hopefully, a good Notre Dame education prepares students to do this.

As they pursue the political vocation, religious folk must have some sense of modesty as to what they can accomplish, some limits on what they think they can achieve on this earth and on what they see as the role of government. They should know well that heaven is elsewhere and, while in the Augustinian sense they may work to have the City of God penetrate and overlap the City of Man, this is an ongoing task for each generation, as Pope Benedict XVI notes. When one appreciates the limits of politics one understands that one's task is not to create "heaven on earth." The latter was the approach adopted by the totalitarians of the last century and they succeeded only in creating variations of a disastrous hell. Furthermore, one must understand, as Daniel Patrick Moynihan pointed out in the commencement address he gave at Notre Dame in 1969, what "government cannot provide." The future senator clarified that "it cannot provide values to persons who have none, or who have lost those they had. It cannot provide a meaning to life. It cannot provide inner peace. It can provide outlets for moral energies, but it cannot create those energies."

Possessing a realistic grasp of the role and possibilities of government usually helps folks of religious outlook appreciate that they will not agree on all the details of policies. *Gaudium et Spes* says in rather formal Vatican "document-speak": "Christians should recognize that various legitimate though conflicting views can be held concerning the regulation of temporal affairs." So it is that good folk can differ—and quite markedly and passionately—on a variety of matters. We might all be able to agree that our religious tradition calls for us to care for "the poor and the weak, the widow and the orphan," but that doesn't mean that all need agree on what precisely should be done with Social Security or entitlement spending and the like.

That said, there are some issues of fundamental importance, especially the life questions, where moral absolutes rather than prudential judgments are involved. Of course, one's conscience must ultimately be one's guide, but it must be a properly formed conscience and one guided by basic precepts of Catholic teaching. There are moral truths, and they must be acknowledged. Everything is not relative. There are some matters, such as abortion, where saying one is "personally opposed" but unwilling to impose one's views on others is deeply flawed.

While the focus here is on the place of religion in the public sphere for politicians, it should go without saying that one's faith should also be a guide to one's private morality. Honesty, integrity, fidelity, and generosity should be personal qualities of those who would publicly refer to their religious convictions. Faith is to guide one's whole life, both public and private.

Let me offer a final encouragement for good people to enter public life. Politics is a noble calling in a democratic society. *Gaudium et Spes* holds that "the church regards as worthy of praise and consideration the work of those who, as a service to others, dedicate themselves to the welfare of the state and undertake the burdens of this task." Those who sense a call to the political vocation should pursue it but always as "a service to others." Perhaps the second Catholic president—and an unapologetic one at that—will be a Notre Dame graduate! In the end, all aspiring politicians would do well to remember St. Thomas More's worthy attitude: he was the king's good servant, but God's first!

## Keep the Faith, Make a Difference
## 2011

*Each year Notre Dame welcomes a new class of approximately two thousand eager students. They are subjected to a weekend of orientation activities of all sorts and are forced to listen to speakers of one sort or another counseling them on how to make the most of their "Notre Dame experience." I succumbed to the temptation to offer advice to the Class of 2015 when invited to do so by the editor of the* Irish Rover. *I hope and pray some members of the class found my comments of benefit. An edited version follows.*

Members of the Class of 2015, I am very glad to welcome you to Notre Dame. I assume that you will hear many times during the orientation activities not only that you are a wonderfully talented class (indeed, perhaps even the best ever), but also that you will accomplish great things at Notre Dame. I hope the latter will be so, although my own deeper hope for each of you is simply that your best and true self will emerge here, the truly crucial part of you that is ready to learn, able to fashion real friendships, willing to serve others, and eager to witness to your faith. There are no absolute guarantees in college, however. Much of what you "get" from Notre Dame will depend quite directly on what you "give" here. Let me offer you some advice based on my quarter century of teaching here and my past associations with many good and able students. Perhaps some of what I say might be of interest and, hopefully, even of help in allowing you to flourish here.

I must encourage you to engage your studies seriously. Please do justice to your studies and your professors. Learn as much as you can from those who teach you. Don't be like those numbskulls who just cram before a test in order to get a certain grade but who aren't engaged by real learning. They should have gone to a different school.

Be men and women who respect yourselves and others. Show a special regard for all those folk at Notre Dame who serve you in one way or another—the wonderful folk who staff the various offices and the generous people who cook for you and clean up after you. Never pass up an opportunity to say thank you. More especially, you must show respect to each other. Now, sadly, too much drinking takes place at Notre Dame. It seemingly "fuels" *some* of what passes for social life here where relations between young men and women can devolve into the superficial and exploitative, "hook-up" culture, where casual sexual relations are treated as the norm. Hold your ground and avoid the disrespect of yourself and others fostered by that behavior. Be authentic and true to your best values, and avoid the pressure to act like a lemming because "everyone else is doing it." They aren't, and neither should you.

It seems that a surprising number of young people today emerge from their undergraduate years feeling rather empty and insecure as well as a bit confused and quite anxious. They studied and got their degrees, but it appears that they missed out on crucial life lessons in the process. I hope your experience at Notre Dame will be different. Indeed, I pray that Notre Dame will allow you to clarify well what really matters in life.

Please don't waste your time at Notre Dame by focusing too much on yourself. Commit yourself to larger causes and good works based on two fundamental elements of Catholic social teaching: respect for the dignity of each human life and work on behalf of the common good. I want to encourage you to hold strong to (or begin to develop) your pro-life convictions. You must be part of that "new generation of builders" of which Blessed Pope John Paul II spoke, who "learn to build brick by brick the city of God within the city of man."

In the end, I pray that you don't just drift along here at Notre Dame, but that right from these early days you begin a quest to follow the path God calls you to travel. God has a distinct plan for you and you must use your time at Notre Dame to discern it and to prepare for your life vocation. Don't be timid during your time here, but be brave and willing to ask the toughest of questions, both within your academic classes and beyond them. Allow me to pose one good question for you to consider: "Good Teacher, what must I do to share in everlasting life?" (Mark 10:17). This was the rich young man's question to Jesus. This individual declined the Lord's invitation to full discipleship and left sad because deep within himself he knew that he had refused to be what God called him to be. May you avoid a similar sadness. Instead, may each of you resolutely keep the faith and truly make a difference.

# Section VI: Priesthood and Holy Cross

## Crisis in the Priesthood: Some Ways Forward
## 2002

*The clergy sexual abuse crisis proved the most damaging episode to beset the Catholic Church in the United States in recent decades. My own location to experience the sexual abuse crisis was as rector of Moreau Seminary, the principal formation site of the Congregation of Holy Cross in North America. I assumed my duties as rector in 2000 with no knowledge that the Catholic Church was about to experience what George Weigel has called "the Long Lent of 2002." I did my best in my work at the seminary to confront the issues raised by the sexual abuse crisis in an honest way. I tried to provide for the seminarians under my direction a formation that would assure that the behaviors revealed in the abuse crisis would never be repeated. I poured my energies into my work at the seminary and did not see myself as an expert who should speak or write about these issues. I made an exception when I was asked to participate in a panel at the 2002 fall conference of the Notre Dame Center for Ethics and Culture under the theme "From Death to Life." I addressed some of the issues raised by the crisis in hopes of offering constructive measures to strengthen the priesthood.*

I am grateful for the opportunity to speak today and honored to share the podium with two such thoughtful and committed Catholics as Sidney Callahan and Jorge Garcia. I am also very glad to be here with our local ordinary, Bishop John D'Arcy, whose resolve and leadership on this issue has been important in guiding this local church through the recent and trying times, as we have faced what we know as the clergy sexual abuse crisis.

I come to this panel and topic from the stance and outlook of a seminary rector and as a priest in the Congregation of Holy Cross. I seek to help train good priests to serve God's people, priests who, in the words of the Second Vatican Council's "Decree on the Life of Ministry of Priests," will go forth "as co-workers united in the single goal of building up Christ's body" ; priests who will commit themselves to what Pope John Paul II has termed the "New Evangelization," and who are ready to proclaim, "Christ: Yesterday, Today & Forever." And let me say up front that nothing that has happened in the past nine months regarding the clergy sexual abuse crisis has altered my objectives or commitment.

I want to try to say a few words on how I view the current "crisis"—if that be the term—and to offer a few thoughts on some ways forward, as the subtitle of our panel topic suggests.

Surely Pope John Paul II spoke for us all in stating: "The harm done by some priests and religious to the young and the vulnerable fills us all with a deep sense of sadness and shame." Those emotions are unavoidable if one faces the reality of the pain and betrayal of trust involved in the clergy sexual abuse issue. We should keep clearly before us that concern for victims and for potential victims must be foremost. This is crucial.

In this regard it seems important that the Church try to draw attention to the reality that sexual abuse of minors is a far greater problem in American society than revealed in the number of cases linked to relatively few priests. I have seen referenced by Fr. Andrew Greeley the research of University of Chicago scholars Edward O. Lauman and Robert T. Michael that asserts that up to seventeen percent of Americans (equally men and women) were sexually abused before puberty (approximately forty million people). I don't presume to have the competence to evaluate such research findings, but if they are anywhere in the ball park, what we have is an enormous problem, one that causes much pain and likely much personal and social dysfunction and so forth. Clearly, this is not a priest problem but a human problem and one that plagues both men and women. The Church must provide firm guarantees of child protection and safety in its institutional settings. This is a given. The Church must work further to encourage more research and understanding of the pathology of pedophila and ephebophilia, the impact of the pathology, the extent to which it exists within American society, the cultural influences that continue to generate it, and how to treat best the victims of such abuse. This is noted in Article 16 of the Dallas Charter. I trust it won't be forgotten.

Now, without in any way seeking to minimize or diminish the work that must be done, I do want to take some issue with the label given to our panel, "Crisis in the Priesthood." I appreciate full well that the clergy sexual abuse issue has led some to call for a public reevaluation of the nature and value of the Catholic priesthood. And yet, I want to suggest that the crisis is not understood well if it is seen as a priesthood crisis.

As we try to get some perspective on this painful matter, it seems clear to me that the fury which drove this issue was fueled by the outrage expressed at bishops who reassigned offending priests (in a *few* cases reassigned them repeatedly) from parish to parish, giving them renewed opportunity to abuse more children. I daresay that if *this* analysis is correct the nub of the issue is poor leadership and proper accountability and credibility of leaders.

Would we be having this discussion now if *all* the bishops had adopted appropriate standards and procedures, if not after the Louisiana case in the mid 1980's, then at least after the Porter case in Fall River in the early 1990's? Would we be on this panel if the sound judgment of Bishop D'Arcy had been pursued in the case of John Geoghegan in the archdiocese of Boston in 1984?

That said, I recognize fully that as we move forward there are important changes that must be made in the areas of (1) leadership and trust; (2) transparency/openness; (3) accountability. The Dallas Charter certainly focused on these areas.

I want to go in a different direction. Drawing on the ideas and suggestions of a number of thoughtful individuals let me note the following matters (however briefly) as contributing to the process of purification that will bring us through this sad saga as a stronger church:

1    Renewed Commitment by Priests to Their Essential Ministry
2    Sound Seminary Formation
3    Re-emphasis on the Meaning of Celibate Chastity and Its Value for the Whole Church.
4    Fostering of an Appropriate Priestly Fraternity
5    Shaping a Church of Forgiveness, Reconciliation, and Compassion

I mention the failures of leaders and the problem of account-ability as a preface to saying that as the clergy sexual abuse issue developed under the media's hot pursuit somehow all priests and the priesthood seemed to get tarnished. It was "guilt-by-association." The "priest-pedophile" became a term of common currency—a label besmirching all priests. Celibacy somehow or other got branded as a "problem." The suggestion was made that those willing to live it must be dysfunctional. In some cases the priesthood was presented virtually as a "pathology." Even those who didn't go that far pointed to: "a closed clerical cul-ture" which "infects the priesthood." This seemed to make all priests compliant in the scandals. In all of this attention was focused on the one to two percent of offenders. The 98% of priests faithfully pursuing their ministry tended to be passed over and ignored. This is the group, termed by Pope John Paul as the "vast majority of dedicated and generous priests and reli-gious whose only wish is to serve and do good." Further, there was no acknowledgment of the important work that had been done over the past decade to address the problem of clergy sex-ual abuse. (So it goes! I guess the *New York Times*, the *Boston Globe*, and CNN owe the Catholic priesthood no favors.)

*Renewed Commitment by Priests to Their Essential Ministry*
It is to this group, however, (i.e the 98% toiling daily in the Lord's vineyard), that the responsibility of repairing the

tarnished reputation of the priesthood falls. It cannot be done quickly or easily.

The trust will be restored when good priests continue doing what good priests have done for centuries: proclaiming the Word of God and preaching about it with authenticity, ministering the Sacraments, especially the Eucharist, and speaking words of forgiveness, consolation, compassion, and encouragement, thereby sharing the life of Christ with others and so building the Christian community. In doing this priests have some factors going their way. First, Catholics have not abandoned their priests in the wake of endless media reports of scandal. They still hold regard for their faithful pastors. They extend support and encouragement. May I say thanks to lay men and women here for that. Secondly, priests still rather like being priests. Whatever the temporary challenge to priestly morale brought on by the clergy abuse scandals, priests enjoy presiding at the liturgy, preaching and teaching, and working alongside their lay sisters and brothers.

It would be wonderful to have some easy "fix" for the reputation of priests and the priesthood in the society at large but I don't see one beyond hard work and faithful commitment to ministry.

### Sound Seminary Formation

Obviously if a "way forward" is encouraging priests to be faithfully committed in ministry, a corollary is that the training of priests should lead to the ordination of men prepared to *serve* this way. In this regard I think the news is quite hopeful. Much has been done in seminary formation in recent years, especially in the years following the Vatican visitation of seminaries in the 1980's headed by Bishops Marshall and Wuerl.

No doubt seminary formation can be improved, and I welcome the kind of assistance that might be rendered in this regard by the new apostolic visitation to seminaries and religious houses of formation. This visit will focus on the question of human formation for celibate chastity. We want to prepare good, mature, and holy priests. I respectfully assert that that is what we have been doing.

The seminarians I work with know that their best selves will be discovered only when they pass beyond self-centeredness and selfishness and truly follow Christ in giving of themselves to others. They are generous, faith-filled, and prepared to explore their religious and priestly vocation in an atmosphere which provides few external supports for this. Careful procedures are pursued in the screening of applications. Programs have been developed which deal directly with sexuality and celibacy, with developmental human maturity, with appropriate pastoral boundaries in relationships. Seminarians are regularly evaluated both personally and in terms of pastoral performance. There is a greater focus on the meaning of the priesthood and the identity of the priest. Undoubtedly more can be done. But it is well to remember that most of the notorious cases of clergy sexual abuse have not involved priests ordained during the last decade or so.

In speaking of seminarians, let me also say a word about vocations and simply repeat the words of Pope John Paul at the closing Mass of World Youth Day in Toronto in 2002: "And if in the depths of your hearts you feel the same call to the priesthood or consecrated life, do not be afraid to follow Christ on the royal road of the cross! At difficult moments in the Church's life, the pursuit of holiness becomes even more urgent." This is surely such a moment.

### *Re-Emphasis on the Meaning of Celibate Chastity and its Value for the Whole Church.*

One of the more important ways forward is to re-emphasize the importance of celibate chastity and to clarify its value for the whole Church.

Growing up in my working class milieu in Australia, good ordinary folks understood at a gut level that celibacy was about serving others—that it was a way of loving and serving many people deeply, but in a manner that a priest or religious would be unable to do if he were in a single/primary relationship. Celibacy meant full availability for apostolic service. I still think this functional view is valid, but clearly celibacy has been targeted by many of the commentators as somehow a source of the problem and some folks seem confused about it.

We need to assert anew the value of celibacy for the Church. Celibacy is a charism, a gift of the Spirit. Those who live it well can be a sign of hope. They can teach with their lives that all will be fully and definitely taken up in Christ and that one can live a life focused on the kingdom to come. In the end, celibacy must be about more than service, for it must be a lesson that "the kingdom has not fully arrived and that earthly life is a transitory one awaiting a fulfillment which is yet to come." Priests living this celibate commitment well must not only serve God's people on the earthly journey toward the kingdom but also "must sacramentalize in their own lives the hunger and hope of the community for the Kingdom to come."

### Fostering an Appropriate Priestly Fraternity

I do not advocate or seek to defend what some have labeled a "clerical culture" in which priests "think of themselves as an entitled class whose members can act in terrible ways against all they say they believe, and still be protected by the silence of other priests and the compliance of bishops." But despite the egregious and truly disgraceful cases which have been well noted, I want to suggest that the way forward involves a deepening and enriching of priestly fraternity.

Priests in the present time must resist the tendency to see their ministry as a kind of private practice. Priests are linked in crucial ways. Their priestly ministry cannot be understood apart from the bishop, nor can it be seen apart from the universal priesthood. Clear priestly identity involves thinking of oneself as part of the presbyterate. Both in the "big picture" and on the level of day-to-day living priests need each other. Priests can give each other support, encouragement, and challenge through a fraternity rooted in shared faith, deep friendship, and common experience. Too many of the priests who leave the active ministry or get into trouble of some sort have felt lonely, isolated, unappreciated, and disconnected.

*Shaping a Church of Forgiveness, Reconciliation, and Compassion*

A number of observers have rather safely argued that the present moment in the Church (as it grapples with the scandals) requires more than ever that the call to holiness be lived more intensely by every member of the Church. It is hard to disagree with that. Our faith clarifies that the holiness of the Church is founded on the holiness of Christ, not the behavior of individual church members, including its priests. But the Church does call each of us to be holy, and if holiness is to be enfleshed in the Church surely we must play our part.

There is a need for us to be understanding and compassionate, to reach out to those who are hurt and to provide real support and care. We also should extend care and forgiveness to perpetrators of abuse. As members of a Church founded on forgiveness which is rooted in redemption we cannot simply banish people from our sight. This may be challenging but it is crucial. There is much to be done. May the Lord guide us along right paths.

# Configured to Christ
## 2007

*In 2007, James Gallagher, Peter McCormick, Gregory Haake, and Stephen Koeth were ordained to the priesthood at Sacred Heart Basilica at Notre Dame. They constituted the class that had begun their initial year of studies in the year that I began my service as rector of Moreau Seminary, and I have always felt a special bond to them. I was deeply honored when they asked me to preach at our Lucenarium service, held on the evening prior to the ordination ceremony. I reflected on the text from the Letter to the Hebrews, which is included below. I also reviewed their time in formation and then drew heavily on Pope John Paul II's apostolic exhortation* Pastores Dabo Vobis. *This homily afforded me an opportunity to express my own deep convictions about the priest-hood, convictions I seek to live by as I pursue my ministry at Notre Dame.*

*For every high priest chosen from among men is appointed to act on behalf of men in relation to God, to offer gifts and sacrifices for sins. He can deal gently with the ignorant and wayward, since he himself is beset with weakness. Because of this he is bound to offer sacrifice for his own sins as well as for those of the people. And one does not take the honor upon himself, but he is called by God, just as Aaron was. So also Christ did not exalt himself to be made a high priest, but was appoint-ed by him who said to him, "Thou art my Son, today I have begotten thee"; as he says also in another place, "Thou art a priest forever, after the order of Melchizedek." In the days of his flesh, Jesus offered up prayers and supplications, with loud cries and tears, to him who was able to save him from death, and he was heard for his godly fear. Although he was a Son, he learned obedience through what he suffered; and being made perfect he became the source of eternal salvation to all who obey him, being designated by God a high priest after the order of Melchizedek.*

*Hebrews 5:1–10*

Tomorrow we will witness the ordination to the priesthood of Jim, Greg, Stephen, and Pete, and we gather here this evening to pray with them and for them.

We know well that they are truly ready to accept this min-istry of service to which God calls them. They have been blessed by God's grace to receive a call to the priesthood—a profound and deep stirring within their beings—and they have respond-ed.

Every priestly vocation is a matter of God's grace, and the powerful reality of God's call is foundational. Our reading tonight reminds us that even Christ, the model of all ministries, realized that the Father had called him, and he gave everything in his response.

This graced call from and full response to God lies at the

heart of the four priestly vocations we celebrate tonight. And yet, we know further that the bountiful grace that undergirds their call has been channeled through men and women whom they have encountered on their respective journeys right down to the very eve of their ordinations.

Of course, we think especially of their families and what a fortunate group these men are. They have been shaped by the love and molded by the example of their parents, who truly were for these men the first and best teachers in the ways of faith, and who still teach them. We give thanks here tonight to Bill and Mary Gallagher, to Charlie and Jeanne Haake, to Leo and Margaret McCormick, and to Richard and Andrea Koeth for being such great instruments of God's grace by training your sons through word and deed to serve others.

We give thanks for all their family members and friends who aided them—in ways that sometimes might not have been directly apparent—in their response to God's call in their lives.

We also give thanks for the Catholic parishes and elementary and high schools on Staten Island, in South Bend, Kansas City, and Grand Rapids that these men attended, and for the good priests and teachers they met there. Those places are truly crucial incubators of faith. We hope and pray they are still encouraging new vocations today.

With their fine college educations behind them these men showed up at Moreau Seminary around mid-August 2000, having been recruited to Holy Cross, in one way or another, by the then vocations director, Fr. Jim "the Duke" King. Their candidate year coincided with my own initial year as rector, and I knew from the start that Moreau was fortunate to have such good men here, men who would help carry this place in good times and in challenging times.

But they too were fortunate to be guided by the candidate team led by the thoughtful, authentic, and (sometimes) humorous Fr. Pat Neary, our present rector. I got to know these men better later that year in a course I taught them known as *Faith and Traditions*. Here I came to appreciate the learning disposition that characterized them as a group and the deep love for the Church that they possessed.

Perhaps it was when discussing that renowned Australian-Irish classic television drama "Brides of Christ" that I sensed that these men wanted to understand better the changes that had taken place in our Church since the Second Vatican Council and to appreciate the wonderful opening of our Church to the world that these changes brought about. At the same time they were eager to hold strongly to those essential tenets of our faith that have guided us from the time of the Apostles—from the time when the Letter to the Hebrews was written. They valued both continuity and change and aimed to get to the heart of what really matters.

Of course, they still had much to learn, although just ever so occasionally they might have thought otherwise! They are of course intelligent men, and what seminarian worth his salt has not at times thought he could do a darn better job than the formation staff (just ask the aforementioned Fr. Jim King about this!).

Next these men with all their goodness left for the novitiate in beautiful Cascade, Colorado, where they benefited greatly from the attentive care of Fr. David Guffey. There they learned an essential lesson that must guide them every day of their lives as priests: in the words of our Constitutions, "That to serve [the Lord] honestly we must pray always and not give up!"

They returned to Moreau Seminary and entered their formal theology studies in the Master of Divinity program. They were well-trained by their professors in the theology department at Notre Dame and did well in their studies, but more telling for me of their call to serve as priests was their engagement with their colleagues in the lay ministry program. These terrific folk—co-workers in the Lord's vineyard—also did their part to guide and to support their four seminarian brothers in their vocations.

Not all training for the priesthood takes place in the seminary or the classroom, and these men have been fortunate to get valuable hands-on training in a whole series of ministry placements.

And they have been privileged to have great mentors along the way, wonderful supervisors, ministry colleagues, and spiritual directors, who have aided them in ways large and small.

Of course, given their engagement in such a wide variety of pastoral activities and given the complex social and cultural conditions of our modern or post-modern world it is easy to understand that priests risk a loss of their focus amidst the great variety of demands and requests they face. But these men have read Pope John Paul II's *Pastores Dabo Vobis*, his exhortation *I Will Give You Shepherds*. They have benefited from the insights of Cardinal Avery Dulles in his book *The Priestly Office*. They know well that the priest must be a preacher of the word, a minister of the Sacraments, and a builder of the community.

They have prepared diligently to undertake these tasks ; they are skilled preachers eager to play their part in proclaiming the Gospel and moving into the forefront of the evangelization that proclaims, "Christ—Yesterday, Today and Forever."

They are ready to preside at the Eucharist and to officiate at the other sacraments: they know the rubrics and so forth. I daresay they know the flow of the various liturgies better than some older priests—even some ordained, say, close to twenty years! They are well equipped to speak words of forgiveness, consolation, and encouragement and so to build up the Christian community. They undoubtedly have the "skills" to serve well, and being the good men they are they want to place their gifts, talents, and training in the Lord's service. They know well that they must resist the temptation to think their ministry is about them. They must recognize daily that they are to labor in the vineyard in the name and person of Christ.

This is what good priests have done for centuries. There are well-marked footprints into which these men can step. Exercising their gifts, utilizing their training, and applying their skills for ministry is all part of them serving well as priests. This more functional description of what a good priest does, however, hardly captures the central essence of the calling into which these men will be ordained tomorrow.

Friends, here I must address a subject that received relatively little attention when I came to Moreau Seminary 25 years ago. It was occasionally touched upon in joking remarks about the likely impact of "ontological change" on certain of the rough-edged seminarians. We were, I fear, still a bit too close to the turbulent years explored in "Brides of Christ" to focus carefully on this matter. In the necessary and crucial post-conciliar effort to enhance the role of the laity in the Church, there was some pressure to downplay the essence of the ordained priesthood.

I must speak plainly to my four treasured brothers, these men whom I love and who are a source of such hope (and whom I trust will visit me when I am old and in Holy Cross House). I must tell each of you that you are not to be appointed as some kind of church functionary tomorrow.

You are not to be ordained into *your* priesthood tomorrow. Rather, you are to be ordained into Christ's. In our faith there is only one priest: Christ! The ordained priesthood is not something separate, but rather is a sharing in his one priesthood. Jesus is priest because, as the Letter to the Hebrews attests, he is the mediator between God and humanity. He brings about, through his sacrifice, the restoration of the world to God.

Through the sacrament of Holy Orders which you will receive tomorrow your very character and being will be *configured* to Christ's priesthood. You, as priest, will be an *alter Christus* (another Christ) who acts *in persona Christi capitis,* that is, in the person of Christ the Head. As such you are charged, as *Pastores Dabo Vobis* beautifully explicates, to make present the very sacrifice of Christ in the Eucharist, to make known the forgiveness of Christ, and his victory over sin and death.

As you pursue your sacred mission in the Church, take Pope John Paul II's exhortation to heart and be priests who participate in Christ's shepherding of the people of God through your service. You must be as the one true shepherd, who "came not to be served but to serve and give his life as a ransom for many" (Mk 10:45). Your priesthood must be oriented to serve the priesthood of all the baptized. Once sacramentally united with Christ you must pursue his ministry of mediation and bring God to men and women near and far.

It is an awesome responsibility that you are willing to undertake. You have not earned it, and no special personal holiness is guaranteed to you by it. Indeed, you are not worthy of it—none of us ordained are! We are all dependent on God's grace.

And so each of you sets forth tomorrow on your priestly journey not knowing what combination of joys and sorrows and of successes and disappointments the future has in store for you. Who knows what you might be called upon to do over the years? Who knows in what measure continuity and change will occur in our Church and in the world around us? However all that may be, know that tomorrow you will be changed in your character and being in such a way that you are marked as a priest for life.

As such a priest you receive from Christ the very treasures of salvation so that, whatever the circumstances, you must pour yourself out and distribute them among the people to whom you are sent. People are starving and thirsting for Christ today. Meet their hunger. Quench their thirst. Bring them Christ. Be Christ for them.

So then, dear family members and friends of our *ordinandi*, let us truly pray for our dear brothers tonight. And let us continue our prayers for them long after the applause that will greet them this weekend is but a fading memory. You in your different ways have been instruments of God's grace in their lives thus far. You must continue to be so in the years ahead so that these men may be great priest-witnesses to Christ and further his saving mission and so to help restore our dear world to God.

## Fr. Moreau and Fr. Sorin
### 2008

*Blessed Basil Moreau, who was beatified in 2007, founded the Congregation of Holy Cross in 1837. One of his early and most talented recruits to the order was the young priest Edward Sorin. Fr. Sorin brought the Congregation of Holy Cross to the United States in 1841 and founded the University of Notre Dame the following year. The complex and difficult relationship between Moreau and Sorin is well told by Rev. Marvin R. O'Connell in his superb biography,* Edward Sorin. *Whatever their difficulties, Moreau and Sorin possessed a deep conviction that they must share Christ with others. Each was deeply committed to the education apostolate as a way of pursuing that fundamental call. Each was a true educator in the faith. The following edited reflections, drawn from* The Cross, Our Only Hope, *speak to the commitments of the two men, and they should speak to Christian educators today.*

*"Imitating Christ is not a matter of knowing Jesus Christ, his teaching and his life as we pride ourselves on knowing the story of some famous person. More than this, we must study the details of the Savior's life and know the love which inclined him to act. We must be filled with the spirit of his example."*

*Fr. Basil Moreau*

Our founder Fr. Basil Moreau deemed Jesus Christ to be the indispensable figure of history. Of course, Moreau knew well that Jesus died as an outcast, clearly dispensable to the civil and religious authorities of his time. But our founder knew more than this—much more. Moreau understood from his own lived experience that Jesus Christ was different from and more than great figures from the past, whatever their accomplishments on earth. Moreau profoundly grasped that the fulfillment of Jesus' life on earth came when he freely and obediently chose to suffer and to die so that we in turn might live. Moreau's heart burned with the knowledge that Jesus Christ was "the resurrection and the life." He wanted all who would follow him in Holy Cross to share his central passion and conviction and to root their lives in the close following of Christ.

Fr. Moreau calls his followers today to know Christ so deeply that they cannot choose but to share him with others. In order to do this with any authenticity and conviction we must deepen our own relationship with Christ. Christ must be alive in us and we must know him truly as savior and also as brother and friend. He is the one who walks with us on life's journey, the one we turn to in times of doubt, challenge and difficulty.

We can study a lot about Christ, read a lot of books about him, and think through our own personal Christology. But Christ is not bound within the covers of books, no matter how learned their contents. He lives beyond the books and out among us in the Church and in the world. And he eagerly wants to live within each of us. He graciously invites us to know and relate to him. Our relationship is deepened and strengthened when we spend time with him in prayer and when we seek him out amidst the poor, the sick, and the abandoned in our world. This relationship is confirmed when we not only read the Gospels but live them out as faithful disciples of Christ.

Whatever your particular spiritual and personal place right now, I hope you will take the chance to look anew at your relationship with the Lord Jesus so that you can allow his life to live more fully within you. We cannot sequester Christ into the category of some worthy figure from the past, but must allow him to enter our lives this very day and so to guide us along his loving way.

*"Today, more than ever before, Catholic education . . . means for our youth a knowledge of Divine truths, more comprehensive and developed, more visibly sustained by daily Christian practices, cheerfully accepted and faithfully observed by them as an indispensable evidence of their initiation to a Catholic life, of which they may well feel proud all their life."*

*Fr. Edward Sorin*

Edward Sorin, the extraordinary Holy Cross priest who founded the University of Notre Dame, hardly qualifies as a great educational theorist or intellectual. He was neither a regular teacher nor a serious scholar. He contributed relatively little to discussions regarding the curriculum as the school he founded in northern Indiana slowly evolved into a genuine institution of higher learning.

Sorin, instead, was an ambitious institution builder and a decisive leader. His courage and iron will assured that Notre Dame survived and eventually prospered despite damaging fires, a terrible cholera outbreak, and a series of financial crises. Yet Sorin was much more than this: he was a man of deep faith and piety who believed that God and Our Lady (Notre Dame) had summoned him across the Atlantic Ocean to undertake a crucial work in Catholic education. He was a missionary eager to spread the Catholic faith in his newly–adopted nation through this educational mission.

From the very outset Sorin hoped that the college he founded would develop as a "most powerful means for good" in the United States by preparing young Catholics to go forth and serve well in the world. He understood that Catholic education was not only about training minds but also about forming character and shaping souls. Sorin was no great educational theorist, but he assuredly got to the heart of the matter.

Catholic educators today at every level might draw inspiration from his insights and example. Our most important contribution to our students is to nurture them in the ways of faith, to provide them with appropriate catechetical and theological formation, to celebrate our faith with them in prayer and liturgy, and to guide them to express it through service of neighbor in the world. We serve our students best when we educate them in the faith.

## Holy Cross Heroes in the Pro-Life Movement
## 2010

*The pro-life movement is truly one of the most exceptional grassroots movements in modern American history. It emerged out of the refusal to accept* Roe v. Wade, *the United States Supreme Court's flawed decision legalizing abortion. In many ways the movement has been largely led by laymen and women doing their part to shape a decent and just society in which the dignity of every person is respected. My own order has contributed to the pro-life cause in a variety of ways, and I was asked to reflect on some key Holy Cross contributors in a piece for our Holy Cross vocation website. I called attention primarily to the efforts at Notre Dame. I trust that the Holy Cross engagement with the pro-life cause will grow ever stronger in the future, on this campus and far beyond.*

I want to share some thoughts with you about the involvement of the Congregation of Holy Cross in the pro-life cause. The Supreme Court decision *Roe v. Wade* brought the modern pro-life movement into existence and Holy Cross has been part of it from the very start.

The heroes in the pro-life efforts within Holy Cross have not always been the most prominent members of the community, but there have been true heroes from the outset. Brother John Lavelle, c.s.c., was a tireless worker for the pro-life cause at Notre Dame throughout the 1970's and 1980's. His wonderful work with college students inspired many young people to carry on his mission. The St. Joseph County Right to Life organization even named an award in his honor to recognize exemplary pro-life students enrolled in local colleges and universities like Notre Dame, Saint Mary's College, and Holy Cross College. Other pioneers in the pro-life movement in those early years included such wonderful priests as Fr. Edward O'Connor who led students in prayer and encouraged their efforts for a deepened respect for human life.

In recent years the pro-life efforts of Holy Cross have been expressed in numerous ways, by numerous individuals, not only in parishes through various life-sustaining initiatives, but also through assistance to a variety of organizations that assist women in crisis pregnancies. I think, for example, of Fr. Paul Doyle who is a longtime member of the board of Hannah's House here in South Bend, a maternity home that provides shelter and support of various kinds for the physical, emotional, and spiritual well-being of pregnant young women. I think also of the wonderful seminarians who, over the last two decades, have done pastoral placements at the Women's Care Center in South Bend. There they have provided direct counseling to young women to persuade them to choose life for their babies.

I must confess that my own direct involvement in pro-life efforts is of rather recent vintage. Of course, I have always preached and written against the evil of abortion, and have presented this as the great moral issue of our time, one that demands our engagement and commitment. I've also tried in meaningful ways to assist women who are pregnant and to influence them to have their babies. Furthermore, I have tried to build "a culture of life" as Pope John Paul II encouraged each of us to do.

Recent events here on campus, however, have prompted me to become more closely involved in pro-life efforts at Notre Dame. In doing so I am following in the footsteps of great Holy Cross priests like Fr. Kevin Russeau and Fr. Jay Steele. Such priests have led the way in supporting the deeply committed students of Notre Dame Right to Life, a group which I now serve as chaplain.

My efforts at Notre Dame have focused especially on working with my faculty colleagues. I have been involved in forming a Notre Dame chapter of the University Faculty for Life organization, a national association promoting the pro-life cause on university campuses. At the present time I serve as the president of our local chapter. We have over 30 formal members (which makes us one of the largest chapters in the country), but there are well over 200 faculty and staff members on our listserv. They are supportive colleagues in the growing pro-life efforts at Notre Dame. We are seeking to do our part through spiritual, academic, and social endeavors to help build support for the pro-life cause on campus and beyond. We want to support our wonderful students in their efforts and to walk beside them in defending life from conception to natural death.

What is truly heartening is that more and more of the younger priests and seminarians in Holy Cross are deeply committed to the pro-life cause. They have heard Pope John Paul II's call to proclaim "the Gospel of Life." Rest assured that we will be well -represented at the March for Life in Washington, D.C. in January. If you are present at the march perhaps you might seek us out and join us. We want more and more men to join us who share our pro-life convictions—men who want to affirm God's gift of life and who resolve to allow all others to share it.

# Section VII: Tributes

## A Man of Faith: Ralph McInerny
## 2010

*Ralph McInerny began teaching at the University of Notre Dame in 1955 and is among the most distinguished Catholic intellectuals to have graced the university. He served as director of the Medieval Institute for seven years and then as director of the Jacques Maritain Center for over a quarter of a century. Throughout his career, he published extensively as both a scholar and fiction writer. His many publications include* Aquinas on Human Action, The Very Rich Hours of Jacques Maritain, *and his memoir* I Alone Have Escaped to Tell You: My Life and Pastimes. *His Gifford Lectures, delivered in 1999–2000 were published as* Characters in Search of Their Author. *Of course, he is the author of the Fr. Dowling mysteries and a series of mysteries set at the University of Notre Dame. This extraordinary scholar was a devoted husband and father and a great friend to many. I got to know him well only during the latter years of his career at Notre Dame, yet that proved a great privilege for me. I visited him during his illness. I was honored to concelebrate at Ralph's funeral Mass at Sacred Heart Basilica at which his great friend, Fr. Marvin O'Connell, presided. I offered this brief reflection at the reception after the funeral, where a number of Ralph's friends had the chance to speak about him and his many gifts.*

I am very grateful to the McInerny family for inviting me to say some words here today. We have heard already the powerful eloquence of Fr. Marvin O'Connell at Mass, and soon others who have known Ralph McInerny much longer and better than I knew him will speak of his wonderful contributions as a brilliant

Catholic intellectual and as a pillar of Notre Dame for over half a century. I must speak of him as a faith-filled man who lived with true fidelity those crucial vocations of husband and father.

I speak here as a priest-friend of Ralph's—and, dare I say, as one who has read more of his detective fiction than of his impressive scholarly works. During my seminary days I did take Ralph's course on the "Thought of Aquinas." He always led off class with a prayer ; that was simply the way he thought things should be done at Our Lady's University. I marveled at his teaching style which seemed to be that of relaying to his students some mere tidbits which he recently gleaned from St. Thomas during one of their frequent conversations!

Ralph taught Holy Cross seminarians for over fifty years at Notre Dame and always with generosity and good spirit. I daresay this was largely because he loved the priesthood, while recognizing all too well the human limitations and faults of those who served in this office in the Church. Though he had left the seminary himself, he knew well that the priest stood "in persona Christi Capitis" and especially at the sacrifice of the Mass.

Ralph's devotion to the Eucharist was deep and real. He attended Mass daily over his many years at Notre Dame. He wanted to be nourished at the Lord's table. This remarkable writer and wordsmith wanted to drink in *the* Word, and he hungered for the very body and blood of Christ. Ralph understood so well that through this sacrament we receive the essential food for mind, heart, and soul so as to become more like Christ, indeed one with Christ. Ralph's devotion to the Eucharist was central to his living out his vocation as a follower of Jesus Christ.

Of course, subsumed within that vocation was his treasured calling as husband and father. Ralph was a blessed and deeply fortunate man, but surely most fortunate in having Connie as his wife and his great partner in life for fifty years. What a home they created on Portage Avenue where they raised their wonderful family. They shared their joys and their sorrows together, especially the sorrow of their son Michael's death. We can take some consolation that Ralph is reunited with Connie and with Michael right now. We can expect that Connie might be clarifying a few things for him as he settles in.

Ralph was justifiably proud of all his children. In his *I Alone Have Escaped to Tell You* he wrote "My daughters have grown into beautiful women and it takes great discipline not to blurt out to others how I love and admire them and my sons." I know he would want me to emphasize this point today and to note also his love for their wonderful spouses and his terrific grandchildren of whom he was so proud. I must note also just how much Ralph's love for his children has been reciprocated by them, as has been especially obvious over these past months of his battle with cancer and its aftermath.

Ralph McInerny was a great husband and father *and* a true man of faith. He seemed to me especially blessed by the gifts of the Holy Spirit. He assuredly possessed those gifts of wisdom and understanding, of counsel and knowledge, of fortitude, piety and fear of the Lord. He deeply desired what is right and good, and his life was a quest to discern the truth and to live a holy life. He was ever vigilant to the needs of the Church and he knew in profound ways—and especially in his final days—that he must trust in divine providence and in God's loving mercy. We all know well that Ralph—whatever his sins may have been—could never be accused of the sin of sloth. He never grew weary of pursuing the Christian life of virtue and of fulfilling his daily round of duties and responsibilities. Indeed, just a few days before his death he expressed an eagerness to return to his writing, for there was more he wanted to share with others.

As Ralph's children, like Mary and David and Dan, and his great friends like Marvin O'Connell and David Solomon know well, Ralph lived his faith to the full right to the end. They were not easy days for him last week. But we can say of him, to borrow from St. Paul, "he fought the good fight, he finished the race, and he kept the faith" (2 Timothy 4:7). We must celebrate his life today and give thanks to God for his gracious presence among us. And may his witness inspire us to live to the full our own vocations.

## Sixty Years at Notre Dame:
## Vincent De Santis as Scholar, Teacher, and Friend
## 2010

*Vincent De Santis is the person most responsible for my coming to Notre Dame for graduate studies. I met him in Australia in 1976 when he held a Fulbright Fellowship at the University of Queensland, where I was completing a master's degree in history. He guided my doctoral studies at Notre Dame and proved a true friend to me in all circumstances. I was able to visit him in a hospice in Victoria, British Columbia just a week before his death in May of 2011. I had the great privilege of presiding at his funeral Mass in his hometown of Birdsboro, Pennsylvania in June of that year. The brief piece below was carried in the* Irish Rover *to mark the completion of his extraordinary career as a teacher at Notre Dame.*

Vincent De Santis took up his initial appointment as an instructor in history at Notre Dame in the fall of 1949. He completed sixty years of teaching here last fall at the rank of emeritus professor when he offered his popular course on "American Presidents from F.D.R. to Clinton." Very few faculty have matched his remarkable record of sixty years of dedication and service to his students and colleagues at this university.

Born and raised in Birdsboro, Pennsylvania, and deeply proud of his Italian heritage, De Santis developed his life-long passion for history at an early age. He majored in the subject at West Chester State College, graduating in 1941. Immediately upon graduation De Santis joined the United States Army, in which he served until December 1945. He rose from private to captain, and as a member of the Nineteenth Infantry Regiment of the Twenty Fourth Infantry Division he saw considerable action in the Southwest Pacific Theater, deploying through

Australia on his way to fierce fighting in New Guinea and in the Philippines. He maintained a diary during these difficult years and occasionally read from it to his Notre Dame students.

After the war the brave soldier became a gifted teacher and a first-rate historian. The G.I. Bill enabled him to study American history at Johns Hopkins University where he worked with C. Vann Woodward, one of the most talented of the brilliant post-war generation of historians. He and Woodward entered into a fifty-year friendship which reached a pinnacle when Woodward came to Notre Dame in 1995 to toast the many accomplishments of his one-time student at a conference held in honor of De Santis.

Guided by Vann Woodward's counsel and example, De Santis gravitated to political history and devoted much of his scholarly work to exploring American political developments during Reconstruction and the Gilded Age. He produced important books such as *Republicans Face the Southern Question* (1959) and *The Shaping of Modern America: 1877–1916* (1973, rev. 1989). These established him as an important figure in the field. His fine reputation led to his being enlisted to join wonderful scholars like David Potter, Carl Degler, and Arthur Link in producing *The Democratic Experience*, a renowned textbook which went through five editions from 1963 to 1981, and has been recently reissued. De Santis' scholarly work brought favorable attention to Notre Dame. It also led to his being honored in various ways. He won an impressive Guggenheim Fellowship and held Fulbright Fellowships in Italy, Australia, and India. He was elected president of the Catholic Historical Society in 1964, and in 2007 the Society for Historians of the Gilded Age and the Progressive Era established the Vincent P. De Santis Prize to honor the best book published in the field, a fitting recognition of his own important scholarship.

Rev. Thomas T. McAvoy, C.S.C., the legendary history department chair, recruited Vincent De Santis to teach at Notre Dame in 1949. The new faculty member's loyalty to Notre Dame ran deep, and he spent his whole academic career here, aside from his visiting appointments and a year's recall to active military service during the Korean War. He joined an excellent department where good teaching and research were both valued. Eventually, De Santis assumed a leadership role in the department. He was promoted to full professor in 1962, and Fr. Hesburgh appointed him to chair the department from 1963 to 1971. He taught literally thousands of undergraduate students over the decades, carrying in his initial years the standard teaching load of four courses per semester. Students found his courses to be demanding but very rewarding. He eased the rigorous demands of his courses after he earned emeritus status in 1982, but his passion for teaching was not dimmed in the slightest. He relished the opportunity to share his unique and valuable insights with his students. Some students in recent years have marveled that Professor De Santis had lived through the whole period he covered in his course on presidents since F.D.R. They benefited from the personal recollections he shared in class discussions and from his ability to relate earlier historical episodes to contemporary events.

In addition to his fine record as an undergraduate teacher, De Santis proved an excellent and effective graduate mentor. He supervised numerous Master's theses and directed fifteen doctoral dissertations on a range of topics in American political and diplomatic history, including my own. I came to Notre Dame from Australia in 1976 to work with the scholar I then called "Professor De Santis." We have been firm friends ever since, and I often have been the beneficiary of his kindness and generosity. I am not alone. Over his long career Vincent De Santis maintained good friendships with colleagues here at Notre Dame and with a wonderful group of historians whom he regularly met at professional meetings all over the country. He worked always to build up a sense of community within his department and university and within the historical profession to which he so proudly belonged. Vincent's generosity is notably evident in his regular financial support for various activities on campus, as well as in his bequest of a six-figure sum to establish a graduate fellowship which will be named in his honor.

Rather sadly it seems that men and women who contributed much to the growth and development of Notre Dame can be quickly forgotten upon either their departure or their death. Perhaps this is the way it will always be as new generations focus on their contemporary concerns and challenges, and, occasionally, succumb to the temptation to congratulate themselves on all their present accomplishments. Yet surely it does us good to acknowledge that we only build upon the efforts of those who preceded us here. We must regularly acknowledge our gratitude to them, and I am truly glad to recognize here the important contribution made to Notre Dame by my treasured teacher and friend, Vincent P. De Santis.

## Rev. Marvin R. O'Connell:
## Sorin's Biographer and Master Historian
## 2011

*Fr. Marvin O'Connell chaired the history department when I arrived from Australia to begin my doctoral studies. He cut a rather imposing figure at the time and, dare I say, there might even have been moments when I found him a little on the intimidating side. In subsequent years my appreciation for him both as a scholar and as a friend has grown.*

*In May of 2011, I organized a conference at Notre Dame to recognize his remarkable career-long contributions as a scholar and a teacher. This was a wonderful academic convocation at which excellent papers were delivered reflecting on Fr. O'Connell's many important books. Prior to the conference I prepared my own tribute to him.*

Fr. Marvin O'Connell is best known among Notre Dame students and alumni as the acclaimed biographer of Fr. Edward Sorin, Notre Dame's remarkable founder. Perhaps this is understandable, but Fr. O'Connell's accomplishments extend far beyond his vivid portrait of Sorin's life. He stands in the very front rank of distinguished historians who have taught and written at Notre Dame.

Fr. O'Connell first journeyed to Notre Dame in 1956 to study for his doctorate under the direction of the renowned Church historian, Monsignor Philip Hughes. O'Connell had been ordained a priest that very year for the Archdiocese of St. Paul, Minnesota. His notable talents as a historian were already in evidence as he had published a well-researched book, *The Dowling Decade in St. Paul* (1955), a version of his master's thesis at St. Paul Seminary, which examined the Church in the twin cities in the 1920's. It would not be the last time that O'Connell would explore Catholicism in Minnesota, but under the astute guidance of Msgr. Hughes he turned his attention to the history of the Reformation and the Counter-Reformation. He wrote his dissertation on Thomas Stapleton, a prolific figure of the English Counter Reformation. Yale University Press published the revised dissertation in 1964. By this point Fr. O'Connell had returned to St. Paul and began his distinguished tenure as priest, teacher, and scholar at the (then) College of St. Thomas. His reputation as a brilliant lecturer and demanding teacher were clearly established during his years at St. Thomas. During this time he also wrote his wonderful account of John Henry Newman and the Oxford Movement, *The Oxford Conspirators* (1969).

In 1972, to Notre Dame's great good fortune, Fr. O'Connell received his archbishop's permission to return to this university to assume the position previously held by his now-deceased mentor, Philip Hughes. So began well over two decades of exemplary service. His teaching at both the graduate and undergraduate levels was especially noteworthy and challenging. Indeed, I have had fellow priests in the Congregation of Holy Cross tell me that they worked harder but learned more in his course on the Reformation than in any of their theology classes. His rather intimidating physical presence guaranteed that undergraduate students maintained high standards of decorum and commitment in his classroom. From 1974 to 1980 Fr. O'Connell chaired the history department and proved a capable administrator who recruited talented faculty.

During his first year as chair of the history department Fr. O'Connell published *The Counter Reformation, 1559–1610*, a volume in the prestigious Rise of Modern Europe series edited by William L. Langer. This book was well–received and named as a History Book Club selection. O'Connell took special pride in Langer's description of the book as so balanced and fair-minded that a reader could not tell whether it was written by a Catholic or a Protestant. Langer rightly noted that this was a "tribute to the author's depth of understanding and truly unusual objectivity."

While carrying his administrative responsibilities and leading the history department in a characteristically firm way, Fr. O'Connell sought a new vehicle for his always lucid prose and chose to write a novel. He published *McElroy* in 1980, his fictional account of the trials and tribulations of a post-war Minnesota politician (whom some readers thought bore a certain resemblance to Senator Eugene McCarthy, known by O'Connell during his years at St. Thomas). Writing history, however, remained his true passion, as the remarkable books he published over the following three decades clearly illustrated.

First came his masterful biography of the great American churchman and first archbishop of St. Paul, John Ireland. *John Ireland and the American Catholic Church* (1988) was not a narrow study but a true "life and times" portrait which cast essential light on the Americanist movement and the place of Roman Catholics in American political life in the late nineteenth and early twentieth centuries. Upon reading this splendid book Fr. Theodore Hesburgh reached the firm conclusion that he must enlist Fr. O'Connell to write the life of Notre Dame's founder. He knew that Fr. O'Connell could do justice to the experience and accomplishments of Fr. Sorin. Father O'Connell found that possibility of interest but knew he had other projects to complete. The first of these he published in 1994, the year he retired from full-time teaching, as *Critics on Trial: an Introduction to the Catholic*

*Modernist Crisis.* This beautifully written multiple biography offered sympathetic portraits of an array of Catholic modernists and assessed their significance as an intellectual movement.

Soon thereafter came *Blaise Pascal: Reasons of the Heart* (1997) which tracked not only Pascal's spiritual journey but also the religious turmoil of seventeenth century France. On completing that book Fr. O'Connell observed correctly that his various works had allowed him to engage "many of the great issues that have confronted the Church during modern times: the English Reformation, the Counter-Reformation, the Oxford Movement, Modernism, Americanism, and finally, French Jansenism." His was a truly impressive body of scholarly work that revealed his broad interests, covering compelling topics from the sixteenth century forward and on both sides of the Atlantic. Yet, especially for those fascinated by the history of Notre Dame, the best was yet to come.

Fr. O'Connell's magisterial account of the life and times of Edward Sorin, c.s.c., appeared in 2001. He dedicated the book to Fr Hesburgh, whom he deemed the "Second Founder of Notre Dame." *Sorin*, coming in at a mere seven hundred and thirty seven pages, made no genuflection in the direction of hagiography. O'Connell was too gifted a historian to succumb to that temptation. The book recounts in riveting detail the deep clash between Edward Sorin and his religious superior, Basil Moreau, the recently beatified founder of the Holy Cross Order. In revealing the contest between these two complex personalities, Fr. O'Connell addressed the larger issue (as the historian Gerald McKevitt noted) of "the struggle of European institutions—in this case, a religious congregation—to adapt to the American environment."

The book garnered high praise from reviewers, one of whom described its thirty chapters as "thoroughly researched and beautifully crafted with rhapsodic descriptions of place, complex character development, and a fine sense of pacing. It reads like a good novel, partly because Sorin was such a character." O'Connell surely captured the essence of that Sorin character in this memorable description: "Whether sad or happy, however, he simply refused to entertain the possibility of failure. So confident was he in his own powers, so sure of the ultimate righteousness of his goals, and so deep his faith that God and the Virgin Mary had summoned him to America to accomplish a great work, that no obstacle could confound him. He was no saint. He was capable of duplicity and pettiness and even ruthlessness. But for sheer courage and for the serene determination that courage gives birth to, he was hard to match."

Fr. O'Connell made clear that Sorin was primarily a priest and missionary rather than an educator. Notre Dame's founder was determined to more firmly establish Catholicism in this predominantly Protestant nation, and all that he did, especially his building of this university, sought that end. Whatever the setbacks in this undertaking—the struggles, the fires, the deaths—he never gave up. Fr. O'Connell captured all the formidable challenges and the occasional triumphs, and neatly summarized his argument: "[T]he paramount truth remains that Notre Dame survived because Edward Sorin . . . refused to fail." This book remains essential reading for all who would truly understand Notre Dame and seek to guide its present and future.

Fr. O'Connell might have been expected to rest on his laurels after the completion of this major work but his passion to write history remained undimmed. He fulfilled a promise first made to Archbishop John Roach to write a history of his home archdiocese, and so his *Pilgrims to the Northland: The Archdiocese of St. Paul, 1840–1962* was published in 2009. It allowed him to tell the story of the Church which had received his immigrant ancestors from Ireland and which had helped shape him. Now he is at work on another Notre Dame study, this one an exploration of the presidents of our university from Sorin to Hesburgh. It also will be required reading for all those who truly want to know the Notre Dame story.

Marvin O'Connell has utilized his striking talents as a historian as an integral part of his fundamental vocation as a priest. He once described the historian as a veritable "midwife to our faith," who must capture as best the evidence will allow the truth of the past. His work recognizes both that God revealed himself "in an historical person who, at a particular time and place, went from town to town, doing good, who was like us in all things but sin," and that "the life of Christ is extended into the life of his people, the Church." He made the latter his special subject, and understood "the special role in the life of the Christian people" of history and the historian. He has notably filled this role and contributed much to our understanding of the Church's journey over the past five centuries. His mentor, Msgr. Hughes, quietly observing him from a higher place (and no doubt in the company of such worthies as Matthew Fitzsimons, James Ward, and Ralph McInerny) must be deeply proud that the young priest from Minnesota, whom he trained well over a half century ago, developed into the master historian that his colleagues and friends enthusiastically acclaim today.

## Building an Intellectual Community: David Solomon and the Center for Ethics and Culture Fall Conference 2011

*David Solomon founded the Notre Dame Center for Ethics and Culture in the fall of 1999. He developed it into a lively organization that aimed "to provide resources for students and faculty to reflect on fundamental ethical matters, with the goal of their using such reflection to shape their lives in line with the good." The center has contributed mightily to Notre Dame in subsequent years and has reached beyond the campus to serve a broad constituency of students and scholars interested in serious ethical reflection. The center's annual "fall confer-ence" proved a special forum for scholarly exchange on matters of true substance.*

*David's tenure as director of the center came to an end on June 30, 2012. I made the following remarks as a tribute to him at the final fall conference over which he presided. Over six hundred participants attended the conference. David's important contribution to Notre Dame and to serious ethical reflection grounded in Catholic teaching was well–appreciated by each one of them.*

Friends of the Center for Ethics and Culture, thanks to each of you for your participation in this wonderful conference. David Solomon will be coming to the podium momentarily— never fear!

I would like to take a moment this evening to reflect on the importance of this conference and on David's role in inspiring it, organizing it, and sustaining it these past eleven years.

As those of you who were present at the conference last year may recall, David Solomon suggested in his traditional end–of–conference reflection that this year's conference might be the *last* of such gatherings. He worried that what had begun with those two crucial first conferences, focused on "The Culture of Death" and on "The Culture of Life," might conclude with this year's gathering devoted to the exploration of "Radical Emancipation: Confronting the Challenge of Secularism."

As you all know by now, this is not the case. One of the important sheets of paper in your conference folder is the notice to "Mark Your Calendars" for the Center for Ethics and Culture's thirteenth annual fall conference, November 8–10, 2012. I know David will have more to say on this and on the crucial appointment of his successor (Professor Carter Snead) that guarantees an important continuity in the work of the CEC and certainly guarantees a continuation of this conference.

This conference was described by my friend Mike Baxter this morning as four-fold in its dimensions. It is a regular academic conference at which serious scholarly papers are delivered and considered. It is a supportive gathering of a community of friends unashamedly engaged in the pursuit of truth. It is a lively jamboree of some of the best young people in the country gathering to reflect on what really matters. And, lastly, it is one of the great Catholic-Baptist ecumenical gatherings with the forging of the Baylor-Notre Dame links.

There is much to Mike's description and you, no doubt, could add your own to describe this energetic gathering which has brought together almost 650 participants this year. Whatever your description, we cannot let this occasion pass by without some words being spoken in a formal way to thank David Solomon and to celebrate the conference.

I want first to call on Prof. Don Briel, who is a regular attendee of this conference and, of course, the guiding force behind the amazing Center for Catholic Studies at the University of St. Thomas in St. Paul, Minnesota. I have asked Don to share some words as a representative of all those who have traveled here to Notre Dame both this year and in previous years.

[Remarks by Prof. Don Briel.]

Friends, I know you are dying to hear David Solomon—but not just yet! Pour another drink if you can!

Permit me to add a few words to those of Don Briel. The learned Robert Sloan paid a moving tribute to David Solomon during his presentation on the *University Presidents* panel yesterday. I hope you heard it. It brought to my mind David's connection with Baylor University. We are very grateful to Baylor for its contribution to the formation of the CEC and the growth of this conference. Baylor tried to recruit David Solomon to head a Christian ethics center, as Don Schmeltekopf reminded me last night. David was tempted but decided to stay on here when our then-provost, Nathan Hatch, gave him the opportunity to head an ethics center at Notre Dame.

As we all know David Solomon is renowned for his "administrative gifts." He gives lectures on how to be a better manager! This is a man who always responds to his e-mail messages quickly! This is a man who always clears out the phone messages on his cell phone so as to facilitate receiving more! His "follow through" is notable—or maybe not!

Seriously, David proved to be a great leader of the center, whatever his supposed limits as a manager—and these are minor. His leadership was evident in the people he recruited to help him at the CEC, such as those marvelous young women in the early years like Jennie Bradley, Katie Freddoso, and Margaret Watkins. During the important and challenging middle years of the center, David recruited the one and only Elizabeth Kirk, the wise and creative Dan McInerny, and the talented Katherine Wales. And in recent years he has been able to draw on the support of his excellent and hard working team of Angela Pfister, Greer Hannan, and Steve Freddoso. All of them were backed up throughout by the steady hand of Tracy Westlake. Encouraging David throughout his years as director has been his wonderful wife, Mary Lou Solomon, whom we must recognize here tonight.

All these folks have played their parts in one way or another in helping with this conference but each of them would readily concede that the indispensable figure, the conductor of the whole orchestra, was David Solomon. From the earliest days David planned on a big gathering to be held each fall. He inspired it at the outset.

David knows how to bring folks together around matters of importance, and that has been so evident here in these past days. He is a truly good and virtuous man who knows how to laugh and how to encourage others. He knows what real friendship is, and he wanted to make this conference a place for forging and renewing friendships.

David's key insight was that he should root the work of the center and the themes of this annual conference in the Gospels and in the profound and important elements of recent Church teaching, especially the encyclicals of Blessed John Paul II, among which *Veritatis Splendor* and *Evangelium Vitae* hold a special place. David and the center have been unafraid to see the conference as an exercise in the quest for truth. It is a little surprising that "a Baptist from Baylor" and from the University of Texas at Austin should have played such a crucial role in fostering such teaching here at Notre Dame, where such encyclicals were not receiving proper attention.

The team at the Center for Ethics and Culture recognizes David's enormous regard and engagement with Pope John Paul

II and the role of this great pope as an inspiration and lodestar for this conference. So we have a small memento for David, perhaps to be placed in his philosophy department office upon his return to Malloy Hall. [This was an icon of Pope John Paul II.]

Let us truly thank God for the gift of David Solomon and for how he has used his talents so well in assembling these conferences at Notre Dame.

Friends, I give you David Solomon.

# Conclusion:
# The Courage to Be a Catholic
# and the Future for Notre Dame

Notre Dame has crucial decisions to make if it is to develop into a truly great and authentic Catholic university. These decisions will require a deep confidence in the worth of this venture in Catholic higher education, something that has not always been displayed at Notre Dame in recent decades. Such confidence combined with an inner security rightly applied, however, will allow Notre Dame to choose substance over image, principles over ratings, and, ultimately, truth over a false prestige. Notre Dame must pursue a distinct and determined course so as to fulfill its holy calling as a university engaged upon a great quest for truth, goodness and beauty. It must be a university in which its students encounter Christ and in which the Gospel is brought to the world.

Notre Dame must reject the path of conformity that leads to an unimaginative imitation of what occurs on the campuses of supposed "preferred peer" schools. This special university must overcome what one astute observer has deemed its "craven quest for success understood in conventional, and often quite secular, terms." Our Lady's university must instead be an intellectual bastion where what Pope Benedict called "the dictatorship of relativism" does not prevail. It must be a place where its faculty and students resist the blights of materialism and utilitarianism in their academic endeavors and instead devote themselves to bringing faith and reason into dialogue. By so aiding an honest confrontation of the great issues of our day Notre Dame can contribute significantly in the intellectual realm to the crucial work of the new evangelization. It can renew its own mission and purpose and thereby assist in renewing ecclesial life in the United States and beyond.

This task will not be easy. The temptations to conform are notable, and the perceived 'costs' of not accommodating to the dominant secular educational model can seem significant. So one must ask: Will Notre Dame resist worshipping before the "golden calf" of the *U.S. News and World Report* rankings with all that implies? Will it seek obsequiously after the "holy grail" of membership in the American Association of Universities as a way to measure its supposed success in American higher education? Will it adopt as an operating strategy an anxious "me-too-ism" which makes it susceptible to the prevailing and often shallow fads that beset American colleges and universities? Will it seek to appease the forces in American society that aim to diminish and limit the role of the Catholic Church and the significance of its contribution in the public square and to intellectual life? Will it disguise itself as a genuine Catholic university by maintaining the elements of the Catholic 'neighborhood'—residential life and campus ministry et cetera—while allowing the crucial Catholic 'school'—the academic heart of the university—to deteriorate and disappear?

In answering these questions Notre Dame faces a more fundamental question. It is an age-old one that has been regularly confronted from the time of the ancient Israelites: who or what will be worshipped? Will it be the one true God or will it be the "baals" of today. False gods and empty idols are all about. They exert a powerful attraction to the unwary, to those who fail to appreciate what really matters. But if a Catholic university bows down before them it will assuredly lose its heart and soul. It will lose its core identity regardless of what Potemkin structures are erected and maintained to hide that loss. This course cannot be allowed to prevail at Notre Dame. It cannot be a place where Catholicism becomes a mere veneer over a largely secular project.

At the present time a lot of silly talk occurs on campus regarding the supposedly "transformative" moment in which

Notre Dame finds itself as it prepares for another major fundraising campaign. According to this view, the university possesses an opportunity to "re-invent" itself, although the exact details of the recasting are rarely specified. Such specious talk needs to be replaced by a clear-headed and courageous commitment to the renewal of Notre Dame's mission as a Catholic university. As those who have read the essays included in this volume will appreciate, Notre Dame must unequivocally adopt *Ex Corde Ecclesiae* as its essential guide. It must grasp at a deep level that it operates "from the heart of the Church." The declaration of "autonomy" from the Church involved in the Land O'Lakes statement must be permanently shelved and rejected.

An institution guided by *Ex Corde Ecclesiae* will pay close attention to those essential questions involved in the daily operation of universities: what is taught and who teaches it? As it proceeds forward Notre Dame must devote great attention to key matters concerning the curriculum and the composition of its faculty. It must hire faculty—Catholics and non-Catholics—who are deeply supportive of its mission and prepared to provide a genuine Catholic education for its students. Such an education will allow students to grasp the complementary nature of faith and reason, receive a deep understanding and love for the truth, and gain a clear appreciation of the Catholic moral and social vision.

To pursue this course Notre Dame will need to enlist the support of key groups that shape its present and future. It surely requires capable leadership that recognizes the dangerous contemporary realities and moves beyond the ostrich-like denial that characterizes much discussion on key matters like faculty hiring. Firm leadership at the level of the university officers and the deans, however, must be accompanied by strong support from the Board of Fellows and the Trustees. The fellows bear fiduciary responsibility for the Catholicity of the university and lay and Holy Cross fellows alike must never relent in their efforts to fulfill a sacred trust that has come to them. The role of lay trustees is also crucial, and they must be selected for their commitment to Catholic higher education and not merely for their giving capacity. Those either not capable of grasping the central issues at stake or too tepid in support of Notre Dame's Catholic mission should exercise their talents on other boards.

Members of the Congregation of Holy Cross—my own religious community—must renew their commitment to fulfill our charism as educators in the faith. Religious orders in Catholic universities have not navigated recent decades well. Holy Cross, too, faces challenges but fortunately, there is a new generation of dedicated religious emerging who promise to engage vigorously in the work of evangelization at Notre Dame. Perhaps they might serve as a special leaven in the renewal endeavor and help to make Notre Dame a vibrant place of integrated education concerned not only with the mind but also with the heart and soul.

Faculty, as this book makes clear, are crucial to any institution of higher learning. Notre Dame must build upon the presence of committed faculty to recruit more devoted teachers and scholars who want to participate in a distinctive project in American higher education. Only if this task is successfully accomplished will Notre Dame rest secure in its Catholic identity. Likewise, such faculty should find able students hungry for the truth who want the distinctive education that Notre Dame can provide. Students who want more limited vocational training or who want to avoid facing deep questions of meaning and some consideration of the transcendent might normally apply to the many other schools with narrower and less demanding curricula.

At most American universities alumni play a very limited role beyond serving as a source of financial support. Notre Dame is different. The alumni matter, and their love for their *alma mater* must be reflected in their continued engagement with the university. It cannot be simply an episodic engagement over egregious affronts like the honoring of President Obama: it must be constant and informed. In this regard the work of the Sycamore Trust to inform alumni of developments on campus has been invaluable. Those who truly love Notre Dame will call it to be its best self and fully support the renewal of its Catholic character.

These essential stakeholders along with other friends and supporters of Notre Dame must all collaborate to assure that the university rejects the secularist temptation and charts a less-traveled path so that has it may lead a true renaissance in Catholic higher education in the United States. A major course-correction is needed. It is a challenging prospect, but Notre Dame is a place that has faced challenges in the past and emerged even stronger. Damaging fires, a terrible cholera outbreak, and a series of financial crises couldn't break Fr. Edward Sorin's iron will and deep faith. The more subtle but equally dangerous trials of our time—trials that test not the physical existence but rather the essential mission of the university—must not defeat those committed to this special venture in Catholic education.

Surely, even in difficult days, we can take heart in the deeply felt observation of the long-time director of the Notre Dame Alumni Association, James E. Armstrong, "that the University of Notre Dame, from its origin, reflects a supernatural influence, an arrangement of large and small miracles, a common denominator among its peoples of a destiny beyond the academic." But some measure of Sorin's will and faith is still needed among those who will fight to uphold and enhance the Catholic character of Notre Dame. We must not be afraid. Instead, we must follow the dictum of the legendary Frank O'Malley and "be about the work." This is a purpose worth fighting and sacrificing for today and in the years ahead. We must do it for Notre Dame and for her Son.

# Addendum:
# Editorial Note and Listing of Contents Citations

The various articles and addresses collected in this volume are meant to record my effort over the past two decades to defend and promote the Catholic mission of Notre Dame. The pieces included here were either written for or delivered to a public audience. The temptation to include specific personal correspondence has been resisted despite the relevance of it to the issues raised in this book.

The various speeches and talks are drawn from copies of the texts kept in my own files. The previously published works draw upon the sources cited below. They are listed in the order in which they appear in the book. In some cases minor editing has taken place for the sake of clarity and to eliminate repetition. Nonetheless, readers will note that certain key arguments and examples are repeated in the volume. Hopefully, this emphasis on matters such as faculty hiring and adherence to *Ex Corde Ecclesiae* conveys the importance of such issues.

## CITATIONS:

"Meeting the Challenge and Fulfilling the Promise: Mission and Method in Constructing a Great Catholic University," in Theodore M. Hesburgh, ed., *The Challenge and Promise of a Catholic University*. Notre Dame: University of Notre Dame Press, 1994, pp. 209–223.

"The Faculty 'Problem': How Can Catholic Identity be Preserved?" *America*, Vol. 197, No. 6 (September 10, 2007), pp. 26–28.

"The Corporate University: A Catholic Response," *America*, Vol. 195, No. 3 (July 31–August 7, 2006), pp. 14–17.

"An Open Letter on the Vagina Monologues Controversy to Fr. John Jenkins," *The Observer*, (April 11, 2006), p. 9.

"Open Letter by Holy Cross Priests on Obama Invitation," *The Observer*, April 8, 2009), p. 9.

"Honoring Obama, Notre Dame, and American Catholic Life," text of speech given May 17, 2009, included as an appendix in Charles E. Rice, *What Happened to Notre Dame?* South Bend: St. Augustine's Press, 2009, pp. 156–161.

"Saving Notre Dame's Soul," Interview by Kathryn Jean Lopez, *National Catholic Register Online*, July 29, 2011.

"Mr. Notebaert, *Ex Corde Ecclesiae*, and the Future of Notre Dame," *The Irish Rover*, Vol. 9, No 7 (December 2, 2011), p. 1 & p. 9.

"Defending Bishop Jenky," Interview by John Burger, *National Catholic Register Online*, April 27, 2012.

"Civility, Courage, and Conviction at Notre Dame," *The Irish Rover*, Vol. 10, No. 5 (October, 2012), p. 8.

"Some Advice for Future Catholic Politicians," *The Irish* Rover, Vol.8, No 11 (March 25, 2011), p. 9.

"Keep the Faith, Make a Difference," *The Irish Rover*, Frosh-O special edition, (August 19, 2011), pp. 6–7.

Reflections on Fr. Moreau and Fr. Sorin drawn from contributions to Andrew Gawrych, csc and Kevin Grove, csc, eds., *The Cross, Our Only Hope: Daily Reflections in the Holy Cross Tradition*. Notre Dame: Ave Maria Press, 2008, entries for February 23 & March 6.

"Sixty Years at Notre Dame: Vincent De Santis as Scholar, Teacher, and Friend," *The Irish Rover*, Vol. 8, No. 1 (April 26, 2010), p. 6.

"Rev. Marvin R. O'Connell: Sorin's Biographer *and* Master Historian," *The Irish Rover*, Vol. 9, Issue 1 (April 28, 2011), p. 8.

# Index